ROBERT FROST

ROBERT
FROST

A COLLECTION OF CRITICAL ESSAYS

Edited by

James M. Cox, 1925– ed.

A SPECTRUM BOOK

Prentice-Hall, Inc., *Englewood Cliffs, N.J.*

205 p. 20 cm.

(A Spectrum book: Twentieth century views, S-TC-3)

© 1962

BY PRENTICE-HALL, INC.

ENGLEWOOD CLIFFS, N.J.

LIBRARY OF CONGRESS CATALOG NO.: 62-9283

Fourth printing .... March, 1965

PRINTED IN THE UNITED STATES OF AMERICA

C-33150

1. Frost, Robert, 1874-   I. t

Table of Contents

ROBERT FROST

Introduction

by James M. Cox

Though Robert Frost has become such a national institution that he was called on to read a poem at the 1961 Presidential Inauguration, it is still difficult to comprehend just how deep his roots go down into time. When he published "My Butterfly" in the *Independent* in November 1894, Henry James had not yet entered his major phase and Stephen Crane had not published *The Red Badge of Courage*. A year earlier, Yeats had published *The Celtic Twilight,* but *Poems* had not yet appeared, and Conrad, having closed his career in the merchant service, was beginning one as a professional writer. The careers of Lawrence, Joyce, Eliot, and Pound had of course not begun; Fitzgerald, Faulkner, and Hemingway had not even been born.

These facts reveal more than Frost's age. They emphasize that he was writing poetry before modern literature had really begun to happen. In fact, Frost grew up in a time when there was no commanding poetic voice in America. Whitman was still alive, still writing, but the force of his career was spent and he had become the Good Gray Poet. Emily Dickinson, the one vital spirit in American poetry, was significantly enough unheard and unknown, having chosen to write her poetry to posterity instead of addressing it to a contemporary audience. In the wake of the Schoolroom Poets, who were dying one by one, there simply was no poetic audience to listen and no voice to speak during the twenty-six years Frost spent in the nineteenth century.

And yet the remoteness of Frost's beginnings is no more striking than the decisive twentieth-century chronology of his career. Although he had published fugitive pieces in magazines, his first volume of poems did not appear until 1913, when he was thirty-nine years old. It is an extraordinarily late age to begin a career, even in America—where Emerson, Whitman, Hawthorne, Melville, and Mark Twain did not discover them-

1

selves as writers until they were past twenty-five. Yet Frost not only began late; he seems to have gathered his forces deliberately and bided his time until he was sure of not launching himself too soon. According to his own claim, by the time of his first book he had accumulated a large enough body of work to fill two and a half volumes of poetry. There is no evidence that he has ever lost that original edge.

The existence of such a margin has enabled Frost to discover his books in much the same way as he discovered the poems they contain. He has not completed poems to make his books but has made his books from completed poems. He once defined the initial delight of making a poem as the "surprise of remembering something I didn't know I knew." And in a letter to Whit Burnett, who had asked him to pick his own best poems, Frost disclosed the basis upon which he built his books:

> I have made this selection much as I made the one for my first book, *A Boy's Will,* and my second book, *North of Boston,* looking backward over the accumulation of years to see how many poems I could find towards some one meaning it might seem absurd to have had in advance, but it would be all right to accept from fate after the fact. . . . In other words could anything of large design, even the roughest, any broken or dotted continuity or any fragment of a figure be discerned among the apparently random lesser designs of the several poems?

The design of which Frost speaks is no plan laid out in advance, but an order which emerges as the poet moves and which he in turn discovers as he reviews his progress. Form is for Frost identical with the act of creation and every poem is by virtue of its form a deed. That is why he entitled the short essay prefacing his *Complete Poems* "The Figure a Poem Makes."

As volume has followed volume, each with its own principle of organization, it is not surprising that Frost's *Complete Poems* (1949) discloses its own larger design. From the invitational lyric "The Pasture," which opens the volume, to the two masques which conclude it, the figure the poems make is the figure of Robert Frost in a New England landscape. The figure and the scene are finally identical, for the poet's language *personifies* his region, making it an extension of himself and converting what was mere geographical space to personal property. Frost's New England is not the alien virgin wilderness occupied by savages and subdued by Puritans; instead it is second growth timber come back to claim land which has been lived over and left behind within the memory of living men; it is thus a grand metaphor for all the past which man throws aside as being at once unpromising and unprofitable. The poet literally enters this abandoned human landscape—human because it has been not only explored but also experienced, still retaining the domestic scars beneath its wilderness—and reclaims it for us all. The result of this imaginative enterprise which converts space to property is a relentless self-possession, bringing into the full range of consciousness as much of that half-remembered life as possible.

The direction of Frost's life provides an analogue to the direction his poetic imagination has taken. Born in San Francisco in 1874, he went to New England at the very time everyone was leaving it and woods were rushing back to fill what had been meadow and pasture. In this New England, Frost spent his young manhood; he married, farmed, taught, and had four children. Yet for all his involvement in the business of supporting a growing family, Frost did not really settle down. At the very moment when it became clear that a career awaited him in teaching (the state superintendent of schools had called him the best teacher in New Hampshire), he withdrew from New England, taking his family with him to Old England. And it was from England that he launched himself as a poet, publishing his first two volumes of poetry there—*A Boy's Will* in 1913, *North of Boston* in 1914. Thus, at the precise moment when the nineteenth-century political order was collapsing into the violence of the twentieth century, Frost emerged from obscurity into the foreground of American poetry, where he has remained for almost fifty years.

Upon emerging, Frost's direction in space was once again counter to the drift of things. If in 1885 he had unwittingly come eastward to New England in the face of westward migration, thirty years later in 1915 he went westward toward New England just when America was about to be drawn out of itself and back toward the Europe which had originally dreamed it. Since this return, although he has wandered from campus to campus as poet in residence and as star guest lecturer, Frost has never really left the New England into which his poetic imagination drew him. Instead, his boy's will has in a long succession of creative gestures converted all that region North of Boston into the Realm of Robert Frost.

II

The discrepancy in age between Frost the man and Frost the poet, his emergence during the interlude between the collapse of the old order and the beginning of the new, and his own poetic strategy of returning to the wilderness of abandoned experience—all serve to indicate Frost's ambiguous position in relation to what we call modern literature. Though his career fully spans the modern period and though it is impossible to speak of him as anything other than a modern poet, it is difficult to place him in the main current of modern poetry. This difficulty may seem to be a problem of recent origin; actually it existed from the moment Frost achieved fame. When *North of Boston* appeared, both William Dean Howells, the aging patriarch of American letters, and Ezra Pound, the eccentric and rebellious exponent of the new poetry, reviewed and praised it. Howells saw the volume as being "unaffectedly expressive of rustic New England" and went on to remark, "Amidst the often striving and straining of the new poetry, here is the old poetry as young as ever; and new only in extending the bounds of sympathy through the recorded to the unrecorded knowledge of humanity." Pound, on the other hand, after attacking the blindness of American editors who had ignored Frost, congratulated the poet for breaking away from "stilted pseudo-literary language" and daring to write in the "natural speech of New England."

During the period between the two world wars, the essential complexity of Frost's poetic identity was forgotten by his partisans and opponents alike in favor of inviting but nonetheless inadequate simplifications. Part of this process is graphically dramatized by the diverse fates of Frost and Pound. While Frost came to be praised and published by the very editors against whom Pound had railed, Pound pursued his embattled way to become one of the chief forces of modern literature. As Frost became more closely identified with a large and relatively unsophisticated audience, Pound increasingly alienated himself from his American origins and by dint of effort and imagination helped create a relatively small but highly disciplined and articulate audience of his own. What Pound, and particularly Eliot after him, succeeded in doing was to create a poetry which aroused new attitudes toward poetry itself. By being critics as well as poets, they inspired a generation of new poetry and new criticism.

Eliot became the figure around whom the force of the new poetry mobilized. Both his poetry and his critical pronouncements had about them an authority which by 1930 dominated the literary scene. Though Frost wrote steadily and reached a wider and wider range of listeners, he remained outside the passionate ring of new believers. Unlike Eliot, who seemed to undergo evolution and reorganization with each new poem, and unlike Pound who concentrated all his disparate self in a devotion toward a single poem of epic scope, Frost seemed to harden into a static figure. Though every one of his poems might be a new creation of himself, it was always the same self being created—the old "character" who had first appeared in "Mending Wall," the opening poem of *North of Boston*. It is not surprising that this character who emerged, but who could not develop and who seemed curiously untouched by the drift of modern poetry, should have come to seem almost quaint and old-fashioned by 1930.

During the Twenties, Eliot—creating the illusion that he was moving through stages on a journey toward some kind of truth—had left the emptiness of Prufrock's world, passed through *The Waste Land,* and turned from the poetry of "despair" toward the poetry of "belief." In the same period, Frost, in *New Hampshire* (1923) and again in *West-Running Brook* (1928), began to create the illusion of a New England farmer poet writing the poetry of opinion. While Eliot was discovering symbols for his age in the ancient myths of creation and fertility, Frost was creating the myth of Robert Frost.

When, during the Thirties, poetry discovered a whole new reality in the political liberalism of the time, Frost became even more removed from the intellectual center of things. He seemed stubbornly—even querulously—conservative, going so far as to raise a dissenting voice against Franklin Roosevelt and the New Deal, sounding in "Build Soil" (1932) like a member of the Republican Party, and directing more and more Yankee wit against socialism in government. At the very moment when the New Criticism gained enough momentum to achieve a distinct identity, Frost seemed farthest from the wave of the future. This divergence between Frost and the intellectuals in the years before World War II resulted not so much in harsh criticism of Frost's work as in complete absence of criticism. He was simply ignored or dismissed as being unworthy of serious consideration. There are many survivors of that era who still have difficulty believing that he is a poet, insisting that he is really nothing more than a cracker-barrel versifier speaking with a pronounced New England accent. They remember with a resentment which the years have not assuaged the hostile attacks upon modern poetry launched in the name of Frost's poetry—and indeed Frost's defenders did incline to use his poetry as a defense perimeter within which to find solace. Not without reason, many who had failed to fall under Frost's spell did come to see the Frost contingent as a cult of unreasoning worshipers seeking protection from an indulgent god.

This is not to say that the early criticism of Frost lacked all semblance of clarity and insight. Amy Lowell, Gorham Munson, Sidney Cox, Mark Van Doren, and Edwin Muir were among the critics who offered valuable estimates. Yet when Richard Thornton in 1937 made the first collection of Frost criticism he wisely entitled the volume *Recognition of Robert Frost.* The collection, essentially a commemorative one honoring Frost's twenty-five years of achievement, was nevertheless fairly representative of the criticism he had received. It showed that during those twenty-five years, though he had been recognized as a poet, his poetry had yet to be appraised.

III

In the following collection I have presented what seems to me the best criticism written on Frost. Readers familiar with the large body of writing on Frost's poetry no doubt will wish that an essay or portion of a book not included had displaced a particular choice I have made. There are certain essays, certain passages from books, and certain explications which I have regretted omitting; but since including them would have meant cutting and patching all the selections, I decided in favor of fewer essays in an unmutilated form. I have arranged the selections in chronological order for two reasons. First, each essay will easily establish its own identity; second, the chronology of the selections accurately reflects a new phase or second stage of Frost criticism, the nature of which I shall attempt to clarify.

The oldest selection in the volume—the chapter from Lawrance Thompson's *Fire and Ice*—appeared in 1942, thirty years after the publication of *A Boy's Will*. Thompson's book is, it seems to me, the first authoritative study of Frost's poetry. Two notable advantages were offered him by history. Between the appearance of Thornton's collection and Thompson's book, Frost had come into sharper perspective, having published his second *Collected Poems* (1939) and *A Witness Tree* (1942). Moreover, Thompson brought with his own considerable ability the inheritance of an age of literary criticism, and he looked at Frost's poetry with an informed scrutiny which no previous writer had accorded it. Instead of attitudinizing about how true Frost's poetry was, instead of recording his impressions, he tried to give an extended description of the body of Frost's poetry. The chapter from *Fire and Ice* included in this selection provides a point of departure for all that follows. In defining Frost's theory of poetry Thompson exemplifies the requisites esential to the critic. He is first of all informed, showing extensive knowledge and command of his subject. Secondly, he is intelligent, simultaneously showing a capacity to relate Frost's poetry to a tradition and an ability to discriminate between the two. Thus he is able to distinguish between Frost on the one hand and Wordsworth and Emerson on the other— poets with whom Frost had often been uncritically associated. Finally, he shows no disposition to distrust his reason, instinctively realizing that the mystery of poetry is discovered and enhanced—not imperiled—by rigorous analysis. His book threw light on Frost's forms, his substance, and on poetry in general. Before Thompson there had been little more than insights and attitudes; after him genuine criticism was at once more possible and more necessary.

The seven selections which follow Thompson's chapter reflect a prevailing division of opinion as to the merits of Frost's poetry. Malcolm Cowley, Yvor Winters, and Harold Watts all emphasize Frost's limitations. Cowley opens the case against Frost with what is in effect a distillation of the misgivings which had accumulated between the world wars concerning Frost's political and psychological conservatism—a conservatism which, Cowley shrewdly argues, prevented Frost from reaching out toward society or in toward the wilderness of the self. By standing safely at the edge of the woods and refusing the risks of town *and* forest, Frost surrendered the responsibility that goes with greatness. He followed neither the individualism of his New England predecessors Emerson and Thoreau nor the humanitarianism and expansiveness of Whitman; instead he pursued a cautious poetic policy which involved the sacrifice of a major talent to the making of a minor poet.

Different though Winters' critical approach is from Cowley's, the spiritual drifter he deplores is essentially the uncommitted figure Cowley objects to. Both authors make their judgments by setting Frost against a norm of moral and social values which they set up in advance. To Winters, Frost represents a morally irresponsible figure whose evasion of issues has rendered him incapable of meeting problems seriously or seeing them clearly. Insisting that the voice of the poet is essentially identical with the voices of the poems, Winters discerns in Frost a poet who fails to convey any wisdom because he has refused the poet's sacred responsibility of telling the truth. Thus Frost, who possesses a considerable lyric ability, is at his worst in didactic or satiric poetry—in which truth, morality, and principle do count—because his own principles are either misguided, misinformed, or simply negligible.

Watts makes a fundamental contribution to the description of Frost's spiritual disengagement. Frost is not, he observes, completely adrift; he is actually only half-disengaged from the world, for he maintains an intimate relationship with natural process, and he even tries to establish communication with society. His social dialogue, however, is tentative and incomplete—a reluctant and whimsical conversation in which Frost is too often content to indulge in stereotyped wisecracking and skepticism. Although Frost's dramatic narratives do reflect an awareness of the complexity of human affairs, his characters are usually discovered in isolated rather than in social situations. The shrewd aspect of Frost's poetic voice is a reflection of the attention he gives to keeping open an avenue of retreat to natural process from his interrupted dialogue with society.

The essays by W. G. O'Donnell, John Napier, and Marion Montgomery, while not directly contending with adversaries of Frost, clearly
rest on the assumption that Frost's achievement far surpasses his limitations. Moreover, without specifically intending to offer counter-argu-
ments to Cowley, Winters, or Watts, they provide balance weights to the
judgments made against Frost. Thus against Cowley's assertion that
Frost withdraws from social issues, O'Donnell presents the whole of
Frost's New England as an image of his awareness of the social history of
a people and a landscape. Locating his standard of value in descriptive
realism rather than in moral seriousness or social involvement, O'Donnell
attempts to establish Frost's concern with history and society.

Marion Montgomery's essay pursues the same issue which absorbed
Watts: Frost's relation to man and nature. There is no dialogue with
society and there is really no dialogue with natural process, Montgomery
claims. Instead, there are only barriers everywhere—between man and
God, man and nature, man and man—which each man is constantly discovering, erecting, and destroying for himself. Man thus begins as a
stranger to his world, his life, and God; the whole business of living
involves a series of accommodations by which man adjusts himself to
the barriers on every side of him. Recognition of the barriers is part of
the whole principle of sanity, leading eventually to respect for man and
God.

John Napier's discussion could well be read in reply to Winters' complaints about Frost's didactic poetry. Following Susanne Langer's definition of the poem as a unitary symbol which creates the illusion of
virtual experience, Napier discusses the ways in which Frost's later
poems present a semblance of reasoning. Instead of finding "West-
Running Brook" and later poems marred by spiritual drift, Napier believes that in the contemplative poetry Frost, almost alone among modern
poets, is carrying out Wordsworth's prophecy that the true poet will
work with, not against, the man of science, "carrying sensation into the
midst of the objects of the science itself."

Randall Jarrell's criticism is in a class by itself. Written in the form of
an appreciation, it is an entirely different appreciation from the old
"recognitions" of Frost. It is a new recognition offered by a member of
the new generation rhetorically exploiting what he knows is the anomaly
of his position. Chiding his readers for their feeling of complacent superi-
ority, Jarrell argues that they are as blind to Frost's greatness as Frost's
rampant admirers once were to Eliot. Jarrell's enthusiastic abandon is
convincing not because it is merely "different" from ordinary criticism
but because he has the rare wit, taste, and intelligence to sustain his
reckless appreciation. When he regrets his inability to quote and com-

ment upon more poems, his rhetoric remains persuasive because his treatment of quoted passages shows a fine discrimination as well as a total imaginative grasp of and response to poetry. Anyone who has heard Jarrell read with running commentary Frost's longer poems knows—and regrets—how much he *did* leave out of the essay. Jarrell's essay represents a conscious awareness of the failure of the new criticism to do Frost justice. His "outrageousness," predicated upon the fact of Frost's neglect by an entire literary contingent, pleads for a re-vision of Frost.

Lionel Trilling's speech at Frost's eighty-fifth birthday celebration is not a plea but a confession marking the surrender of that hard core of resistance which gathered against Frost during the Thirties. At least it was an offer of surrender—somewhat reluctant perhaps, with an attempt to carry the white flag proudly and even a touch aggressively, but a surrender nevertheless. The sudden eruption of all the emotion latent in the scene emphasizes how much history and how much antagonism had gone into the making of the drama. Recalling as it does the famous Whittier birthday dinner in 1877 at which Mark Twain's performance produced such repercussions, this entire incident—which Trilling rightly calls a cultural episode—deserves much closer examination than it has received. It should tell in its own way as much about the literary history and culture of our time as the Whittier dinner tells about the literature and society of the Gilded Age.

Trilling's speech, Frost's apparently troubled reaction to it, and the attack upon it launched by J. Donald Adams all reveal the reluctance of parties on both sides of the issue to abandon positions in which so much intellectual and emotional capital has been invested. There remains a strong tendency to assume former attitudes in an effort to preserve a reality which they no longer possess. Thus even after Frost has received the honor of reading "The Gift Outright" at a presidential inauguration, some petulantly complain of the honors critics have denied him. Equally absurd complaints from an opposite quarter are made by those who cannot comprehend Frost's rural scene because of their urbanity. The last two selections in this book give evidence that criticism can neither sustain nor be sustained by such worn-out attitudes. The selections—themselves conclusions to books published in 1960—provide an appropriate conclusion to this second stage of Frost criticism.

George W. Nitchie, measuring Frost against major twentieth-century poets, presents what is unquestionably the most coherent and responsible statement of the case against Frost. Since his entire book is devoted to a patient construction of this case, a summary of his argument is perhaps the best introduction to his concluding chapter. Nitchie's central contention is that Frost's simplified rural world results in an ultimate reduction of human values in the poetry. The Frostian man in that alien natural world either creates nature in his own image in an anthropocentric imaginative act, compromises and bargains with its powers in a series of prudent gestures, or stares upon its indifferent face in contemplative regard. Whichever alternative he chooses, the human situation as Frost presents it remains relatively solitary, simple, and antisocial: its morality involves mere acts of choice made by a lonely self; its politics relies on a negative concept of freedom—freedom from restraint instead of freedom to achieve—and is thus essentially conservative; its myth is essentially regressive and Edenic; its philosophy is improvised along a line of shrewd aphorisms instead of resting on a systematic and coherent body of thought; and its poetics, rather than showing commitment to the unity of metaphor, falls back on simile and whimsy. These are the limitations which cause Nitchie to find Frost's stature quite diminished as compared to the figures of Yeats, Eliot, and Stevens.

Probably the best answer to Nitchie's reasoned reservations is John F. Lynen's *The Pastoral Art of Robert Frost,* the concluding chapter of which is the last selection in this volume. As Lynen sees it, Frost's poetry does have a coherent myth—a myth of New England expressed through a pastoral structure in which an entire region is evoked through the speech and actions of a character or characters. This structure establishes a duality of vision by constantly implying a comparison between an explicit rural and an implicit urban world. In addition to defining an implicit urban world, the remoteness and calculated simplicity of the rural world transform Frost's New England into a symbolic vista. The extremely stylized voice which creates the scene becomes itself a symbol, its colloquial characteristics immediately suggesting a richly controlled range of associations. In his last chapter, instead of setting Frost against modern poets, Lynen puts him with them and yet demonstrates his clear individuality—showing that though Frost's style seems strangely familiar, the very strangeness of that familiarity reflects the genuinely new thought which the poetry embodies. To support his argument, Lynen gives a fine analysis of Frost's "Beech," comparing it to a sonnet by Dylan Thomas and showing the peculiarly modern characteristics of each poem.

It is no coincidence that Nitchie and Lynen should publish in the same year studies which arrive at almost precisely opposite estimates of Frost. In the light of the preceding selections it is clear that a generation of criticism has contributed to the formation as well as substance of their arguments. This does not mean that their conclusions are mere summaries of preceding discoveries. Instead, their work seems to be a fulfillment—a completion—of the dominant tendencies in the criticism which preceded them. Reading their concluding chapters, one is able to see what the second stage of Frost criticism has accomplished and what remains to be done.

IV

If the first phase of Frost criticism was rightly termed the recognition, the second can with equal precision be called the appraisal and acceptance of Robert Frost as a modern poet. Nitchie and Lynen are saying very different things in their conclusions, but they are doing the same thing: they are estimating Frost's stature in relation to modern poetry. They treat Frost's poetry as if it were a body of work deserving the same patient attention which has long been accorded Yeats, Eliot, Pound, and Stevens. In brief, they accept Frost as a modern poet and appraise his work accordingly. The very seriousness of Nitchie's effort to define Frost's limitations is a greater recognition of and compliment to Frost's poetic stature than many a perfunctory hymn of praise.

As a matter of fact, the history of Frost criticism is part of Frost's identity. The criticism and the poetry mutually define each other. In the case of Eliot and modern poetry in general, criticism began with interpretation largely because this was the requirement the poetry placed upon the reader. Explanation and paraphrase became so much a part of modern criticism precisely because, in the absence of literal statement and logical syntax, reconstruction of the "meaning" of the poem became imperative. Despite critical insistence that paraphrase is a "heresy" and that a poem "must not mean but be," the chief irony of modern criticism lies in the fact that it interprets, explains, allegorizes, and paraphrases more than any literary criticism in English history. Frost's poetry, however, invariably produces a different critical response. Basically narrative and dramatic in structure, his poems seem astonishingly clear at first encounter, so clear that the two aspects of his form which always invite attention are the speaker and his "story." It was almost inevitable that early criticism should have been drawn to Frost's "personality" to the extent of ignoring his art, whereas later criticism has been almost exclusively concerned with disclosing Frost's "thought."

If Eliot criticism began with attention to form and meaning, criticism of Frost is going to end there. The pressure for interpretation is beginning to be felt, as the steadily accumulating explications of particular poems attest, yet Lynen's book is the first extended study whose argument is advanced by a series of analyses of individual poems. Here again an aspect of Frost's identity helps to account for the delay.

Where Eliot's poems mark crises and turning points in the development of his career—the critic goes instinctively to *The Waste Land,* then to *Ash Wednesday,* and on to *Four Quartets* to chart the poet's progress and direction—Frost has no crises, no turning points, and no apparent center. His long poems seem no more important than his short ones, and it is hardly an accident that his most explicated poem is "Stopping by Woods on a Snowy Evening." Explication as a means of approach to a career so atomically structured seems at first glance to offer nothing more than a series of endlessly repeated exercises.

Yet much rigorous analysis will be required before the full nature of Frost's achievement begins to emerge. A close look at a neglected poem such as "Putting in the Seed" will reveal something of the Frost who is yet to be discovered:

> You come to fetch me from my work to-night
> When supper's on the table, and we'll see
> If I can leave off burying the white
> Soft petals fallen from the apple tree
> (Soft petals, yes, but not so barren quite,
> Mingled with these, smooth bean and wrinkled pea;)
> And go along with you ere you lose sight
> Of what you came for and become like me,
> Slave to a springtime passion for the earth.
> How Love burns through the Putting in the Seed
> On through the watching for that early birth
> When, just as the soil tarnishes with weed,
> The sturdy seedling with arched body comes
> Shouldering its way and shedding the earth crumbs.

Many readers have no doubt grasped the poem without realizing how much they held. How many have noticed, for example, that it is a combination of Shakespearean sonnet and dramatic monologue? To see this is to begin to comprehend how the poem is a complete fusion of form and action. The very power of the poem lies in the way the speaker's colloquial idiom, working casually and unostentatiously through two traditional structures to seize upon the most primal passion, recapitulates his action of incidentally converting barren apple blossoms into a substance enriching and nourishing the seeds he plants. This wedding results in a renewal of form—a daring extension of the sonnet's range into social and physical regions which the traditional love sonnet did not begin to touch. This renewal is nothing less than a revolution—a revolution so quiet that the reader hears only the sound of a new voice in the poetry, a revolution so clear that the reader cannot realize the radical way in which poetic experience has been reorganized.

The foregoing remarks are offered not as a "reading" of the poem—they do not begin to touch its full complexity—but as a preliminary attempt to define the relationship which Frost's poetry establishes with the reader. There is first the encounter and recognition, in which the poem is casually grasped; the easy familiarity of language and action are the invitation constituting the premise of the relationship, and it is hardly accidental that Frost should have prefaced his *Complete Poems* with the invitational lyric "The Pasture." The second phase of the relationship, particularly for a reader familiar with modern poetry, is likely to be an uncertainty about the significance of the poem. Lacking any ambiguity, the poem seems to obscure its art behind the baldness of its statement. Certainly there seems little reason to "interpret" so straightforward a poem, and a reader trained to deal with Eliot or Stevens understandably might have to convince himself that the poem had any "depth" or newness. But in the final stage of the relationship—reached after the poem has been casually passed over or cursorily read a dozen times—the reader discovers with surprise how totally organized the experience of the poem has been. Only then does he perceive the masterful control which carries the poem from the absolutely colloquial idiom and action of the first two lines through the fanciful mingling of blossom and seed on to the point where, in the tenth line, the action becomes a pure figure.

Criticism of Frost has accomplished only the first two stages of the relationship: recognition and acceptance. It has at last arrived at the threshold of the third, the phase of understanding and full discovery. It will enter, for the poetry will make its way and create the third stage of criticism. Though it is impossible to anticipate exactly the discoveries and evaluations of the coming phase, it may not be impossible to anticipate its general direction.

A serious study of Frost's poetry will, I believe, discover how much its structure emerges in terms of a central character—the poetic figure of Robert Frost. This character cannot redefine himself, cannot really change; if he could he would cease to be a "character." In a letter to Elizabeth Shepley Sergeant, Frost set forth the nature of his personality:

The one thing I boast I can't be, is disillusioned. Anything I ever thought I still think. Any poet I ever liked I still like. It is noticeable, I go back on no one. It is merely that others go back on me. I take nothing back. I don't even grow. My favorite theory is that we are given this speed swifter than any stream of light time or water for the sole purpose of standing still like a water beetle in any stream of light time or water off any shore we please.

Unable to change, the character emerges into the light, revealing aspects of himself which were really there all the time. There are no creations of new worlds, only discoveries of land that has been known but forgotten. Thus in writing a poem, the poet is remembering what he didn't know he knew.

Discovery and definition of this character will actually mean a careful study of all aspects of the poetry in a new light—for all aspects will be the related "characteristics" which describe the character at the center and create the powerful illusion of his existence. Indeed, Frost the public figure may come to seem more the creature than the creator of the poetry, a "sayer" demanded by poems which create the illusion of a spoken language. And the wisdom, or "thought," of the poetry, which is at turns enigmatic, oracular, and platitudinous, will be treated as part of the character's style, not separately as a body of truth or philosophy. It is worth noting here that Lynen's book is the first study which begins to establish any kind of dynamic touch with Frost's style and structure. Past critics have been content to drop little more than a few remarks about the speech of New England.

With a fuller understanding of the central character, the comic dimension of Frost's genius should receive genuine critical attention. The "character" by his very nature tends toward comic rather than tragic development; for if he becomes tragic he would have to incline toward recognition scenes, self-discovery, and commitment to transcendent reality. Frost, however, has clearly moved toward comedy and wit—from lyric through narrative toward satire, and finally to masque. Failure to recognize Frost's comic genius has resulted in criticism which laments his failure to realize the "tragic" potentiality of *North of Boston,* or which dismisses the whole comic machinery of Frost's art by indiscriminate use of the term "whimsy." Actually, Frost's much deplored whimsy is a kind of characteristic poetic fancy by means of which the character, rejecting the transcendental machinery of his New England predecessors, projects his consciousness into nature.

Finally, Frost's enigmatic skepticism will emerge as the character's style of belief, for it is actually a tendency toward cautious skepticism which makes everything the character does and thinks contribute not to any substance or reality outside himself but to the constant enlargement of his own reality. Thus has Frost the man been remarkably assimilated into the figure of Frost the poet; the two are inseparably wedded to create the character—the living body—of the poetry. In the world of the poetry, man and poet and poem are one. The grand design reveals the poet saying poems; his poetry is the *play* which he cannot help performing. It is the myth of Robert Frost.

Robert Frost's
Theory of Poetry

by Lawrance Thompson

A poem begins with a lump in the throat; a home-sickness or a love-sickness. It is a reaching-out toward expression; an effort to find fulfilment. A complete poem is one where an emotion has found its thought and the thought has found the words. . . . My definition of poetry (if I were forced to give one) would be this: words that have become deeds.[1]

(Robert Frost)

In a literary age made nervous by the tugging conflicts of factions, Robert Frost has been able to win the admiration and respect of opposed individuals even while he has stoutly refused to take sides in the controversies. Almost miraculously he has moved about in the conflagration unscathed—like one of those figures in the fiery furnace. A glance at his sojourn among poets will reveal the paradox of his friendships. Before the turn of the century his early verse was praised by Richard Hovey; before the first World War, he had earned and returned the warm affections of such English poets as Edward Thomas, W. W. Gibson, and Lascelles Abercrombie. In 1913 that American renegade in London, Ezra Pound, had sent to his countrymen an enthusiastic review of *North of Boston*—and Harriet Monroe printed it in *Poetry*. Returning home, Frost found that he had been praised warmly in an early issue of the *New Republic* by Amy Lowell, leader of the free-verse Imagists. More understandably, Edwin Arlington Robinson sent a letter of rich praise in 1917. Poets so diverse in method as Ransom, MacLeish, and Hillyer revealed their obligation to Frost's poetry in their early work.

"Robert Frost's Theory of Poetry," from *Fire and Ice: The Art and Thought of Robert Frost* by Lawrence Thompson. Copyright, 1942, by Holt, Rinehart and Winston, Inc. Reprinted by permission of Holt, Rinehart and Winston, Inc. *Fire and Ice* has been recently reprinted by Russell & Russell, Inc.

[1] Robert Frost's definitions of poetry, printed on the dust jacket of *West-Running Brook* (New York: Holt, Rinehart & Winston, Inc., 1929).

And in 1936 an English edition of his *Selected Poems* was issued with introductory essays by a curious foursome: W. H. Auden, C. Day Lewis, Paul Engle, and Edwin Muri. The secret of Frost's wide appeal seems to have been that his poetry, from the beginning, caught fresh vitality without recourse to the fads and limitations of modern experimental techniques.

The problem of the experimentalists was to determine how free poetry should be if it were to escape the threadbare conventionalism of an outworn tradition. Naturally the emphasis was on new forms, in this declaration of poetic independence, for freedom of the poet's material has always existed, together with certain abiding limitations of the poet's method. Frost carried on his own distinct experiments, emphasizing speech rhythms and "the sound of sense." He has called attention to "those dramatic tones of voice which had hitherto constituted the better half of poetry." In Frost's theory of poetry, the self-imposed restrictions of meter in form and of coherence in content stand not halfway down the scale of grace. He has made many casual references to the general quality of those limitations which work to the advantage, not to the disadvantage, of new and lively poetry.

The restrictions of the experimentalists, ironically seeking liberation, have amused Frost. With pleasant banter he has teased his contemporaries by jesting about their desperate "quest for new ways to be new." Behold the fantastic variety of restrictions in their freedom, he said: "Poetry, for example, was tried without punctuation. It was tried without capital letters. It was tried without any image but those to the eye. . . . It was tried without content under the trade name of poesie pure. It was tried without phrase, epigram, coherence, logic and consistency. It was tried without ability. . . . It was tried premature like the delicacy of unborn calf in Asia. It was tried without feeling or sentiment like murder for small pay in the underworld. These many things was it tried without, and what had we left? Still something." [2]

There were other kinds of restrictions which amused Frost, such as those of overemphasis. Perhaps poetry could be used to purge the world of wickedness and bring heaven down to earth in the form of an international brotherhood. This was a shift of emphasis from one type of pure poetry to another type of pure poetry! Frost offered his own anecdote for comment:

"I had it from one of the youngest lately: 'Whereas we once thought literature should be without content, we now know it should be charged

[2] Robert Frost's introduction to Edwin Arlington Robinson's posthumous *King Jasper* (Toronto: The Macmillan Company, 1935).

full of propaganda.' Wrong twice, I told him. Wrong twice and of theory
prepense. But he returned to his position after a moment out for
reassembly: 'Surely art can be considered good only as it prompts to action.'
How soon? I asked him. But there is danger of undue levity in teasing
the young. . . . We must be very tender of our dreamers. They may seem
like picketers, or members of the committee on rules, for the moment.
We shan't mind what they seem, if only they produce real poems." [3]

The restrictions which Frost accepts in his theory of poetry save him
from the dangers of two extremes: nothing of content (pure art) and
nothing except content (pure preaching). He is also unsympathetic with
those who think they may set up as goals of perfection the expression of
thought or emotion in the form of abstractions: sound merely for the
sake of sound, or inner agitation which becomes wildness with nothing
important enough to be wild about. The danger of this last experiment,
he says, is that "we bring up as aberrationists, giving way to undirected
associations and kicking ourselves from one chance suggestion to another
in all directions as of a hot afternoon in the life of a grasshopper." [4] So
much for those who have imitated that beauty of free association in
thought or emotion which the impressionistic Symbolists established as
a fad in poetry. Furthermore, Frost hates to see poets use their medium
as a vehicle for shrieking frustration and disgust. Grievances he would
willingly restrict to prose, so that poetry might concentrate on griefs, on
"woes, woes immedicable"; might be permitted to go its way in tears.

These, then, are some of the restrictions which Frost considers to be
of false value in poetry, popular as they may have been among the
straining experimentalists. But this process of paring away at the non-
essentials does not bring us in to any kernel, any simple answer which
Frost has as to the nature of poetry. To him the mystery, the wonder, the
virtue, the magic of poetry is its heterogeneity of elements somehow
blended to a single autonomous unit. The problem of the poet is to
achieve this integration, this fusion. The difficulty of calling on a poet
to explain is that we call on him to reverse the process and resort to
deliberate analysis, disintegration, diffusion. Such a task, repugnant to
Frost and to many poets, is left to the analysis of the critics. But the gulf
between integration and analysis is one which criticism has never succeeded in bridging, nor is there much hope that even our specialized
scientific approaches through the terms of psychology, philology, and
metaphysics will bridge the gulf. Fortunately, the hints and observations

---

[3] "Education by Poetry: A Meditative Monologue," given by Robert Frost at
Amherst College; published in the *Amherst Graduates' Quarterly*, XX, No. 2
(February 1931), 75-85.
[4] Frost, "The Figure a Poem Makes."

thrown off by the poets themselves help us to reach across the gulf until the distance is at least reduced.

Form

Refusing to arrange his observations into any kind of systematic theory, Frost has mentioned several specifics and factors which seem to him important. Rejecting the hard and fast boundaries of definition as too dangerous, he has indicated certain elastic principles which seem not only sensible and salutary but also deeply rooted in the experience of poets in any age. Cautiously, he begins by finding the initial impetus of the poet to rise out of intensely perceived experiences which are given expression because of the hunger, the need for expression, in the Emersonian sense of the word. But he qualifies his use of the word "expression" with some care. How dangerous it might be to suppose that the response to the desire for expression should inevitably produce an artistic utterance. There have been some inartistic screams in modern poetry. But to "gape in agony," he says, and to write "huge gobs of raw sincerity bellowing with pain" are obviously kinds of expression which, be they ever so heartfelt, are too formless to be considered as anything other than mere expression. They lack shape.

Form, then, may be said to be the most important characteristic which Frost finds essential to poetry in any age. But the spread of meaning in that very elastic word must be suggested before such a simple statement is understood. For example, we may start with the great variety of stanzaic forms and then break any of them down to the rich formal relationships of rhyme to rhyme, of line to line, of sentence to sentence, of words which talk back and forth to each other in the poem. When we recall that another characteristic of form is balance and equilibrium, or controlled unbalance, we open up entirely new vistas. Furthermore, form in poetry is modulated also by the relation, the balance, of emotion and emotion, of thought and thought, of emotion and thought, of the image and the metaphor, of the specific and the general, of the trivial and the significant, of the transient and the permanent. All these facets appear to Frost as related aspects of that terse but by no means simple word "form."

To give form in poetry is also to employ that intricate method of conveying organization, shapeliness, fitness, to the matter or substance of context or meaning of the poem. Before meaning finds its place in a poem it must become subordinated to its proper balance with structure. And Frost goes further to assert quite bluntly that another requirement of poetry is that this formal fusion of distinct elements shall achieve the personal idiom of the poet's expression without sacrificing that happy correspondence which must exist between his own experience and the experience of those who come after to read or hear the poem.

Such fundamentals are even more complicated than they seem to be. But it is the duty of the lover of poetry to perceive at least the outer aspects of these fundamentals. And those who have tried to explain have sought different ways of getting at the problem. For example, it may be appreciated that modern critics have with good reason rejected the conventional division of poetry into two simple components: form and content. A peculiar interrelationship is disregarded in such arbitrary separation. Out of the fusion grows a quality which is neither form nor content, but somehow a by-product of the fusion. John Crowe Ransom has described this extra quality as "texture" and is willing to call the fusion which produces it "structure." But this new combination of terms helps only slightly to increase our awareness of the complexity in a good poem. For example, none will claim that meaning or content or context has disappeared because it has become integrated as structure. To the contrary, the process should have increased our acuteness in perceiving the overtones of meaning enriched by the position of meaning in the structure of the poem. Now it happens that many modern poets and critics are willing to assume that meaning, having undergone a peculiar metamorphosis in a poem, is no longer meaning; that it has been translated into something rich and strange. Granted, Frost says, that it has been enriched; still it is meaning. And he is willing to go so far as to say that meaning is the ingredient best able to save poetry from effeteness. He finds variety in poetry more closely allied to many-sidedness of content than to the many-sidedness of form, difficult as it may be to extricate the one from the other in a poem. To me, the odds seem to favor neither the one nor the other. And I believe that Frost's own poetry is at its best when the two elements have become so completely reconciled that they are happily joined in a holy marriage and defy any attempted separation.

The Poetic Impulse

But how does this complicated relationship first begin to take shape? Frost has told us something of his own personal experience as it concerns the genesis, the working out of a poem. Again and again he has said that there is a striking analogy between the course of a true poem and of a true love. Each begins as an impulse, a disturbing excitement to which the individual surrenders himself. "No one can really hold that the ecstasy should be static and stand still in one place. It begins in delight, it inclines to the impulse, it assumes direction with the first line laid down, it runs a course of lucky events, and ends in a clarification of life—not necessarily a great clarification, such as sects and cults are founded on, but in a momentary stay against confusion. It has denouement. It has an outcome that though unforeseen was predestined from the first image of the original mood—and indeed from the very mood. . . . It finds its own name as it goes and discovers the best waiting for it in some final phrase at once wise and sad—the happy-sad blend of the drinking song." [5]

In this aspect of the poet's intent, Frost implies that he finds himself impelled forward as if by faith, so that the poem is somehow believed into existence. "The beauty, the something, the little charm of the thing to be, is more felt than known." As for the source of that initial impetus, he finds it growing out of a flash of recognition; a fresh perception. But there is another kind of recognition which might be called a correlation. Somehow it amounts to a new awareness of self. The present moment serves as a fulminating agent which fires experience lost in the dark of memory and causes that experience to burst into flame. This accident, producing an emotional intensity, might be described as an act which projects the past into the future. Frost has his own striking analogy:

"For me the initial delight is in the surprise of remembering something I didn't know I knew. I am in a place, in a situation, as if I had materialized from a cloud or risen out of the ground. There is a glad recognition of the long lost and the rest follows. Step by step the wonder of unexpected supply keeps growing. The impressions most useful to my purpose seem always those I was unaware of and so made no note of at the time when taken, and the conclusion is come to that like giants we are always hurling experience ahead of us to pave the future with against the day when we may want to strike a line of purpose across it for somewhere." [6]

This kind of inspiration is in no way related to what Wordsworth had in mind when he referred to "emotion recollected in tranquillity." It is more closely related to the recognition-scene, so long a source of surprise and emotional tension in dramatic narratives. In a peculiar sense, the poet's fresh recognition creates an emotional crisis. He is impelled to find release from that crisis—and the resolution of it is the poem.

Frost implies that there are two kinds of recognition which he has experienced as one part of the poetic impulse; two different ways in which this sense of interplay between the past and the present is first motivated and finally resolved in the form of a poem. The first way occurs

[5] *Ibid.*
[6] *Ibid.*

when some experience in the present inspires an emotional recognition that is more a matter of sense impression than of clear mental perception. The emotional tension—the lump in the throat—which is established through such a recognition, impels the poet into the physical act of recording in poetry the details of the immediate moment; the details of that immediate experience which happens to the poet in the physical world, or which is happened upon by the poet in the nonphysical world of his own reverie. Uncertain as to the precise nature of this sudden meeting between past experience and present experience, the poet ventures into the recording of the moment, the capturing of the incident. He proceeds with this recording as an act of faith, without foreseeing the outcome. And as this emotional tension finds its gradual resolution in the poem, the emotion finds its thought. In other words, the mental recognition of meaning in this emotional experience gradually asserts itself on a new plane of metaphorical reference. It may find its expression in a stated simile or it may find its expression merely through that which is implied or suggested.

This first kind of recognition which Frost suggests, as a part of his poetic impulse, may be demonstrated by examining a single poem. The more easily understood the poem may be, the better are the chances of making it serve as an illustration here. For that reason I choose the graceful and familiar "Stopping by Woods on a Snowy Evening." In fair warning, I must confess that I do not know the story as to how Robert Frost happened to write this poem. But my guess, even if it should prove wrong in specific details, may still have validity as a general illustration of that process which I am trying to clarify. The poem is a dramatic lyric which breaks into the middle of an incident, so that there is a drama-in-miniature revealed with setting and lighting and actors and properties complete. At the beginning, the reader finds the curtain going up on a little action which approaches the climax of an experience, real or imagined; that is, an experience which happened to the poet or one which came to the mind of the poet as possible. A rural traveler is the actor whose brief soliloquy describes the circumstances under which he has stopped his horse-drawn sleigh to enjoy, in spite of cold and loneliness, the strange beauty of white snowflakes falling against a background of dark trees. There are many reasons why he should not stop; common-sense reasons which seem to occur even to the traveler's little horse. But the spell of the moment is so strong that the traveler is reluctant to leave, regardless of the winter night and the cold storm. He is impelled to move on by the realization of duties and distances; those "promises" which he must keep and the "miles to go" before he completes his journey. Thus the poem ends, and the images which crowd the statements are direct and unmistakable. Where, in such lines, does the emotional tension resolve itself into the mental focus of a metaphor? If this simple little poem is to be considered as one in which the resolution suggests two planes of reference, the reader must be made aware of words and images which face two ways at once. Considered from the viewpoint of the poetic impulse, it is quite probable that the poet, impelled emotionally to record this real or imagined experience, did not immediately see in it any metaphorical correspondence between the sight of the moment and the insight of the past-in-the-present. Yet a correspondence appears with dramatic clarity in the final stanza. The reader is aware of more than one possible meaning for such words as "promises" and "miles" and "sleep." And it is probable that the poet also came upon these words with a conscious perception and recognition of a rational focus which grew out of this moment first felt vaguely and emotionally in the form of an inner tension. Almost with a sense of surprise the poet may have found a second plane of reference which gave deeper importance to the little incident which became the poem. But Frost's characteristic reticence and shyness, a part of his New England heritage, led him to be satisfied with those three words which suggest, without explanation or elaboration, the rationally perceived focus of this correspondence.

Each reader has no difficulty in making an elaboration from this implied metaphor. In the poem, the specific incident has completely displaced the general analogy. If a reader is satisfied to settle for the specific as satisfactory in itself, there is nothing to hinder him from so doing. On the other hand, if he wishes to continue with the extensions of the metaphor, there is nothing to hinder him from that added pleasure. The most obvious correspondence would suggest the analogy between the specific experience of the rural traveler and the general experience of any individual whose life is so frequently described as a journey; a journey including pleasures and hardships, duties and distances. In the light of such analogies, the other images offer correspondences which are valid. There is even a slightly tragic implication suggested by "the coldest evening of the year." Yet within this bitter cold occurs an elementary revelation of beauty which lays claim on us as existing nowhere else. Regardless of the dark and cold, we are prone to tarry quite irrationally because of this paradoxically somber excitement and recompense. The reluctance to leave becomes an expression of the endless hunger for holding and making permanent a dark moment of pleasurable discovery in a transient experience. But we are impelled forward and away by other and inevitable commitments. There are the "promises" which we have made to ourselves and to others, or which others have made for us. And there are the "miles" we must travel through other kinds of experience before we yield to that final and inevitable commitment: sleep in death.

I am well aware that this kind of metaphorical extension is distasteful to some, and is frequently branded by others as impressionistic nonsense. I am equally sure that any poet who uses metaphors with the deliberate purpose of suggesting more than is stated offers his readers, through the very nature of his method, the freedom to read the poem on as many different planes of reference as may be discovered. The only restriction is that such induced correspondences must not be made if they invalidate the initial relationship of the specifics to each other. The rules of the game are as old as poetry. Children derive much pleasure from playing with those square boxes of different sizes which may be put together, one inside another, until they are contained within a single block. They may be treated without imagination as a single block, but the pleasure begins when they are telescoped outward. In a restricted sense, the pleasure derived from opening up a metaphor may be compared to the pleasure derived from opening up that single block which has so many proportionate identities hidden within it.

I have said that Frost implies a second kind of recognition which he has experienced in the poetic impulse. The second occurs when the emotional pleasure is derived from the sudden mental perception of a thought which comes into sharp focus through the discovery and recognition of a particularly apt correspondence or analogy. The difference between these two approaches to the writing of a poem should be clear. The first begins as an emotional response which gradually finds its resolution in a thought metaphorically expressed; the second begins with the perception of the metaphor, and the rational focus is so pleasurable in its sudden discovery that it produces an emotional afterglow. The first leads the poet to venture into the writing of the poem as an act of faith, without foreseeing the outcome; the second leads the poet to give shape and weight to a rational correspondence which has been perceived clearly before he begins the writing of the poem. Nevertheless, Frost is fond of handling each of these by letting the specific displace the general until the analogy is implied or stated as a kind of climax to the poem.

In selecting an illustration for this second process, I again venture a guess. For reasons which may become clear before I finish, I am willing to suppose that one poem written in this second manner is that entitled "For Once, Then, Something." Here also is a dramatic lyric, with its single actor unfolding, through his brief monologue, a setting which builds directly to a climactic moment. At the beginning, there is an implied reference to other actors who may be considered collectively as the antagonists. Before we go further, let us imagine the manner in which the poet's thoughts may have led him to recognize in the action of this moment the apt incident or metaphor which brought a sense of pleasurable response and emotional tension. Those who have examined Frost's poetry with care are familiar with his increasing fondness for metaphors which make use (or fun) of concepts and problems in systematic philosophy. His own middle-ground position permits him to control an ingrained skepticism in such a manner as to deal playfully with the extremes of affirmation and denial. He has frequently suggested that he is particularly wary of hydra-headed Platonic idealism and of all those glorious risks taken by any who boldly arrive at transcendental definitions. Pleasantly scornful of those who assume too much as to the extent and validity of human knowledge, Frost tells us, he has often shared the longing which inspires philosophers to project their systems beyond the realms of the known and the knowable. He has never grown tired in his own cautious search for truth, yet he has never been tempted to believe that absolute truth could be defined satisfactorily even by the most profound philosophic systems. As he says in his poem entitled "Neither Out Far Nor In Deep," we all will continue forever to watch and hope, "wherever the truth may be." In *A Witness Tree,* he sums up the persistent attempt to resolve the inscrutable, thus:

> We dance round in a ring and suppose,
> But the Secret sits in the middle and knows.

"For Once, Then, Something" is the record of an incident which pleased Frost, apparently, as a happy analogy which might serve to state the paradox between his own watchfulness and his own skepticism. Obviously, the poem is so nicely constructed that the reader may enjoy it on a single plane of reference, without any concern for the epistemological implications. But my supposition is that Frost's experience happened to bring the analogy into sharp focus with his lifelong accumulation of prejudices concerning the extent and validity of knowledge; that he deliberately prepared the incident for interpretation on an epistemological plan of reference, by using one word which is so obviously placed that it stands out like a sore thumb. Here is the poem, complete:

> Others taunt me with having knelt at well-curbs
> Always wrong to the light, so never seeing
> Deeper down in the well than where the water
> Gives me back in a shining surface picture

Me myself in the summer heaven godlike
Looking out of a wreath of fern and cloud puffs.
Once, when trying with chin against a well-curb,
I discerned, as I thought, beyond the picture,
Through the picture, a something white, uncertain,
Something more of the depths—and then I lost it.
Water came to rebuke the too clear water.
One drop fell from a fern, and lo, a ripple
Shook whatever it was lay there at bottom,
Blurred it, blotted it out. What was that whiteness?
Truth? A pebble of quartz? For once, then, something.

As soon as that naked word "Truth?" asserts itself with whimsical and teasing boldness at the beginning of the final line, the reader is made aware of a new kind of game. One may enjoy trying to examine the bottom of a well through water, but only a poet would look there for truth. So the reader turns back to the beginning of the poem to examine the images and phrases in the light of that single word. Do the images corroborate the implication of such a brazen hint? The first line immediately becomes an oblique reference to the long-standing quarrel between the speaker as a skeptical relativist and his antagonists as believing absolutists. Next we come to the nature of the taunt: the speaker has been ridiculed as an egocentric who can do no better than perceive the absolute being as the reflection of his own not-too-pathetic human image. Then a further correspondence is suggested between the specific search below the surface of the well-water and the general search below the surface of human experience for some meaning which will satisfy human yearnings for certainty. Having perceived this general connotation, the reader finds an easy addition in the description of the speaker who is also taunted by his more idealistic, possibly religious, friends because he has hindered his own search by taking his position "always wrong to the light"—and suddenly the religious extensions of the word "light" fall naturally into the pattern of this second plane. Once, however, the poet humorously suggests that his endeavor seemed to permit a passing glimpse of something. Perhaps he had caught sight of the hidden mystery itself. But too soon the spell was broken by a seemingly deliberate accident and a rebuke. It seemed as though there might be some intelligence which intended that this human being and others should never have more than a glimpse.

Thus the incident of the traveler in the snowy woods and of the spectator peering down into a well are two examples which help to explain Frost's remarks concerning his own experience in analyzing that mysterious process which has to do with the poetic impulse. Wordsworth took pleasure in turning from the present to find an emotional excitement and inspiration in happy memories of the past. Paradoxically, Wordsworth's pursuit of ultimate reality in the impulses from a vernal wood became a form of escape from the unpleasantness of the momentary and transient actuality. Frost's method is diametrically opposed. He takes pleasure in ignoring the ultimate reality of the philosophic and religious absolute; takes pleasure even in turning his back on the past, until a momentary experience is illuminated with richer value by that which his past experience accidentally brings to the present. And Frost's quest of the present moment as the greatest reality becomes a pursuit in the Emersonian sense; it becomes implicit with newly perceived aspects of an evident design in the universe. Always, the past cuts across the present moment to reveal and illuminate the moment by transforming it into a metaphor which has for him beauty and meaning. It may be valuable to reconsider his own statement here:

"For me the initial delight is in the surprise of remembering something I didn't know I knew. I am in a place, in a situation, as if I had materialized from a cloud or risen out of the ground. There is a glad recognition of the long lost and the rest follows. Step by step the wonder of unexpected supply keeps growing. The impressions most useful to my purpose seem always those I was unaware of and so made no note at the time when taken, and the conclusion is come to that like giants we are always hurling experience ahead of us to pave the future with against the day when we may want to strike a line of purpose across it for somewhere."

But in the process of that resolution from the moment of poetic impulse to the final completion of the poem, there arises the persistent need for cunning and artistry. Frost does not imply that the poem writes itself. The poet must establish a careful balance between the personal intimacy of the experience and the separation of the experience through statement which gains perspective without loss of intensity. The thoughtful statement of the relationship between the present experience and the remembered experience balances the emotion. Equilibrium is truly a large part of what is meant by artistry. "Keeping the thing in motion," Frost has said, "is sometimes like walking a rolling barrel." Again he feels it analogous to riding an untamed horse: "The great pleasure in writing poetry is in having been carried off. It is as if you stood astride of the subject that lay on the ground, and they cut the cord, and the subject gets up under you and you ride it. You adjust yourself to the motion of the thing itself. That is the poem." [7]

---

[7] "The Poet's Next of Kin in a College," a talk given by Robert Frost at Princeton University on October 26, 1937; published in *Biblia*, IX, No. I (February 1938).

Accidentally, a poet may lose one kind of equilibrium, fall off, and continue his journey to the end of the poem in a truly pedestrian fashion. Then the critical reader becomes painfully aware of the accident and is able to point out the place: "This is where he fell off." To Frost this loss of balance was a part of what Poe meant when he said that there was no such thing as a long poem; that he could show any reader of a long poem where the rider fell, and how far he limped before he again managed to climb astride his Pegasus.

There is a pertinent paradox in the poet's craving for the intimacy of experience which gives insight and, at the same time, his longing for separation which permits objectivity and perspective. As a part of the poet's preparation, Frost has often hinted at this problem. The dark woods seem to become a symbol of that withdrawal from life for the sake of clarification. The first poem in his first book, "Into My Own," sang the yearning for lostness in "dark trees" that "stretched away unto the edge of doom," because such lostness would lead to self-discovery. One might not do violence to "Birches" by discovering in the final passage a reflection of the poetic hunger for withdrawal which might permit swift and exciting return, with grace and without effort, to a new sense of life:

> I'd like to get away from earth awhile
>
> .   .   .   .
>
> And climb black branches up a snow-white trunk
> *Toward* heaven, till the tree could bear no more,
> But dipped its top and set me down again.
> That would be good both going and coming back.

In the response to poetic materials and poetic insight the deliberate and conscious craftsmanship must be combined with a sense of surrender to the material which has been possessed. "You adjust yourself to the motion of the thing itself." The muscular assertiveness of the will defeats its own purpose. The poet as rider finds his curious animal to be tender-mouthed. Or it might be said that the poem which succeeds has the casual grace of the dancer completely responsive to the rhythm of the music and concerned only with an almost reflexive expression of the emotion thus inspired. The shrewdness of the poet is to remain true to the mood and true to the material at the same time. We may not like Plato's metaphor of the perfect image concealed in the untouched block of marble. But in the nature of poetic response to a moment and situation in time and space, the poet is responsible in a strange way to elements which he may distort only at the peril of destruction and loss. I find a happy analogy, regardless of the original intent, tucked away at the heart of Frost's poem, "The Ax-Helve":

> He showed me that the lines of a good helve
> Were native to the grain before the knife
> Expressed them, and its curves were no false curves
> Put on it from without. And there its strength lay. . . .

So the perfection of the poem arises out of the poet's pleasure in discovering words, images, metaphors, phrases, "native to the grain" of the emotion, the thought, the situation.

There is a peculiar satisfaction which Frost finds from the ultimate resolution, release, or completion of a poem. Out of the chaotic confusion of daily impressions and thoughts the poet captures a moment with his words and achieves a kind of crystallization which gives to his chaotic raw materials not only shape but weight. And this metamorphosis creates that sense of stability which Frost refers to when he speaks of "a momentary stay against confusion." His poem "West-running Brook," which furnished the title for his fifth book, is built around an elaborate metaphor which has a particularly happy connotation if one interperts it in the light of the poet's intent. The metaphor is built around the image of one wave which rides forever above a sunken rock: permanence in transience. "The stream of everything that runs away" is able to create the illusion, but only the illusion, of "not gaining but not losing" because of the black water "flung backward on itself in one white wave." It suggests to the poet the analogy of existence:

> And it is time, strength, tone, light, life and love—
> And even substance lapsing unsubstantial;
> The universal cataract of death
> That spends to nothingness—and unresisted,
> Save by some strange resistance in itself,
> Not just a swerving, but a throwing back,
> As if regret were in it and were sacred.
> It has this throwing backward on itself
> So that the fall of most of it is always
> Raising a little, sending up a little.

We may go on to play the age-old game of analogies and say that the poet's hunger for creating a sense of stability and of crystallization from the flux of things has in it a sacred regret of its own—and a sense of triumph in his accomplishment, for this very reason. From the viewpoint of the artist, Frost hints that we all know that sense of comfort and pleasure because it is also derived even from the most humble achievement of form in our lives.

Meaning

If we may return a bit, Frost's image of experience hurled into the future, as if by intuitive foreknowledge of the eventual need, is very closely related in spirit to Emerson's theory of poetry. The flash of recognition is a happy response to that union of impressions present and past. But the gradual elaboration of the thing felt with delight leads naturally to a statement of the larger understanding, the half-sad, half-happy wisdom of the conclusion. In quite a different context of associations, Emerson once spoke of the way in which the thoughts of the present gave to the thoughts of the past a new arrangement in the mind of the perceptive individual, so that the utterance was fresh. He continued: "It came into him life; it went out from him truth. It came to him short-lived actions; it went out from him immortal thoughts. It came to him business; it went from him poetry. It was dead fact; now, it is quick thought. It can stand, and it can go. It now endures, it now flies, it now inspires. Precisely in proportion to the depth of mind from which it issued, so high does it soar, so long does it sing."

We may recognize a further relationship between the theories of Emerson and Frost. One speaks of dead fact becoming quick thought; the other speaks of a "clarification of life" which grows out of poetry. We are back to the problem of meaning, and of its importance to the poem. Is meaning in a poem a means to an end or is it an end in itself? Each would say that there is no pat answer to such a question. There are several different planes of thought on which the question may be considered. On the first plane, each would say that beauty is its own excuse for being; that the delight is the goal. On a higher plane, there is a new by-product analogous to that which is created when the material merges with the shape the poem gives it. There is a difference between making poetry a means to an end and in finding, at the conclusion of a poem, that something more than pleasurable emotion has been created. I am convinced that both Frost and Emerson have sometimes confused these differences in their own poems, but I am sure that in theory their awareness of the difference is demonstrable. On this higher plane of reference, there is a pleasure which arises from a deeper understanding. Let the poem start and finish ever so playfully; it will touch and illuminate experience. Robinson put it thus:

The games we play
To fill the frittered minutes of a day
Good glasses are to read the spirit through.

The little game, the poem, is in no sense a picture of life as it actually exists. It is not a key to the poet's philosophy of life. It is more closely akin to a momentary glimpse which is at once a distillation and an elaboration of a moment. Yet somehow in the preservation of that transience the poet touches on the permanent. Relationships are the essence of metaphor and of poetry to Frost. And Emerson calls the poet "the Sayer" not only because he is namer of beauty but also because he is "a perceiver and dear lover of the harmonies that are in the soul and in matter—and specially of the correspondences between these and those."

The first concern of the poet is with that substance which he wishes to express. And he must have enough drive in an emotional sense to encompass and relate the parts. If he is able to possess his material with an intensity which gives artistic validity to the material, he may then take pleasure in the shapeliness of the poem, the autonomousness of the creation. In that shapeliness is its excuse for being. But this does not inhibit either artist or reader from finding another kind of pleasure in the meaning.

Because a poem subordinates meaning to its proper balance in structure, one is not able to test the validity of a poem's morality by the standards either of religious creeds or of scientific fact. What may be true for a poem may be false when tested by the average rules of good conduct. For example, Eliot's ironic poem "The Hollow Men" may outlast all his other poems. It is an excellent poetic epitome of pessimism and disillusionment. As such, it has its own validity, its own truth, its own morality, even though its meaning is plainly opposed to the idealism of Christian morality or to the facts of human nobility and heroism in the face of a tragic world. Quite obviously a poem is able to succeed and have its entity without recourse to these standards. Yet, because the material of poetry is so deeply rooted in life and living, that material inevitably relates itself to, and is colored by, the larger affirmations of human morality. And it would seem to be one characteristic of lasting poetry in any language, in any age, to reaffirm in its independent fashion the various aspects of strength in human courage, human love, human aspiration. Because fear, hatred, despair, and negation are equally aspects of human experience, these also demand their place as materials for poetry.

It is the poet's virtue to develop that insight and wisdom which enable him to recognize and represent the apparent conflict between the constructive and destructive elements, the good and the bad, in nature and in human experience. Those elements, so inextricably related to each other, furnished the basis for dramatic conflict in Greek tragedy. Again, the all-inclusiveness of Shakespeare's insight, with its recognition of the good in the bad, the bad in the good, and triumph of constructive forces only at great cost and waste of good, tallies with our own experience after more than three hundred years, and helps to give his poetry permanence. Obviously, the possession of insight and wisdom in perceiving these spiritual relationships is not enough to create poetry; but it seems to be one of the essentials of lasting poetry. And at the risk of being called didactic in his affirmations, Robert Frost has subscribed to such a general rule, such a limitation if you wish, in the writing of his poetry.

It has been said that "in the high artist, ethics and aesthetics are one." How true—and how dangerous. The test is a familiar one: does the artist handle his ethical and moral observations in such a way as to make them implicit? If he does not, he has failed in a very serious way. Robert Frost's poetry frequently takes that risk, and does not always succeed in keeping the thoughts implicit. When the ethical or the moral content becomes explicit, it threatens to destroy the artistic structure, which may not be strong enough to contain it. Such an accident does not invalidate the ideas or concepts, but it does invalidate the position of these ideas or concepts in a poetic frame. No matter how noble or profound the thought, it fails to justify the shortcomings of intended artistry. There have been few poets who could set out bluntly, like Milton, "to justify the ways of God to man"—and proceed to subordinate, or to keep implicit within the structure of the poem, such an overpowering goal. Most of the Puritans were more bold than talented in their attempts to prove that art is concerned with directing the individual to apprehension; that art is therefore a means to knowledge and truth. It would seem to me that any aesthetic theory which begins by reducing art to a means is doomed to failure; but the double handicap of Puritan theory was that the end, in their eyes, was redemption from human depravity. And such an end was so important to them that the intended balance was often sacrificed almost eagerly!

Robert Frost's poetic theory, quite at odds with Puritan aesthetics, is nevertheless colored by his Yankee heritage of Puritan teaching. His own belief in poetry as "a clarification of life" seems to have close relattion to the ideas of that other New England individualist who was not ashamed to find certain virtues in Puritan concepts, provided they could be inspired with flexible vitality. Emerson said that the poet's creative power was derived from his passionate craving to express the existence of harmonies and correspondences which are discovered between the present and the past, the seen and the unseen, the material and the spiritual. And Frost's personal description of his poetic intent seems closely related to this explicit statement from Emerson:

"For it is not metres, but a metre-making argument that makes a poem,—a thought so passionate and alive that like the spirit of a plant or an animal it has an architecture of its own, and adorns nature with a new thing. The thought and the form are equal in the order of time, but in the order of genesis the thought is prior to the form. The poet has a new thought; he has a whole new experience to unfold; he will tell us how it is with him, and all men will be the richer in his fortune."

But there are nice differences between the Puritan desire to redeem the individual from his human depravity, the Emersonian desire to interpret "harmonies" as proofs of human divinity, and the Frostian desire to make poetry "a clarification of life." The Puritan argument is as debatable as the Emersonian argument. Frost prefers to leave to prose those questions suitable for debate; he finds poetry at its best when its statements and observations touch realms of spiritual values where there is no room for argument: sorrow, aspiration, loneliness, love. Songs are built around everlastingly perceived values which are true for us all. It is not the poet's function to argue that "in Adam's fall we sinnèd all" or that in Christ's death we were all saved. There are still a few of us who consider these as subjects for controversy. And Frost points out that we don't join together in singing an argument. But in human nature there are certain enduring qualities and everlasting truths which permit us to join in hymns of joy or threnodies of sorrow. Let a poem be written on these themes and it will last, says Frost, for "it will forever keep its freshness as a metal keeps its fragrance." So he has generally avoided venturing into poetic argument. Poetry deals with a meaning and truth which may clarify the mingled goodness and badness of life without growing too optimistic over the existence of the one or too pessimistic over the existence of the other. And these overtones of significance, implicit in the poem, are permissible as subject matter for connotation on that higher plane of poetry. This is Frost's answer to those who ask how poetry can become a "clarification of life" without making meaning an end in itself.

The Poem and the Reader

We are now in a better position to consider that aspect of a poem which faces outward to find response from the reader. The poet's aim and purpose represents one plane of the poem; but when he has achieved release from the need which prompted his utterance, the test of the poem has just begun. For the poem, "twice blest," faces not only toward the poet and his intent but also toward the reader and the understanding which the reader brings to it. And the difference between these two planes of reference is obviously the difference between the poet's experience and that artfully limited expression of the poet's experience which is projected in the content of the poem so that it may be shared by the reader. Thus the content must risk the danger of being further restricted by the reader's experience and perceptivity. These determine the degree to which the poem's inherent merit and meaning may be appreciated. Thus considered, the poem is something more than a mere expression of release for the poet; its function is not fulfilled as an autonomous unit if it has merely satisfied the poet. For the poem must be able to establish a basic correspondence between writer and reader. If it fails to contain statement intelligible at least to the intelligent, and intelligible to the degree that there is a common ground in experience for general agreement as to its denotation, then it does not succeed as a poem, no matter how certain the poet may be that his intent is stated. A good example of such failure is Eliot's most famous poem, "The Waste Land," and Eliot acknowledged its failure on this score when he felt obliged to supplement it with his erudite and esoteric footnotes. Such a solution of the problem through the trappings of explanation invalidates the required autonomy of the poem and delivers it immediately into the arms of the snobbish or the academic readers who may keep it limping about on flimsy crutches of praise and elucidation. The simple fact remains: the poem, as such, fails to satisfy the initial requirement of autonomy, regardless of its curiously ingenious pastiche craftsmanship.

But the reader's recognition of correspondence between himself and the poet in that denotation which is essential to autonomy may readily be seen to constitute only the first step in appreciation. It might be called the foundation on which are built higher levels of perception. For it is the nature of poetry to convey or suggest moods and meanings apart from the explicit and recognized meanings. And this difference between that suggested and that stated is the difference between connotation and denotation. Although connotation may be made in several different ways, Robert Frost has concentrated in theory and practice on his two particular favorites: on the tone or sound of words themselves or in their relation to each other—and on the symbolic meaning of words and phrases. To him these seem to be the basic elements in the poetry of any age and remain today the most fecund of the "old ways to be new." The first of these he has elaborated as "the sound of sense," as opposed to the more limited poetic theory concerning the musical sounds. To Frost, as we shall see in the following chapter, this phrase of his tends to deprecate the *merely* musical: the sensuously titillating, at one extreme, or the spiritually moving, at the other extreme. And it will be seen that his theory of "the sound of sense" is quietly antipathetic to that particular attitude toward sound in poetry which was the preoccupation of Poe or to Lanier's theory of musical notation in verse.

The connotation of words and phrases in their double meaning is, of course, related to the age-old poetic use of comparisons, implied or stated. But Frost has developed his theory of the metaphor in a manner peculiar to his poetry. And this development will also be considered at length in a subsequent chapter.

It is essential to remember that these different aspects of poetry which have been considered separately in this analysis of Frost's theory are completely merged in the artistic expression so that they become inseparable parts of the whole. On consideration, the reader may be conscious of the manner in which the content of the poem faces inward toward the poet's experience and outward toward the experience of the reader. And our enjoyment may be heightened by the hints at experiences greater than those which find their way into the poem. This is part of the charm of poetry. But no reader is fair to the poem if he insists on crowding the poet with questions as to what is "back of it." Frost is willing to laugh at anyone "who stands at the end of a poem ready in waiting to catch you by both hands with enthusiasm and drag you off your balance over the last punctuation mark into more than you meant to say." His answer is always ready: "If I had wanted you to know, I should have told you in the poem."

The Case Against Mr. Frost

by Malcolm Cowley

Robert Frost has been heaped with more official and academic honors than any other American poet, living or dead. Although he was never graduated from college, having left Dartmouth after two months and Harvard after two years (and more credit to his dogged independence), he holds by the last count seventeen honorary degrees. He was twice made a Master of Arts (by Amherst and Michigan), three times a Doctor of the Humanities (by Vermont, Wesleyan and St. Lawrence) and twelve times a Doctor of Letters (by Yale, Middlebury, Bowdoin, New Hampshire, Columbia, Williams, Dartmouth, Bates, Pennsylvania, Harvard, Colorado and Princeton). He has been chosen a Phi Beta Kappa poet by Tufts, William and Mary, Harvard (twice) and Columbia. He has been a professor at Amherst; a poet in residence and a fellow in letters at Michigan; a Charles Eliot Norton professor, a Ralph Waldo Emerson fellow and a fellow in American civilization at Harvard, all these being fairly lucrative appointments. He has been awarded four Pulitzer Prizes, one more than E. A. Robinson and two more than Stephen Vincent Benét, the only other poets to be named more than once. He has also received the Loines Prize for poetry, the Mark Twain medal, the gold medal of the National Institute of Arts and Letters and the silver medal of the Poetry Society of America. His work has been the subject of at least two full-length critical studies, many brochures, pamphlets, bibliographies and a memorial volume, *Recognition of Robert Frost,* not to mention hundreds of essays which, some discordant notes in the early years, have ended as a vast diapason of praise.

And Frost deserves all these honors, both for his poetry in itself and for a long career devoted to the art of verse. In a country where poets go to

Malcolm Cowley, "The Case Against Mr. Frost," *The New Republic* (September 11, 1944), pp. 312-13; (September 18, 1944), pp. 345-47. Reprinted by permission of the author and *The New Republic.*

seed, he has kept his talent ready to produce perfect blossoms (together with some that are misshapen or overgrown). It is a pleasure to name over the poems of his youth and age that become more vivid in one's memory with each new reading: the dramatic dialogues like "The Death of the Hired Man" and "The Witch of Coös," besides half a dozen others almost equally good; the descriptions or narrations that turn imperceptibly into Aesop's fables, like "The Grindstone" and "Cow in Apple Time"; and, best of all, the short lyrics like "The Pasture," "Now Close the Windows," "The Sound of the Trees," "Fire and Ice," "Stopping by the Woods on a Snowy Evening" (always a favorite with anthologists), "To Earthward," "Tree at My Window," "Acquainted with the Night," "Neither out Far Nor in Deep," "Beech," "Willful Homing," "Come In" . . . and I could easily add to the list. One of his best lyrics was written in 1892, when Frost was a freshman at Dartmouth; three or four others were included in his latest book, *A Witness Tree,* published just fifty years later; and these recent poems show more skill and density of expression than almost anything he had written before. This same volume and the one that preceded it—*A Further Range,* published in 1936—also contain bad poems that have been almost equally admired: long monologues in pedestrian blank verse, spoken as if from a cracker barrel among the clouds, and doggerel anecdotes directed (or rather, indirected) against the New Deal; but a poet has the right to be judged by his best work, and Frost at his best has added to our little store of authentic poetry.

If in spite of this I still say that there is a case against him and room for a dissenting opinion, perhaps I chiefly mean that there is a case against the zealous admirers who are not content to take the poet for what he is, but insist on using him as a sort of banner for their own moral or political crusades.

We have lately been watching the growth in this country of a narrow nationalism that has spread from politics into literature (although its literary adherents are usually not political isolationists). They demand, however, that American literature should be affirmative, optimistic, uncritical and "truly of this nation." They have been looking round for a poet to exalt; and Frost, through no fault of his own (but chiefly through the weaker qualities of his work), has been adopted as their symbol. Some of the honors heaped on him are less poetic than political. He is being praised too often and with too great vehemence by people who don't like poetry. And the result is that his honors shed very little of their luster on other poets, who in turn feel none of the pride in his achievements that a battalion feels, for example, when one of its officers is cited for outstanding services. Instead Frost is depicted by his admirers as a sort of Sunday-school paragon, a saint among miserable sinners. His common sense and strict Americanism are used as an excuse for berating and belittling other poets, who have supposedly fallen into the sins of pessimism, obscurity, obscenity and yielding to foreign influences; we even hear of their treachery to the American dream. Frost, on the other hand, is depicted as loyal, autochthonous and almost aboriginal. We are told not only that he is "the purest classical poet of America today"—and there is some truth in Gorham B. Munson's early judgment—but also that he is "the one great American poet of our time" and "the only living New Englander in the great tradition, fit to be placed beside Emerson, Hawthorne and Thoreau."

But when Frost is so placed and measured, his stature seems greatly diminished; it is almost as if a tough little Morgan horse, the best of its breed, had been judged by the standards that apply to Clydesdales and Percherons. Height, breadth and strength: he falls short in all these qualities of the great New Englanders. And the other quality for which he is often praised, his utter faithfulness to the New England spirit, is not one of the virtues they knowingly cultivated. They realized that the New England spirit, when it stands alone, is inclined to be narrow and arithmetical. It has reached its finest growth only when cross-fertilized with alien philosophies.

Hinduism, Sufism, Fourierism and German Romanticism: each of these doctrines contributed its own share to the New England renaissance of the 1850's. Even Thoreau, who died almost in sight of his birthplace, said that he had traveled much in Concord; he spoke of bathing his intellect "in the stupendous and cosmogonal philosophy of the Bhagvat-Geeta. . . . The pure Walden water," he said, "is mingled with the sacred water of the Ganges." And Hawthorne, who told us that "New England is quite as large a lump of earth as my heart can really take in," was eager for any new ideas that might help to explain the nature of New Englanders as individuals or as members of society. The books he borrowed from the Salem Athenaeum during the ten lonely years he spent at home included the complete works, in French, of Rousseau, Voltaire (several times), Pascal, Racine (several times) and the "Essais" of Montaigne, as well as a great number of volumes on science, philosophy, general history and the past of New England.[1] Some of his weaker contemporaries were quite unbalanced by the foreign learning with which they overloaded their minds; but the stronger ones assimilated

---

[1] These facts about Hawthorne are taken from F. O. Matthiessen's *American Renaissance* [*American Renaissance:* Art and Expression in the Age of Emerson and Whitman (New York: Oxford University Press, 1941)], a book that has never been sufficiently praised. —M.C.

everything and, in the end, reasserted their own New England natures, which had become immensely richer.

And even Frost, as purely Yankee as his character seems today, was partly formed by his three years abroad. The turning point in his life was when he sold his first New Hampshire farm (which his grandfather had bought for him on condition that he live there at least ten years) and when, in 1912, his wife said, "Let's go to England and live under thatch." In England he made the reputation that enabled him to continue his career as a poet (and also as a "poet in residence"). In England, too, he had the experience of meeting other poets who understood what he was trying to say: Lascelles Abercrombie, Rupert Brooke, Wilfred Wilson Gibson and Edward Thomas. They were willing to learn from him, and Frost, in a sense, learned even more from them: that is, he learned to abandon the conventional language of the Late Victorians and to use his own speech without embarrassment. It is interesting to compare *A Boy's Will*, published in London but written in New Hampshire before his English journey, with "Mountain Interval," published after his return to this country in 1915 but written chiefly in England. The poems in *A Boy's Will* gave his own picture of the world, but in the language of the genteel poets; they were full of "maidens pale," "sweet pangs" and "airy dalliance." The poems written in the English countryside used the language that is spoken north of Boston. Once it had been regarded as a mere dialect only to be used in ballads like "Skipper Ireson's Ride" and in satirical comments like "The Biglow Papers"; but Frost in England had done what Hemingway would later do in Paris: he had raised his own idiom to the dignity of a literary language.

It was after his return that he carried the process further. Having learned to write New Hampshire, he also began to think New Hampshire, in the sense of accepting its older customs as immutable laws. . . .

II

In spite of his achievements as a narrative and lyric poet . . . there is a case against Robert Frost as a social philosopher in verse and as a representative of the New England tradition. He is too much walled in by the past. Unlike the great Yankees of an earlier age, he is opposed to innovations in art, ethics, science, industry or politics. Thus, in one of his longer blank-verse monologues, he bridles when he hears a "New York alec" discussing Freudian psychology, which Frost dismisses as "the new school of the pseudo-phallic." Elsewhere he objects to researches in animal behavior (which he calls "instituting downward comparisons"), to new inventions (saying that ingenuity should be held in check) and

even to the theory of evolution—or at least he ridicules one farmer who
speaks of it admiringly, whereas he sympathizes with another who stops
him on the road to say:

> The trouble with the Mid-Victorians
> Seems to have been a man named John L. Darwin.

New ideas seem worse to him if they come from abroad, and worst
of all if they come from Russia. He is continually declaiming against
the Russians of all categories: the pessimistic Russians, the revolutionary
Russians, the collectivistic Russians, the five-year-planning Russians: he
seems to embrace them all in a global and historical dislike that extends
from Dostoevsky to Dnieperstroy. He is horrified by the thought that
New England might be exposed to the possibility of adopting any good
or bad feature of the Russian program. Thus, after reading about a
project for rural rehabilitation, he hastened to write:

> It is in the news that all these pitiful kin
> Are to be bought out and mercifully gathered in
> To live in villages next to the theatre and store
> Where they won't have to think for themselves any more;
> While greedy good-doers, beneficent beasts of prey,
> Swarm over their lives, enforcing benefits
> That are calculated to soothe them out of their wits,
> And by teaching them how to sleep the sleep all day,
> Destroy their sleeping at night the ancient way.

Sometimes Frost decides that it would be a relief "To put these people
at one stroke out of their pain"—these people being the marginal farmers;
then next day he wonders how it would be if someone offered to put an
end to his own troubles. The upshot is that he proposes to do nothing
whatever, being satisfied with the New England countryside as it is—
or rather, as it was in his early manhood—and outraged by anyone who
tries to improve it.

Yet there are other poems in which he suggests that his faithfulness
to "the ancient way" is more a matter of habit than conviction. In "The
Black Cottage," he remembers an old woman who had lost her husband
in the Civil War and who used to say (in her "quaint phrase," as Frost
calls it) that all men were created free and equal. The old woman was also
an orthodox Christian, and her presence in church kept the minister from
changing any phrases in the Creed. The minister says, recalling "her
old tremulous bonnet in the pew":

> I'm just as glad she made me keep hands off,
> For, dear me, why abandon a belief
> Merely because it ceases to be true.
> Cling to it long enough, and not a doubt
> It will turn true again.

Although the minister is speaking, he seems to express Frost's attitude toward the old New England standards. The poet is more conventional than convinced, more concerned with prudence than with virtue, and very little concerned with sin or suffering; you might say that he is more Puritan, or even prudish, than he is Christian. All the figures in his poems are decently draped; all the love affairs (except in a very late narrative, "The Subverted Flower") are etherealized or intellectualized; and although he sometimes refers to very old adulteries, it is only after they have been wrapped in brown paper and locked away in cupboards. On the other hand, there is little in his work to suggest Christian charity or universal brotherhood under God. He wants us to understand once and for all that he is not his brother's keeper:

> I have none of the tenderer-than-thou
> Collectivistic regimenting love
> With which the modern world is being swept

—and the ancient world was also swept, in the first centuries after Christ. There is one of his narratives, "Two Tramps in Mud Time," that has often been praised for the admirable lesson with which it ends; and yet a professor told me not long ago that his classes always seemed vaguely uncomfortable when they heard it read aloud. It was first published in 1934, and it deals with what seems to have been an incident of the depression years. The poet tells us that he was working in his dooryard on an April day between winter and spring; he was splitting great blocks of straight-grained beech with a lively sense of satisfaction. Two tramps came walking down the muddy road. One of them said, "Hit them hard," and then lingered by the roadside, suggesting wordlessly that he might take the poet's job for pay. The poet assumed that they had spent the winter in a lumber camp, that they were now unemployed and that they had slept "God knows where last night." In life the meeting may have had a different sequel. Perhaps the poet explained to the homeless men that he liked to split his own wood, but that he had other work for them to do; or perhaps he invited them into the kitchen for a slab of home-baked bread spread thick with apple butter. In the poem, however, he lets them walk away without a promise or a penny; and perhaps that explains why a college class—west of the Alleghanies, at least—cannot hear it read without feeling uneasy. Instead of helping these men who wanted to work, Frost turns to the reader with a sound but rather sententious sermon on the ethical value of the chopping block:

> But yield who will to their separation,
> My object in living is to unite
> My avocation and my vocation
> As my two eyes make one in sight.
> Only where love and need are one,
> And the work is play for mortal stakes,
> Is the deed ever really done
> For heaven and the future's sakes.

The meter and tone of the passage remind us of another narrative poem written in New England almost a hundred years before; but "The Vision of Sir Launfal" had a different moral to point:

> Not what we give but what we share,
> For the gift without the giver is bare;
> Who gives himself with his alms feeds three,
> Himself, his hungering neighbor and me.

What Frost sets before us is an ideal, not of charity or brotherhood, but of separateness. "Keep off each other and keep each other off," he tells us in "Build Soil." "We're too unseparate out among each other. . . . Steal away and stay away." In some of his poems he faintly suggests Emerson, and yet he is preaching only half the doctrine of self-reliance, which embraced the community as well as the individual. Emerson said, for example, "He only who is able to stand alone is qualified for society," thus implying that the self-reliant individual was to use his energies for social ends. Frost, on the other hand, makes no distinction between separateness and self-centeredness. In his poems, fine as the best of them are, the social passions of the great New Englanders are diverted into narrower channels. One cannot imagine him thundering against the Fugitive Slave Law, like Emerson; or rising like Thoreau to defend John Brown after the Harpers Ferry raid; or even conducting a quietly persistent campaign against brutality on American ships, as Hawthorne did when he was consul at Liverpool. He is concerned chiefly with himself and his near neighbors, or rather with the Yankees among his neighbors (for although his section of New England is largely inhabited by Poles and French Canadians, there are only two poems in which these foreigners are mentioned). He says when splitting his straight-grained beech blocks:

> The blows that a life of self-control
> Spares to strike for the common good
> That day, giving a loose to my soul,
> I spent on the unimportant wood;

—and one feels that these blows might symbolize the inward or backward turning of energies in a region that once had wider horizons.

And Frost does not strive toward greater depth to compensate for what he lacks in breadth; he does not strike far inward into the wilderness of human nature. It is true that he often talks about the need for inwardness. He says, for example, in "Build Soil," which for all its limitations of doctrine is the best of his long philosophical poems and perhaps the only one worth preserving:

> We're always too much out or too much in.
> At present from a cosmical dilation
> We're so much out that the odds are against
> Our ever getting inside in again;

—yet still he sets limits on the exploration of himself, as he sets them on almost every other human activity; here again he displays the sense of measure and decorum that puts him in the classical, or rather the neo-classical, tradition. He is always building defenses against the infinite, walls that stand "Between too much and me." In the woods, there is a pile of rocks and an iron stake to mark the limit of his land; and here too:

> One tree, by being deeply wounded,
> Has been impressed as Witness Tree
> And made commit to memory
> My proof of being not unbounded.

The woods play a curious part in Frost's poems; they seem to be his symbol for the uncharted country within ourselves, full of possible beauty, but also full of horror. From the woods at dusk, you might hear the hidden music of the brook, "a slender, tinkling fall"; or you might see wood creatures, a buck and a doe, looking at you over the stone fence that marks the limit of the pasture lot. But you don't cross the fence, except in dreams; and then, instead of brook or deer, you are

likely to meet a strange Demon rising "from his wallow to laugh." And
so, for fear of the Demon, and also because of your moral obligations,
you merely stand at the edge of the woods to listen:

> Far in the pillared dark
> Thrush music went—
> Almost like a call to come in
> To the dark and lament.
>
> But no, I was out for stars:
> I would not come in.
> I meant, not even if asked,
> And I hadn't been.

But Hawthorne before him, timid and thin and conventional as he
was in many of his tales, still plucked up his courage and ventured into
the inner wilderness; and Conrad Aiken's poems (to mention one
example of New England work today) are written almost wholly from
within that haunted mid-region. To explore the real horrors of the
mind is a long tradition in American letters, one that goes back to our
first professional novelist, Charles Brockden Brown. He said in one of his
letters, quoted in a footnote by Van Wyck Brooks, "You, you tell me, are
one of those who would rather travel into the mind of a plowman than
into the interior of Africa. I confess myself of your way of thinking." The
same tendency was continued by Poe and Melville and Henry James, and
it extends in an almost unbroken line into the late work of Hemingway
and Faulkner. But Frost, even in his finest lyrics, is content to stop
outside the woods, either in the thrush-haunted dusk or on a snowy
evening:

> The woods are lovely, dark and deep.
> But I have promises to keep,
> And miles to go before I sleep,
> And miles to go before I sleep.

If he does not strike far inward, neither does he follow the other great
American tradition (extending from Whitman through Dos Passos) of
standing on a height to observe the panorama of nature and society. Let
us say that he is a poet neither of the mountains nor of the woods,
although he lives among both, but rather of the hill pastures, the
intervals, the dooryard in autumn with the leaves swirling, the closed
house shaking in the winter storms (and who else has described these
scenes more accurately, in more lasting colors?). In the same way, he

is not the poet of New England in its great days, or in its late-nineteenth-century decline (except in some of his earlier poems); he is rather a poet who celebrates the diminished but prosperous and self-respecting New England of the tourist home and the antique shop in the abandoned gristmill. And the praise heaped on Frost in recent years is somehow connected in one's mind with the search for ancestors and authentic old furniture. You imagine a saltbox cottage restored to its original lines; outside it a wellsweep preserved for its picturesque quality, even though there is also an electric pump; at the doorway a coach lamp wired and polished; inside the house a set of Hitchcock chairs, a Salem rocker, willow-ware plates and Sandwich glass; and, on the tip-top table, carefully dusted, a first edition of Robert Frost.

Robert Frost and New England:
A Revaluation

by W. G. O'Donnell

Kierkegaard remarks somewhere in his *Journals* that widespread popularity in a contemporary author must be viewed with a certain amount of suspicion, for contemporary fame often indicates that a writer is basically superficial or that he is being misread by his own generation. If Kierkegaard's observation is taken literally, no modern American poet (above the level of such rhymesters as Edgar Guest) can be held suspect; for none has attained the type of popularity that has been won by a dozen or more modern novelists. Among our contemporaries generally accepted as poets, Robert Frost probably comes closest to fame. A few of his writings, at least, are known to a fairly large number of people and are enjoyed without the support of any special critical notation. Of course, there are critics who dismiss Frost as a talented bard, a homespun verse philosopher who has attracted undue attention by means of a painfully direct and diluted poetry. Partly for these reasons and partly because we now have before us what would appear to be his full range, a reappraisal of Frost's work may be in order.

Before that is attempted, it should be said that Frost happens to possess great gifts aside, if not wholly separate, from his poetry. Outstanding to those who have talked with him privately is a personality of extraordinary charm and integrity. There is also his ability as a public entertainer. The lecture tours undertaken by poets and novelists often turn out to be embarrassing failures, since literary men rarely seem to be very happy in front of a large audience. Not so with Robert Frost. Of the thousands throughout the country who have seen and heard him, not many are likely to forget the impression they received of a man of wisdom and unfailing humor. As he appears today on the platform, they see a rugged-looking old man with a couple of books and notebooks in

W. G. O'Donnell, "Robert Frost and New England: A Revaluation." From *The Yale Review* (Summer 1948), pp. 698-712. Copyright 1948 by the Yale University Press. Reprinted by permission of *The Yale Review*.

his hand. They notice the rumpled white hair and unusual face. Though he may wear the conventional evening dress, the clothes seem loose and natural, as if the man could go out to fetch the calf or clean the pasture spring in the same outfit. After the introduction and the applause, he begins in quiet, conversational tones and before long says something that makes those in the front row laugh aloud; and the rest listen with renewed concentration. The speaker is extremely sensitive to his audience, and their reactions lead him on to unplanned digressions and asides—or so it seems. A few minutes later he usually gives up the pretense of delivering a lecture and reads one of his own poems—something in manuscript or possibly an old stand-by such as "Birches" or "Mending Wall." He reads in a firm and resonant voice that sounds like the inevitable medium for transmitting the poetry. More talk follows; then more poems in the same voice full of curious overtones. But the performance on the stage, though a work of imagination in its own right, contributes more to Frost's reputation as a poet than to an acute understanding of the poetry itself. For his significant revelations, one must turn to his eight published collections.

It should also be said that Frost, like any other important poet, must be rescued from the unavoidable distortions of the anthologies if his full stature is to be recognized. He should be read in an edition that will include every poem he has written for publication. Although the anthologists have always represented Frost extensively, they have no choice but to give undue prominence to the briefer lyrics at the expense of the longer pieces in blank verse. Limitations of space may justify this arbitrary method of selection, but the procedure eliminates some of Frost's best poems and obscures the changes in thought and style that have taken place in Frost's writing since his earliest efforts in the 1890's.

We do not understand a poet until we recognize the principle of development at work in his creation. Yeats and Eliot concern themselves (a trifle self-consciously) with the interesting question of their own development, and they go to elaborate lengths to document their various crises and conversions. W. H. Auden, though still this side of middle age, has had his periods delimited and his spiritual evolution charted. Robert Frost, however, has declined to furnish any obvious signposts by which one may read the progress of his inner changes. He has given the world the poetry itself—no notes, no extended prose essays directly analyzing himself and his art. Some readers have professed to find no change at all in Frost: he made up his mind about life at an early age, they say, and since then he has only become more contentiously sure of all he thought was true.

In actual fact, basic changes have been taking place in Frost all along, but from the beginning the clarity of his verse has obscured the complexities of his development. His lucidity is such that he who runs may read; there is always an easily grasped meaning or image for the reader—some perception of nature, some comment about bent birches, blueberry patches, or deep woods filling up with snow. Were there nothing in Frost below this superficial level, he would certainly have to be set down as a simple bard with a gift for versifying.

Herein Frost presents a striking contrast to Eliot's more difficult poems. There are passages in *The Waste Land, Ash Wednesday,* and *Four Quartets* that have no easily apprehended meaning on the surface. Such passages often possess startling imagery, and they may be built upon sincerely felt rhythms, to which anyone, even an illiterate person, can respond readily enough. But before one can come to grips with writing of this type, one must pierce through the subtleties of a complicated and somewhat personalized symbolist mode of communication. And even after prolonged analysis of the text the most penetrating critics—to say nothing of ordinary readers—are still left with a residue of irreducible ambiguity, a few lines and images that communicate no experience.

The great advantage enjoyed by an Eliot is that he has developed a method of making a creative use of his difficulty and complexity. His readers will of necessity be perceptive and discriminating; and if they can pass through the initial ordeal of learning to interpret the symbols with which the poet is concerned, they will discover that the poetry has become vital and deeply experienced. Eliot will have fit audience, though few. Frost's subtlety is of a quite different order: it becomes more apparent with continued reading. Since Frost does not regard explicit statement as an artistic blemish, one is not faced with an overwhelming obscurity to begin with. The type of art practiced by Frost possesses some advantage in aiming immediately at human experience. It does not result in a clean-cut division of potential readers into an understanding elite and an unknowing mass; for it is based upon the premise that imaginative literature can convey depths of experience to the few though it has some meaning on a more elementary level for the many. And a unique quality in Frost is that the primitive understanding of his writing—the type of response the poet himself tries to evoke in his lectures—does not do violence to the ultimate understanding which comes only after the reader has been familiar with the poetry for years.

Frost's first volume, *A Boy's Will,* published in London in 1913, is a failure as a collection. At its best it can stand comparison with the later volumes. But the book lacks unity of tone; it represents the first gropings of a writer in search of a personal idiom. At its worst it echoes the accumulated poetic diction of the past: the poet dwells in a vanished abode with his strangely aching heart; his sorrow talks, and he is fain to list; he walks afield at dusk, carrying a worn book of old-golden song.

In spite of this weakness, however, *A Boy's Will* had a genius of its own that announced to a small circle of discerning critics the arrival of a new voice in poetry. One distinctive quality of the volume is the scene it reveals, for Frost had already decided to give his writing a local habitation and a New England name, to root his art in the soil that he had worked with his own hands for a decade before his sojourn in England. Not since Thoreau had anyone responded so sensitively to the particularities of a rural landscape. Aspects of the New England countryside flash through *A Boy's Will,* through the good poems and the trivialities. The reader finds himself in the midst of the wooded valleys and the wooded hills; he hears the blue jay's screech and the whimper of hawks beside the sun; he comes upon the purple-stemmed wild raspberry, the sodden pasture lanes of late fall, and the abandoned cellar holes gradually being reclaimed by nature.

All these carefully selected details do not add up to a totality of impression, however. *A Boy's Will* tends to place a special value on the native detail as an end in itself, for Frost had not yet developed his later ability to make the local truth in nature an integral part of the over-all purpose of a poem. The book contains brilliant phrases in isolation and delicately etched aspects of the New England country, but it fails to utilize these resources so as to disclose the mind of the poet or the character of the people who made the scene what it is. Not until subsequent volumes did Frost's genius for portraying the landscape become a functional part of his writing.

North of Boston, the second volume, is by all odds the major achievement of Frost's career. It was there that he cast aside the adopted talents of *A Boy's Will,* oriented himself to his chosen background, and came into his own. Although the shorter lyrics in other volumes may be unsurpassed as separate poems, *North of Boston* is the collection that adds power and strength to Frost's effort, and it is pre-eminently the collection to which readers will return in any attempt to define Frost's significance.

The rural New England from which Frost emerged when he sold. his farm in New Hampshire was not the region of vital accomplishment that had once predominated in the American scene. In the opinion of Henry Adams the influence of New England was sharply curtailed after 1815, when the South and West began adding an aggressive, expansionist tone to American society. Perhaps Adams was too pessimistic about his Yankees; but the New England that literary historians are now commemorating with nostalgic solicitude was in the grave with Emerson and his contemporaries long before Robert Frost began to write. *North of Boston* reflects a hinterland in a time of declining prosperity. The people in Frost's book have never known the culture of a mid-nineteenth-century Concord. They are caught up in a struggle with the elementary problems of existence—holding a farm together, paying off a mortgage, dragging through the routine of the daily chores, and at the same time not breaking under the strain of anxiety, isolation, and overwork.

The term "Indian summer" has been used to designate certain phases of latter nineteenth-century New England, but that image is hardly an accurate evocation of life as it actually was in the hill towns and on the isolated farms. After reaching a climax in 1860, their development began to decline within a decade. Marginal land and farms were abandoned almost immediately, bridges went unrepaired, and old roads disappeared vaguely in the middle of a woods. Within twenty years, maple trees and birches were back again in fields that had once been plowed every spring. When the Civil War commenced, 12,000,000 acres were under cultivation in New England; fifty years later there were only 7,000,000 acres. During that half century of shrinking agriculture the population of the region doubled. In short, New England became largely urban and industrialized. As the strength of the village culture diminished year by year, the cities were expanding with a steady influx of immigrants who spoke no word of English and knew nothing of native customs.

North of Boston should be read against this background of social and economic disturbance, for it was this that led Frost to paint the bleakest picture of life to be found in his collected poetry. Those accustomed to think of Frost as one of the few affirmative voices in the midst of a disillusioned America between wars should reread "Home Burial," "The Fear," "The Housekeeper," and "A Servant to Servants." These poems, together with "The Hill Wife," "An Old Man's Winter Night," and a few others written during the same decade, would almost lead one to think that Frost may have been contemplating a complete break with the environment he was later to be identified with in the public mind.

Frost has consistently declined to take up arms in defense of the genteel tradition, and in this respect alone he has risen far above the average run of novelists and poets who are writing about New England today. Frost knows how to look objectively as well as imaginatively at the region which has been the object of his scrutiny for half a century, and when occasion demands he can make a reckless choice in thoroughly non-Yankee fashion. His father before him had rebelled against the native folkways by sympathizing with the South at an inappropriate moment and by crossing the continent to become a journalist in San Francisco. Frost himself, a returned Yankee with a heightened love of the upland farms and the naked pastures, broke through the conventional pattern by taking his wife and children across the Atlantic and publishing *North of Boston* from the opposite pole of the English-speaking world.

The book is at once an artist's necessary and salutary rebellion against a way of life and a mature adjustment to an environment. This complicated double movement of rejection and acceptance is the heart of the experience. It saved the affirmations in the later Frost from changing to the accents of sentimentality and nostalgia. And it allowed him to write honestly about the society of the country village without evoking the woebegone folk of a Spoon River cemetery.

Abnormal people abound in *North of Boston*—unbalanced people like the overwrought mother in "Home Burial," who is cracking up under a burden of grief over her child's death; or the common-law wife in "The Fear," who unconsciously disguises her desires as obsessions. Most abject of all is the ghastly lunatic in "A Servant to Servants," who makes life a hideous mockery for himself and his relations. In this poem, more than in Edith Wharton's *Ethan Frome* or in Eugene O'Neill's *Mourning Becomes Electra* or *Desire under the Elms,* one gets an insight into what had gone wrong in certain sections of New England. Hard work and a stony soil had combined to bring about nervous prostration instead of heroic response to the challenge of difficult circumstances. The integrity of an older age had deteriorated into an attempt to maintain a false self-respect, and everything had conspired to make the disaster of insanity a lasting corrosion. Frost saw that these morbid disorders cropped up somewhat too frequently in the remote rural districts, and he suggested that something in the land and the way of life seemed to breed such diseased minds.

But he saw other people, as well, neighbors of the unfortunate ones he portrayed so vividly, and sound people tip the scales back in favor of normality. There are farmers like the one in "The Death of the Hired Man," who discovers the meaning of home—"something we somehow haven't to deserve"—and learns that everyone needs at least one place of refuge where the demands of strict justice are tempered by a spirit of charity. Then there are the characters whom Frost allows us to see through the eyes of a humorist. "A Hundred Collars" has the genial, bibulous collector, Vermont Democrat, a hulking fellow continually moving into a size-larger shirt; he is a poet in his perceptions, and he shares his creator's enduring love of the Vermont landscape—"The lay of different farms." The unpretentious "Blueberries" has Loren, the fatherly, and his brood of young Lorens, poor as a pasture full of steeplebush, but determined not to be poverty-stricken, not asking anything of anyone, just taking what nature is willing to give—and surviving.

Throughout each poem in *North of Boston* Frost insistently projects the theme of alienation, of man's isolation from his fellow man. The old-style farmer in "Mending Wall" not only refuses to pull down the useless barriers but, to make matters worse, insists upon having the last word: "Good fences make good neighbors." The Yankees in "The Generations of Men" pry into their past, look suspiciously at the incoming newer races, and decide that, when all is said and done, there are really no names quite like the old ones. In "The Black Cottage" the world passes by the best in an earlier New England that took the phrases of the Declaration of Independence seriously. The husband and wife of "Home Burial" cannot share the grief which, more than anything else in their experience, should make them one in feeling; they irritate a raw spot with every syllable they utter and thus unfit themselves for any return to a normal existence.

Nothing could be farther afield than to conclude that Frost admires this alienation which he interprets so vividly, or that he hopes to see it prevail. There are those who hold that a writer should cap every such perception of fact by a fiery denunciation. But in *North of Boston* Frost is a poet, not a pamphleteer. And he must in any case be himself; one cannot expect him to adopt the rhetoric and the explicit method of Whitman. Democracy and America find representative voices in both Frost and Whitman; both writers are concerned with brotherhood and fellowship, although each approaches the problem in an individual fashion. Whitman responds to the question of the attainment of democracy by writing the vague and formless song of the open road, by spreading out his arms in a universal embrace that gathers in North and South, black, white, yellow, and red, good and evil, the prude and the rake. Others may be divisive, selective, or exclusive, but Walt Whitman accepts everyone and with romantic gusto loudly affirms all aspects of life in America. Robert Frost believes no less strongly in the value of affirmation, but looking at the world more realistically than Whitman does, he knows that if alienation could be overcome by the repeated affirmation of fellowship, it would have disappeared a long time ago.

Frost recognizes the existence of a force that sends a powerful groundswell under the barriers between man and man. But in *North of Boston* he is content to portray these barriers and make a dramatic projection of the theme of isolation. He dislikes isolation as much as any man of wisdom does, but he sees it a fact that everyone must face in one form or another. In short, *North of Boston* is Frost's tragic discovery. "Going for Water," one of the lyrics in *A Boy's Will*, sets forth the poet's youthful happiness in the days before the transition from innocence to knowledge; with his companion at his side, the reliant bride who shares the experiences of the early poetry, he goes about his commonplace tasks, and the simplicities of the rural world are transformed in the light of the happiness of a young man and a young woman sharing the solitude of house and wood:

> We ran as if to meet the moon
>   That slowly dawned behind the trees,
> The barren boughs without the leaves,
>   Without the birds, without the breeze.
>
> But once within the wood, we paused
>   Like gnomes that hid us from the moon,
> Ready to run to hiding new
>   With laughter when she found us soon.
>
> Each laid on other a staying hand
>   To listen ere we dared to look,
> And in the hush we joined to make
>   We heard, we knew we heard the brook.

In later years these youthful accents seldom recur in Frost's writing; a mature realism entered the poetry with *North of Boston*. Frost had become one acquainted with the night, although he did not propose to live in the darker regions. Having made the tragic discovery, the poet will in some obscure way be happier knowing the truth than not knowing.

In *A Witness Tree*, the seventh volume, published in 1942, there is a poem called "Happiness Makes Up in Height," which deals with the same scene found in "Going for Water," the rural retreat with house, wood, and a couple in solitude. This time, however, it is not a young man talking; the youthful, accented rhythms are gone, and one hears instead the voice of a man who has lived many years beyond the tragic discovery and is now looking back upon life. He did not go bounding through existence from one happiness to another. When he considers the apparent predominance of tragedy and sorrow in the world, he wonders why he has ever been happy. And he finds an objective correlative for the experience—the one day of perfect radiance in a lifetime of days swirled around with mist and cloud:

> . . . that one day
> No shadow crossed but ours
> As through its blazing flowers
> We went from house to wood
> For change of solitude.

He is happy because of a radiant experience that transfigured everything and acted as an insight into the strength of man's spirit that can suffer evil yet remember good. The two lyrics point the way of Frost's development.

T. S. Eliot, who also went to England as a young man but stayed much longer than Frost had done, revisited the United States in September, 1932, for the first time in eighteen years. After landing in Canada, he came down across what he refers to as the beautiful, desolate country of Vermont. Beyond the wooded hills he found the squalor of the dying mill towns—Manchester, Lawrence, Lowell. Surveying the scene, Eliot concluded that the countryside north of Boston gave evidence of a meagre and transitory success, more desperate than the desert. He could see nothing but failure and defeat in a region where a flourishing tradition had long since come to an end and had been overgrown by newer groups who had broken down the homogeneity of earlier times.

Twenty-eight years before Eliot's return to America, Henry James, another eminent exile from the eastern seaboard, came back to spend a few months lecturing and revisiting the scenes of his youth. For two months he lived within sight of the White Mountains—a few miles from Derry, New Hampshire, where Robert Frost was farming and writing his first poems. James meditated on the landscape of New England in its autumn glory: the leaves had ripened to the fall; day by day there was an exquisite stillness in the air, and a sadness, also, as if both the summer and the region had been prolonged far beyond their prime.

At first, as he relates so brilliantly in "The American Scene," he felt as if he were wandering about in Arcadia. Six weeks of Indian summer weather merged to form a gorgeous blur in his consciousness. But the question of the value of New England rises perennially, and he could not ignore it. Why have so few people called this land sterile, bleak, and hostile? Is it possible that the traditional beauty of the countryside is really an illusion? Henry James, who had removed himself from America and could trust the objectivity of his vision, concluded that some sections of New England possess a powerful beauty that one cannot attribute to the charm of nostalgia.

The spell was irresistible in the craggy, rocky, woody places, particularly in New Hampshire, where the shade was very dense, and things were seen in a drizzle of forest light. Wherever he looked, he could find poetry in solution in the atmosphere. But he could not escape the feeling that he was only a pilgrim in the land. Though he had discovered great natural beauty in New England, he had serious doubts about the people themselves. An element of bleakness, of downright ugliness and dinginess, clung to many of the towns; whatever else they had, they lacked the charm and the grace which he found in the older systems and forms of Europe. He failed to see that the scenic beauty, far from being an accident of nature, results in part from a continuing interaction between the land and its inhabitants. In short, he was out of step with Robert Frost's people—the men and women of the hillside farms. He was a little too deeply impressed by the summer folk who lived in their admirable country houses until the end of the season and then left the land to the "quaint" natives. When he discovered Frost's black cottages and abandoned cellar holes—classic symbols of decay—he needed no further proof that an end had come for this particular human experiment.

Robert Frost recognized the failures and defeats that Henry James noted on his leisurely tour through New England in 1904, but he was one of those who decided to come back and resist the supposed verdict of history. Frost described the record of failure with uncompromising realism because he knew from first-hand experience the conditions that Henry James could only observe at a distance. Many of his best lyrics grow out of this knowledge of the facts and express a sense of transience, a realization of the rush of everything to nothingness—the end of a season, the end of a farm or a family or a village culture. But the fact of the decline in New England led Frost to a conclusion diametrically opposed to the one reached by Eliot and James. What impressed Frost most of all was not that much of the older New England had been lost but that something had survived, that a vitality remained which was strong enough to meet the challenge of new and potentially disastrous conditions. If this perception of survival is not true, then America has been in a bad way indeed for many decades.

In so far as Frost is a voice of New England, he is a minor figure in contemporary literature; to the extent that he makes his New England universal in meaning and implication, he is a significant writer. In his ability to portray the local truth in nature he has no peer; but that power, remarkable though it undoubtedly is, has value only when it is allied with an ability to speak in terms of experiences that are valid for those who know New England only as a small territorial division on the map of the United States. Apart from *North of Boston* Frost seldom reaches the plane of universal meaning—to my mind, not more than a score of times in his whole career. But because he has given the language thirty poems and some fifteen hundred lines that convey significant human experience, he can not easily be consigned to the company of the lesser poets. Regionalists are invariably minor writers because they tend to adopt elegiac moods not in accord with the facts of the life around them. Frost himself has occasionally lapsed into this fault. In "A Brook in the City," "A Roadside Stand," and "Build Soil," for example, he sets up an unpleasant antagonism between the country, with its rugged virtues and its manly independence, and the teeming megalopolis, with its chaos and ugliness; and such poems speak for a nonexistent America. But Frost reaches the plane of universal experience in his book of people, *North of Boston,* and in "The Hill Wife," "An Old Man's Winter Night," "October," "Now Close the Windows," "The Oven Bird," "Birches," "Stopping By Woods," "To Earthward," "Spring Pools," "Acquainted with the Night," "Happiness Makes Up in Height," and "Directive."

It is in these poems that Frost's non-declamatory voice comes through most clearly. That style did not grow out of the New England soil, like steeplebush or sugar maples. No amount of pedantic listening to the supposedly racy speech of New Hampshire farmers could have produced this distinctive, unrhetorical language. Frost did not set out to do for his region what John Millington Synge had done for the Aran Islands. If we are to do justice to Frost's achievement and talk intelligently about the process of artistic creation, we must see the style as a deeply personal accomplishment. Frost did not discover a subject matter and then call in the aid of a tangy regional speech. The style is too integral a part of the whole pattern to be removed and given a convenient label such as "New Hampshire." The language is effective not because it has specific connections with a region but because Frost has made his characteristic rhythms and twists of phrase appropriate to the total experience of the poetry.

"Directive," one of the latest poems, first published in the poet's seventy-second year and now included in the most recent collection, *Steeple Bush,* may possibly be a summing up of Frost's attitude towards New England and towards existence in general. In its gnarled and crotchety way this odd but vigorous poem is one of his surest victories over the danger of a lapse into regional mannerism. Once again he is concerned with evidence of an older New England that faded away into nature and was lost. As he writes about the rural scene this time, however, he is aware of the confused present—"All this now too much for us"—and he casts about for a principle of continuity, a source of strength and wisdom. Unusual and highly effective comparisons and conceits become part of the central experience, for the imagination in the poem has a metaphysical quality. The directive sends the reader up an old country road, and one feels the past close by, peering curiously out of the abandoned cellar holes, like "eye pairs out of forty firkins." But Frost is not sending anyone back to the past or the land or subsistence farming or even to the country atmosphere. The destination turns out to be a brook, cold as a spring, the water of the house that once flourished at the top of the hill. It is not the America of the past that counts, but the enduring source of wisdom that created a life full of vitality and happiness. As usual, Frost's directive points to no short cut through current problems. What the poem affirms is the difficulty of finding a true source of spiritual strength. But you must find it. You can't get saved if you don't drink from the mountain brook:

> Here are your waters and your watering place.
> Drink and be whole again beyond confusion.

Robert Frost:
or, the Spiritual Drifter as Poet

by Yvor Winters

Robert Frost is one of the most talented poets of our time, but I believe that his work is both overestimated and misunderstood; and it seems to me of the utmost importance that we should understand him with some accuracy. If we can arrive at a reasonably sound understanding of him, we can profit by his virtues without risk of acquiring his defects; and we may incidentally arrive at a better understanding of our present culture.

A popular poet is always a spectacle of some interest, for poetry in general is not popular; and when the popular poet is also within limits a distinguished poet, the spectacle is even more curious, for commonly it is bad poetry which is popular. When we encounter such a spectacle, we may be reasonably sure of finding certain social and historical reasons for the popularity. Frost is similar in his ways and attitudes and perceptions to a very large number of the more intelligent, if not the most intelligent, of his contemporaries: to the school teachers, the English professors, the more or less literate undergraduates, the journalists, and the casual readers of every class. These people are numerous and are in a position to perpetuate their ways and attitudes; this similarity, therefore, is worth examining.

Frost has been praised as a classical poet, but he is not classical in any sense which I can understand. Like many of his contemporaries, he is an Emersonian Romantic, although with certain mutings and modifications which I shall mention presently, and he has labeled himself as such with a good deal of care. He is a poet of the minor theme, the casual approach, and the discreetly eccentric attitude. When a reader calls Frost a classical poet, he probably means that Frost strikes him as a "natural" poet, a poet who somehow resembles himself and his neighbors;

but this is merely another way of saying that the reader feels a kinship to him and likes him easily. Classical literature is said to judge human experience with respect to the norm; but it does so with respect to the norm of what humanity ought to be, not with respect to the norm of what it happens to be in a particular place and time. The human average has never been admirable, and in certain cultures it has departed very far from the admirable; that is why in the great classical periods of literature we are likely to observe great works in tragedy and satire, the works of a Racine and a Molière, of a Shakespeare and a Jonson, works which deal in their respective ways with sharp deviations from the ideal norm; and that is why literature which glorifies the average is sentimental rather than classical.

Frost writes of rural subjects, and the American reader of our time has an affection for rural subjects which is partly the product of the Romantic sentimentalization of "nature," but which is partly also a nostalgic looking back to the rural life which predominated in this nation a generation or two ago; the rural life is somehow regarded as the truly American life. I have no objection to the poet's employing rural settings; but we should remember that it is the poet's business to evaluate human experience, and the rural setting is no more valuable for this purpose than any other or than no particular setting, and one could argue with some plausibility that an exclusive concentration on it may be limiting.

Frost early began his endeavor to make his style approximate as closely as possible the style of conversation, and this endeavor has added to his reputation: it has helped to make him seem "natural." But poetry is not conversation, and I see no reason why poetry should be called upon to imitate conversation. Conversation is the most careless and formless of human utterance; it is spontaneous and unrevised, and its vocabulary is commonly limited. Poetry is the most difficult form of human utterance; we revise poems carefully in order to make them more nearly perfect. The two forms of expression are extremes, they are not close to each other. We do not praise a violinist for playing as if he were improvising; we praise him for playing well. And when a man plays well or writes well, his audience must have intelligence, training, and patience in order to appreciate him. We do not understand difficult matters "naturally."

The business of the poet can be stated simply. The poet deals with human experience in words. Words are symbols of concepts, which have acquired connotation of feeling in addition to their denotation of concept. The poet, then, as a result of the very nature of his medium, must make a rational statement about an experience, and as rationality is a part of the medium, the ultimate value of the poem will depend in a fair measure on the soundness of the rationality: it is possible, of course, to reason badly, just as it is possible to reason well. But the poet is deliberately employing the connotative content of language as well as the denotative: so that what he must do is make a rational statement about an experience, at the same time employing his language in such a manner as to communicate the emotion which ought to be communicated by that rational understanding of the particular subject. In so far as he is able to do this, the poem will be good; in so far as the subject itself is important, the poem will be great. That is, a poem which merely describes a stone may be excellent but will certainly be minor; whereas a poem which deals with man's contemplation of death and eternity, or with a formative decision of some kind, may be great. It is possible, of course, that the stone may be treated in such a way that it symbolizes something greater than itself; but if this occurs, the poem is about something greater than the stone. The poet is valuable, therefore, in proportion to his ability to apprehend certain kinds of objective truth; in proportion as he is great, he will not resemble ourselves but will resemble what we ought to be. It becomes our business, then, to endeavor to resemble him, and this endeavor is not easy and for this reason few persons make it. Country conversation and colloquial charm are irrelevant to the real issue. The great poets, men like Ben Jonson, Fulke Greville, and Richard Crashaw, have few readers; though some of them, like Milton, are widely admired from a distance. But they offer us, in their best efforts, the finest understanding of human experience to which we have access; some people are able and willing to understand them; and the human intelligence, however precariously, is thus kept alive. If we set up false ideals of human nature, and our best poets judge experience in terms of them and so beguile us into doing likewise, the human intelligence is to that extent diminished.

Frost has said that Emerson is his favorite American poet, and he himself appears to be something of an Emersonian. Emerson was a Romantic pantheist: he identified God with the universe; he taught that impulse comes directly from God and should be obeyed, that through surrender to impulse we become one with God; he taught that reason is man-made and bungling and should be suppressed. In moral and aesthetic doctrine, Emerson was a relativist; his most thorough-going disciples in American literature were Walt Whitman and Hart Crane. In Frost, on the other hand, we find a disciple without Emerson's religious conviction: Frost believes in the rightness of impulse, but does not discuss the pantheistic doctrine which would give authority to impulse; as a result of his belief in impulse, he is of necessity a relativist, but his relativism, apparently since it derives from no intense religious conviction, has resulted mainly in ill-natured eccentricity and in increasing melancholy. He is an Emersonian who has become sceptical and uncertain without having reformed; and the scepticism and uncertainty do not appear to have been so much the result of thought as the result of the impact upon his sensibility of conflicting notions of his own era—they appear to be the result of his having taken the easy way and having drifted with the various currents of his time.

II

I should like first of all to describe a few poems which deal with what in the hands of a more serious writer one could describe as the theme of moral choice. These poems throw more light on Frost as a whole, perhaps, than do any others, and they may serve as an introduction to his work. I have in mind especially three poems from *Mountain Interval*: the introductory piece entitled "The Road Not Taken," the post-scriptive piece entitled "The Sound of the Trees," and the lyrical narrative called "The Hill Wife"; and one poem from *A Further Range:* the poem entitled "The Bearer of Evil Tidings." These poems all have a single theme: the whimsical, accidental, and incomprehensible nature of the formative decision; and I should like to point out that if one takes this view of the formative decision, one has cut oneself off from understanding most of human experience, for in these terms there is nothing to be understood—one can write of human experience with sentimental approval or with sentimental melancholy, but with little else.

"The Road Not Taken," for example, is the poem of a man whom one might fairly call a spiritual drifter; and a spiritual drifter is unlikely to have either the intelligence or the energy to become a major poet. Yet the poem has definite virtues, and these should not be overlooked. In the first place, spiritual drifters exist, they are real; and although their decisions may not be comprehensible, their predicament is comprehensible. The poem renders the experience of such a person, and renders the uncertain melancholy of his plight. Had Frost been a more intelligent man, he might have seen that the plight of the spiritual drifter was not inevitable, he might have judged it in the light of a more comprehensive wisdom. Had he done this, he might have written a greater poem. But his poem is good as far as it goes; the trouble is that it does not go far enough, it is incomplete, and it puts on the reader a burden of critical intelligence which ought to be borne by the poet. We are confronted with a similar critical problem when the Earl of Rochester writes remarkably beautiful poems to invite us to share in the pleasures of drunkenness. The pleasures of drunkenness are real—let no one delude himself on that score—and the Earl of Rochester is one of the most brilliant masters of English verse. But if the pleasures of drunkenness are regarded in what the sentimental critics are wont to term a true perspective, they are seen to be obstacles to other experiences of far greater value, and then they take on the appearance of temptations to sin. Dante would have dealt with these pleasures truly, placing them where they belong in the hierarchy of values; Rochester was not equal to the task, but Rochester gave us a good evaluation of the experience of a man in his predicament as he himself sees it. He is like the demon defined by Aquinas: good in so far as he may be said to exist, but a demon in so far as his existence is incomplete. And like the demon he is also enticing, for he has more than usual powers of persuasion. We are protected against his incompleteness and against his enticements if we understand his limitations, and we can then profit by what he possesses; but without understanding, we may be drawn to emulate him, to form ourselves upon him—we may, in a sense, become possessed by an evil power which is great enough to control us and diminish our own being.

The comparison of Rochester to Frost is unjust in one respect, for Rochester was a consciously vicious man; whereas Robert Frost would not willingly injure anyone. Yet the comparison in other ways is just, for Frost, as I shall show, has willfully refrained from careful thinking and so is largely responsible for his own condition; and his condition is less dramatic and more easily shared by large numbers of his contemporaries than was the condition of Rochester, so that he is probably a greater menace to the general intelligence. Rochester knew himself to be a sinner, and he knew that he would be regarded as one. Frost by a process of devious evasions has convinced himself that he is a wise and virtuous man, and he is regarded as a kind of embodiment of human wisdom by hundreds of thousands of Americans from high school age to the brink of senility. He embodies a common delusion regarding human nature, and he is strongly reinforcing that delusion in the minds of his contemporaries.

"The Sound of the Trees" deals with a longing to depart which has never quite been realized. The trees

> are that which talks of going
> But never gets away.

The poem ends as follows:

> I shall make the reckless choice
> Some day when they are in voice

> And tossing so as to scare
> The white clouds over them on.
> I shall have less to say,
> But I shall be gone.

The poem has the same quality of uncertainty and incomprehension as "The Road Not Taken"; it is written with about the same degree of success, with about the same charm, and with about the same quality of vague melancholy. In considering either of these poems, especially if one compares them even to minor works by sixteenth- and seventeenth-century masters, one will observe not only the limitations of intelligence which I have mentioned, but a quality, slight though it may be, of imprecision in the rendering of the detail and of the total attitude, which is the result of the limitations. Such a poem as Robert Herrick's "Night-Piece to Julia" is as sharp as a knife in comparison. Herrick knew exactly what he was saying and exactly what it was worth. Frost, on the other hand, is mistaking whimsical impulse for moral choice, and the blunder obscures his understanding and even leaves his mood uncertain with regard to the value of the whole business. He is vaguely afraid that he may be neither wrong nor right.

"The Hill Wife" is a less happy specimen than the poems just mentioned. It deals, not with a personal experience of the author, but with a dramatic situation seen from without; and the dramatic crisis is offered as something incomprehensible. The wife leaves her husband because she is lonely on their back-country farm, but there is no clear understanding of her motive; we are told that she is disturbed when the birds leave in the fall, and frightened by a casual tramp, and that a pine near the window obsesses her thoughts. The last section, characteristically entitled "The Impulse," describes her final act as a sudden and unpremeditated one. The poem has an eerie quality, like that of dream or of neurosis, but it has little else. As a study in human relationships, it amounts to nothing, and one has only to compare it to "Eros Turannos" by Robinson to discern its triviality. "The Bearer of Evil Tidings" deals with a similarly casual and sudden decision, although it is a more interesting poem. And one might mention also the poem from *A Witness Tree* entitled "A Serious Step Lightly Taken": the serious step in question is merely the buying of a farm; but the title is characteristic, and the title implies approval and not disapproval—it implies that serious steps ought to be lightly taken. But if serious steps are to be lightly taken, then poetry, at least, is impoverished, and the poet can have very little to say. Most of the world's great poetry has had to do with serious steps seriously taken, and when the seriousness goes from life, it goes from the poetry.

III

I shall consider next some of the more clearly didactic poems, which will reinforce what I have been saying. I should perhaps mention briefly as one of these, a short lyric in *West-Running Brook,* a lyric called "Sand Dunes," of which the clearly stated theme is the Emersonian notion that man can think better if he frees himself wholly from the past. The last poem in the same volume, at least as the volume originally appeared, is called "The Bear." The poem compares the wild bear to the bear in a cage; the uncaged bear is a creature of free impulse and is compared by implication to man as he would be were he guided by impulse; and the caged bear is compared to rational man as he is. The poem is amusing on first reading, but it wears thin with time. The difficulty is this, that satirical poetry is a branch of didactic poetry, for whereas purely didactic poetry endeavors to convince directly, satirical poetry endeavors to convince indirectly by ridiculing what the poet takes to be a deviation from wisdom; and both forms depend rather obviously upon the soundness of the ideas which they expound or assume. Frost tells us in this poem that reasoning man is ridiculous because he appears to labor and to change his mind; and he implies that impulsive man would be a wiser and a nobler creature. The fact of the matter is, however, that impulsive man, if he is restrained, like Frost, by conventions and habits the nature and origins of which he does not understand, is likely to be merely confused, uncertain, and melancholy; and if he is not so restrained may degenerate to madness or to criminality. Within relatively recent years, we have had two tragic examples, in Hart Crane and in Ezra Pound, of what a man of genius can do to himself and to his work by energetically living the life of impulse. It is not foolish to change one's mind; one learns by changing one's mind. Life is a process of revision in the interests of greater understanding, and it is by means of this process that men came down from the trees and out of the caves; and although civilization is very far from what it should be, nevertheless mankind have shown a marked improvement over the past ten thousand years. This improvement is the result of the fact that man is a rational animal, as I believe that a certain Greek once remarked. The uncaged bear, or the unreflective cave-man, is inferior to Thomas Aquinas and to Richard Hooker, to Dante and to Ben Jonson, and to assert the contrary is merely irresponsible foolishness. Frost then is satirizing the intelligent man from the point of view of the unintelligent; and the more often one reads the poem, the more obvious this fact becomes, and the more trivial the poem appears.

Frost expounds the same ideas more directly still in his poem "To a Thinker," in *A Further Range*. The idea in this poem is the same as that in "The Bear," but is even more plainly stated; we have the commonplace Romantic distrust of reason and trust in instinct. The poem ends as follows:

> So if you find you must repent
> From side to side in argument,
> At least don't use your mind too hard,
> But trust my instinct—I'm a bard.

The poem is badly written, but one couplet is momentarily amusing:

> I own I never really warmed
> To the reformer or reformed.

Yet when we examine it more carefully, there is something almost contemptible about it. There are, of course, reformers and reformers, and many of them have been ludicrous or worse. Frost is invoking the image of the soap-box politician or the street-corner preacher in order to discredit reason. But the word *reform* can be best evaluated if one separates the syllables for a moment. To reform means to re-form. And the progress of civilization has been a process of re-forming human nature. Socrates re-formed the human mind; Jesus re-formed man's moral and religious nature; Aquinas re-formed philosophical method and content; and William the Silent re-formed the idea of the state. Frost endeavors to gain his point by sleight-of-hand; he endeavors to obscure the difference between St. Thomas Aquinas and Pussyfoot Johnson.

Even Frost, with his instinct to guide him, is not proof against wavering, however. In the same volume with the poem just described is a poem called "The White-Tailed Hornet," in which Frost describes the activities of a hornet and the errors it commits under the guidance of instinct, and he reprehends mankind for having engaged in "downward comparisons":

> As long on earth
> As our comparisons were stoutly upward
> With gods and angels, we were men at least,
> But little lower than the gods and angels.
> But once comparisons were yielded downward,

> Once we began to see our images
> Reflected in the mud and even dust,
> 'Twas disillusion upon disillusion.
> We were lost piecemeal to the animals
> Like people thrown out to delay the wolves.

Yet we have seen Frost himself engaging in downward comparisons, and we shall see him doing it again. This is the only poem in Frost's works which seems to represent a conscious rejection of his usual ideas, and this poem, as I have said, even occurs in the same volume with the poem which I quoted previously, "To a Thinker." It is possible that Frost shares the contempt felt by Emerson and by Whitman for consistency, or he may be so inexperienced a thinker as to be unaware of his inconsistency; the point is of little importance, for he nowhere else takes up this argument.

Frost has something to say of the relationship of the individual to society. His most extensive poem on this subject is called "Build Soil—A Political Pastoral," and was delivered at Columbia University, May 31, 1932, before the national party conventions of that year. It will be remembered that these were the conventions which led to the first election of Franklin D. Roosevelt, and that the time was one of the darkest periods in the history of the nation. The poem is Frost's most ambitious effort to deal with his social, political, and economic views. As to his economic views, he says that if he were dictator of the country:

> I'd let things take their course
> And then I'd claim the credit for the outcome.

This statement, if it means anything at all, is a statement of belief in an unrestrained laissez-faire system, of the sort that Emerson would have approved; a belief that if things are left alone they must come right. It represents a doctrine of political drifting which corresponds to the doctrine of personal drifting which we have already seen; in practice, it could lead only to the withdrawal from public affairs of the citizen not concerned primarily with personal aggrandizement, and to the surrender of the nation to the unscrupulous go-getter, who, though he may not be a drifter, is not governed by admirable aims. It is similarly an obscurantist doctrine: it implies that this realm of human activity, like others, cannot be dealt with rationally and is better if not understood. As to the behavior of the private citizen, Frost says:

> I bid you to a one-man revolution—
> The only revolution that is coming.

We're too unseparate out among each other—
With goods to sell and notions to impart . . .
We congregate embracing from distrust
As much as love, and too close in to strike
And so be very striking. Steal away
The song says. Steal away and stay away.
Don't join too many gangs. Join few if any.
Join the United States and join the family—
But not much in between unless a college. . . .

The individual is thus advised against any kind of political activity in a time of national collapse. The difficulties of effective political action are obvious; the English-speaking peoples have been struggling with the problems of constitutional government for centuries. But if the reality of the difficulties results in our stealing away from them, society will be taken over, as I have said, by the efficient scoundrels who are always ready to take over when everyone else abdicates. In a dictatorship by scoundrels, the Frosts and the Thoreaus, the amateur anarchists and village eccentrics, would find life somewhat more difficult than they have found it to date. Frost objects in the last passage to the commerce of minds, and he objects to it earlier in the poem:

Suppose someone comes near me who in rate
Of speech and thinking is so much my better
I am imposed on, silenced and discouraged.
Do I submit to being supplied by him
As the more economical producer?
No, I unostentatiously move off
Far enough for my thought-flow to resume.

It does not occur to Frost that he might learn from his betters and improve himself; he can see only two possibilities in his relationship with them—he can be silenced by them or he can ignore them and proceed as before. There is the implication in this passage that his personal "thought-flow" is valuable merely because it is his own, that it should remain uncontaminated. He believes that the man and the nation equally will reach their fullest development through a kind of retreat to passivity, through letting things happen as they may with a minimum of influence from without.

The same sentimental dislike for society, for community of interest, can be found in the poem called "The Egg and the Machine," a poem appended in the *Collected Poems* to the group called *West-Running*

Brook. The poem tells of a Thoreau-like adventurer who is exasperated
to encounter a railroad running through his favorite marsh. After a
locomotive passes him, he proceeds to find a nestful of turtle eggs, and
Frost writes:

> If there was one egg in it there were nine,
> Torpedo-like, with shell of gritty leather
> All packed in sand to wait the trump together.
> 'You'd better not disturb me any more,'
> He told the distance, 'I am armed for war.
> The next machine that has the power to pass
> Will get this plasm in its goggle-glass.'

Here are several familiar Romantic attitudes: resentment at being unable to achieve the absolute privacy which Frost names as a primary
desideratum in "Build Soil," the sentimental regard for the untouched
wilderness (the untouched wilderness would provide absolute privacy
for the unique Romantic), and the sentimental hatred for the machine.
I am willing to admit, in connection with the last matter, that machinery
is sometimes far from beautiful, both in itself and in some of its effects;
but its benefits have been overwhelmingly great, and the literary farmer
in Vermont could scarcely hope to subsist either as farmer or as writer
without its help, any more than he could hope to subsist unless a good
many people faced moral and political realities; and it is curiously unjust
that the locomotive, that patient and innocuous draft horse of civilization, should be selected to symbolize the viciousness of machinery.
Frost's real objection to the machine, I suspect, is its social nature; it
requires and facilitates cooperation, and Frost is unwilling to recognize
its respectability mainly for this reason.

There have been other literary works dealing with resentment at the
machine and the changes it has introduced; the resentment I believe
to be foolish, but in certain settings it may have a tragic if barbarous
dignity. Bret Harte wrote a story called "Maruja," which tells of the
first railroad to proceed through the San Antonio Ranch in what is now
Los Altos, California, and of the resentment of the old Indian overseer
at this destruction of the old order. The Indian, Pereo, whose resentment
against the incoming Anglo-Americans had developed to the point of
paranoia, and who had murdered one of the new-comers by roping him
about the neck from horseback and dragging him to death, rode out
against the first locomotive, roped it, and tried to drag it from the
tracks, and was himself dragged and killed. The negro ballad of John
Henry tells of a "steel-driving man" who broke his back in the attempt

to out-hammer a steam-drill. These actions are naïve and primitive, but they are heroic in a fashion, they at least have the seriousness of honest violence. Frost's protagonist, however, expresses his feelings by threatening to throw a turtle-egg into the headlight of a locomotive. The turtle-egg, of course, may be intended as something more than a simple missile: it is "plasm," raw life, and hence capable of confounding (although only symbolically) the mechanical product of human reason. The trouble is again that the symbols will not stand inspection: the locomotive cannot be equated with human reason, for it is merely something created by human reason to facilitate higher activities; there is nothing either of wisdom or of greatness in the egg of a turtle; and of the locomotive and human reason about equally would be quite unperturbed by the egg of a turtle. As we pursue the symbolism, we are left where we began, with a petulant and self-righteous gesture, a feeble joke.

There is a kind of half dramatic, half didactic poem occasionally, of which I shall mention two examples: "West-Running Brook" and *A Masque of Reason*. The first of these is a brief affair in the form of a dialogue between a young husband and wife who apparently have just established themselves on a farm next to a brook which runs west instead of east; they observe a ripple in the brook, in which the water is thrown upward and apparently backward against the current. The husband, in certain lines which are the chief part of the poem, comments upon the ripple:

> Speaking of contraries, see how the brook
> In that white wave runs counter to itself.
> It is from that in water we were from
> Long, long before we were from any creature.
> Here we, in our impatience of the steps,
> Get back to the beginning of beginnings,
> The stream of everything that runs away . . .
> It has this throwing backward on itself
> So that the fall of most of it is always
> Raising a little, sending up a little.
> Our life runs down in sending up the clock.
> The brook runs down in sending up our life.
> The sun runs down in sending up the brook.
> And there is something sending up the sun.
> It is this backward motion toward the source
> Against the stream that most we see ourselves in,
> The tribute of the current to the source.
> It is from this in nature we are from.

The theology of this passage, if we may call it theology, is tenuous and incomplete; it is what a certain kind of critic would call suggestive, rather than definitive; there is, in brief, very little to it. Frost seems to have suspected this, for he did not let his meditation on the ripple stand alone on its merits; he framed it in the dialogue I have mentioned and made his young people responsible for it. Yet the people are not depicted as characters, and their remarks lead to no dramatic action; the meditation gives the momentary illusion that the characters are more important than they are; the conversational framework gives the momentary illusion that the meditation is more important than it is. Thus the structure of the poem is actually a piece of deception, and the substance of the poem is negligible.

A Masque of Reason is the same kind of poem on a larger scale. The characters are God, the Devil, Job, and Job's wife. The scene is "A fair oasis in the purest desert"; the time is the Day of Judgment. Job and his wife suddenly discover the presence of the Burning Bush. She says:

> There's a strange light on everything today.

Job: The myrrh tree gives it. Smell the rosin burning?
The ornaments the Greek artificers
Made for the Emperor Alexius,
The Star of Bethlehem, the pomegranates,
The birds, seem all on fire with Paradise.
And hark, the gold enameled nightingales
Are singing. Yes, and look, the Tree is troubled.
Someone's caught in the branches.

Wife: So there is.
He can't get out.

Job: He's loose! He's out!

Wife: It's God.
I'd know him by Blake's picture anywhere.
Now what's he doing?

Job: Pitching throne, I guess.
Here by our atoll.

Wife: Something Byzantine.

(The throne's a ply-wood flat, prefabricated,
That God pulls lightly upright on its hinges
And stands beside, supporting it in place.)

This brief passage gives a clue to the nature of the whole poem. Job's first speech above is a piece of remarkable rhetoric: there is nothing else in the poem to equal it. It reminds one of Yeats, especially of Yeats's brilliant but whimsical poem called "Sailing to Byzantium." From that passage onward, through the references to Blake and to the plywood throne, we have details which are offered merely for the shock of cleverness; the details are irrelevant to any theme discernible in the poem. Frost, the rustic realist of *North of Boston,* appears in his old age as a standard exemplar of irresponsible Romantic irony, of the kind of irony that has degenerated steadily from the moderately low level of Laforgue, through Pound, Eliot, Cummings, and their younger imitators. The method is employed throughout the poem.

The poem falls roughly into three parts. The first of these deals with God's first explanation to Job of the treatment Job had been accorded in life. God tells him:

                    You helped me
      Establish once for all the principle
      There's no connection man can reason out
      Between his just deserts and what he gets.
      Virtue may fail and wickedness succeed. . . .
      You realize by now the part you played
      To stultify the Deuteronomist
      And change the tenor of religious thought.
      My thanks are to you for releasing me
      From moral bondage to the human race.
      The only free will there at first was man's,
      Who could do good or evil as he chose.
      I had no choice but I must follow him
      With forfeits and rewards he understood—
      Unless I liked to suffer loss of worship.
      I had to prosper good and punish evil.
      You changed all that. You set me free to reign.

So far as the ideas in this passage are concerned, the passage belongs to the fideistic tradition of New England Calvinism; the ideas can be found in more than one passage in Jonathan Edwards, as well as elsewhere. The carefully flippant tone, however, is something else; it belongs to the tradition of Romantic irony which I have already mentioned, and is used to make the ideas seem trivial. The ideas and the tone together express the Romantic ennui or disillusionment which is born of spiritual laziness, the laziness which is justified by the Romantic doctrine that one can best apprehend the truth by intuition and without labor. One can find the same ennui, expressed in various ways, in Henry Adams, in Laforgue, in Eliot, and in scores of others.

The second passage of chief importance is the one in which God revises his explanation. Job insists that God's explanation is not the true one, that God is concealing something, and God makes the following admission:

> I'm going to tell Job why I tortured him
> And trust it won't be adding to the torture.
> I was just showing off to the Devil, Job,
> As is set forth in chapters One and Two.
> (*Job takes a few steps pacing.*) Do you mind?
> (*God eyes him anxiously.*)
>
> Job: No. No, I mustn't.
> 'Twas human of You. I expected more
> Than I could understand and what I get
> Is almost less than I can understand.
> But I don't mind. Let's leave it as it stood.
> The point was it was none of my concern.
> I stick to that. But talk about confusion . . .

The general idea is the same as in the preceding passage, but the debasement of the attitude toward the idea becomes now a matter of explicit statement as well as of stylistic tone. There is no understanding of good and evil in themselves, of the metaphysical questions involved. Good is submission to an anthropomorphic and undignified God and is made to seem preposterous. Evil is made equally preposterous, and for similar reasons. The poem resembles "The Bear," but is on a larger scale. If these concepts of good and evil were the only concepts available, or if they were the best concepts available, then Frost's satire would be justified. But they are not, and in reading the poem one can only be appalled at Frost's willful ignorance, at his smug stupidity.

In spite of the close relationship between the two passages which I have quoted, however, the poem is far from unified. These two passages are separated by various outbursts of indignation on the part of Job's wife at the way female witches are treated, in spite of the fact that male prophets have always been received with honor; and there are other minor excursions. The concluding pages are devoted to the appearance of the Devil, who is called up by God, so that Job's wife may photograph the three main actors in the old drama as a memento. This passage is in itself an excursion from the main theme, but it is employed to permit subsidiary excursions:

> God: Don't *you* twit. He's unhappy. Church neglect
> And figurative use have pretty well
> Reduced him to a shadow of himself.
>
> Job's Wife: *That* explains why he's so diaphanous
> And easy to see through. But where's he off to?
> I thought there were to be festivities
> Of some kind. We could have charades.
>
> God: He has his business he must be about.
> Job mentioned him and so I brought him in
> More to give his reality its due
> Than anything.
>
> Job's Wife: He's very real to me
> And always will be. Please don't go. Stay, stay .
> But to the evensong and having played
> Together we will go with you along.
> There are who won't have had enough of you
> If you go now. Look how he takes no steps!
> He isn't really going, yet he's leaving.
>
> Job: (*Who has been standing dazed with new ideas*)
> He's on that tendency that like the Gulf Stream,
> Only of sand, not water, runs through here.
> It has a rate distinctly different
> From the surrounding desert; just today
> I stumbled over it and got tripped up.
>
> Job's Wife: Oh, yes, that tendency! Oh, do come off it.
> Don't let it carry you away. I hate
> A tendency. The minute you get on one
> It seems to start right off accelerating. . . .

In this passage, the satire is aimed at the word *tendency*, but the exact meaning of the word is not clear: it may mean a trivial fashion; it may mean an intellectual movement; it may indicate that Frost is unable to distinguish between a trivial fashion and an intellectual movement, just as he is unable to differentiate among reformers. The mutilated fragment from Herrick serves no purpose, but is merely an aimless effort to be funny. The poem as a whole is at loose ends; no single part of it is intelligent or even tries to be intelligent. It is a curious performance to signalize the seventieth birthday of a poet of so great a reputation. It is matched in triviality and general ineptitude by the collection of short poems entitled *Steeple Bush* and published more recently.

The best of the didactic poems is the one called "The Lesson for Today." The poem is for the most part a suavely satirical comment upon that school of contemporary criticism which holds that the modern poet is condemned to mediocrity because of the degeneracy of the age, and to this extent the poem is one with which it is hard not to sympathize. Frost addresses his hypothetical poet of the court of Charles the Great as follows:

> I can just hear you call your Palace class:
> Come learn the Latin Eheu for alas.
> You may not want to use it and you may.
> O paladins, the lesson for today
> Is how to be unhappy yet polite.
> And at the summons Roland, Olivier,
> And every sheepish paladin and peer,
> Being already more than proved in fight,
> Sits down in school to try if he can write
> Like Horace in the true Horatian vein,
> Yet like a Christian disciplined to bend
> His mind to thinking always of the end.
> Memento mori and obey the Lord.
> Art and religion love the sombre chord.
> Earth's a hard place in which to save the soul,
> And could it be brought under state control,
> So automatically we all were saved,
> Its separateness from Heaven could be waived;
> It might as well at once be kingdom-come.
> (Perhaps it will be next millenium.)

From this subject, however, the poem wanders into a brief discussion of mortality in general and the poet's concern with the subject; and after that topic the poem closes on the poet's epitaph for himself:

> I hold your doctrine of Memento Mori.
> And were an epitaph to be my story

> I'd have a short one ready for my own.
> I would have written of me on my stone:
> I had a lover's quarrel with the world.

These two transitions are casual rather than structural, and the poem falls badly apart. The last lines, moreover, are extremely bad. There is a weak sentimentality about them which one perceives easily, but the reason for which deserves mention. There are good reasons for quarreling with the world, or at least with large segments of it; much of the world is evil, and the evil had better be recognized and taken seriously. If the quarrel can be reduced to a lover's quarrel, it is not serious. It is as if one said to a murderer: "After all, you are human, and you have a perfect right to your own opinions, attitudes, and behavior; we are all human and should respect and admire each other." The principle back of the final line is vicious and corrupts the line. And the intellectual vagueness which is responsible for this weak ending is responsible likewise for the fragmentary structure of the poem and for the weakness of the other poems which I have been considering.

Frost, as far as we have examined him, then, is a poet who holds the following views: he believes that impulse is trustworthy and reason contemptible, that formative decisions should be made casually and passively, that the individual should retreat from cooperative action with his kind should retreat not to engage in intellectual activity but in order to protect himself from the contamination of outside influence, that affairs manage themselves for the best if left alone, that ideas of good and evil need not be taken very seriously. These views are sure to be a hindrance to self-development, and they effectually cut Frost off from any really profound understanding of human experience, whether political, moral, metaphysical, or religious. The result in the didactic poems is the perversity and incoherence of thought; the result in the narrative poems is either slightness of subject or a flat and uninteresting apprehension of the subject; the result in the symbolic lyrics is a disturbing dislocation between the descriptive surface, which is frequently lovely, and the ultimate meaning, which is usually sentimental and unacceptable. The result in nearly all the poems is a measure of carelessness in the style, sometimes small and sometimes great, but usually evident: the conversational manner will naturally suit a poet who takes all experience so casually, and it is only natural that the conversational manner should often become very conversational indeed.

It is worth while to mention one other poem in connection with Frost's retreat from the serious subject. The poem I have in mind is called "The Times Table." The poem deals with a farmer who is given

to commenting on death and who is reproved by Frost: Frost remarks
that such comments should not be made

> Unless our purpose is doing harm,
> And then I know of no better way
> To close a road, abandon a farm,
> Reduce the births of the human race,
> And bring back nature in people's place.

We should remember that Frost is a poet and normally speaks with
full consciousness of his role as poet; it is reasonable to assume that this
poem applies to the poet as well as to other persons. The poet, then,
should not deal with death or with comparably disturbing topics, because these topics distress and discourage people. Yet I wish to point
out that all people die, that human life is filled with tragedy, and that
commonly the tragedies accumulate all but overwhelmingly toward the
end. To ignore the tragic subject is to leave oneself unprepared for
the tragic experience; it is likely to lead to disaster and collapse. It is
the business of the poet, let me repeat, to understand his subjects, and
as far as may be the most difficult and important subjects, in rational
terms, and at the same time to communicate the feeling which ought
to be communicated by that rational understanding. The great poet
judges the tragic subject completely, that is, rationally and emotionally;
the nature of the human mind is such that we can enter the poet's mind
by way of his poem, if we are willing to make the effort, and share his
judgment. In this way we may gain both understanding and strength,
for the human mind is so made that it is capable of growth and of
growth in part through its own self-directed effort. This is the virtue of
poetry; in so far as it is good, and we understand both its goodness and
its limitations, it enables us to achieve a more nearly perfect and comprehensive being, to reduce that margin of spiritual privation which is
evil. But Frost advises us to turn away from serious topics, and for the
greater part he confines himself to minor topics. The major topics
impinge upon his personal experience, however, for after all they are
unavoidable; but his treatment of them is usually whimsical, sentimental,
and evasive; and in his later years his poetry is more and more pervaded
by an obscure melancholy which he can neither control nor understand.

IV

Yet Frost has a genuine gift for writing, as I have pointed out, and
this gift emerges more clearly in his later work than in his earlier,

though still hesitantly and momentarily. The view of human nature which we have seen Frost to hold is one that must lead of necessity to a feeling that the individual man is small, lost, and unimportant in the midst of a vast and changing universe. This feeling is expressed in the well-known poem entitled "On Going Unnoticed." The nostalgic love for the chaotic and the dream-like, which Frost inherits from the Romantic tradition, along with an habitual but unreasoned hesitancy or fear, which is the heritage of the earlier New England, keeps Frost looking two ways, unable to move decisively in either direction. He is neither a truly vigorous Romantic, such as Hart Crane, nor a truly reactionary Classicist, such as E. A. Robinson. He cannot decide whether to go or to stay, and the result is uncertainty and increasing melancholy. One may see the same difficulty in "Tree at My Window." Frost sees his own mind as similar to the vague dream-head of the tree, the thing next most diffuse to cloud, and the feeling of the poem is one of a melancholy longing to share the dream-like experience more fully. One can trace the manner in which Frost has arrived at this state of mind, and to that extent the poem is comprehensible. The feeling appears to be rendered more or less truly; that is, it seems to be an acceptable version of the feelings of a man in this predicament. But the poet does not understand the nature or the limitations of the predicament; and to that extent the poem is incomplete and not quite sure of itself. Like "The Road Not Taken" it puts on the reader a burden of critical intelligence which ought to have been borne more fully by the poet; and if the reader is not capable of the necessary intelligence, the poem is likely to draw him into a similar state of mind.

"The Last Mowing" deals with the same subject, and even more beguilingly. It describes a meadow which is being abandoned and is about to be taken over by the wild flowers before the more massive wilderness moves in:

> The place for the moment is ours,
> For you, oh tumultuous flowers
> To go to waste and go wild in,
> All shapes and colors of flowers,
> I needn't call you by name.

The next to the last line of this poem—"All shapes and colors of flowers" —is a curious triumph of rhetoric. Shape and color are named as pure abstractions; no particular shape or color is given; and what we get is an image of the shapeless and the shadowy, of haunting confusion, of longing for something unrealizable, of the fields of asphodel. This poem in its subdued and melancholy, yet somehow violent, abandonment to chaos, is one of the most explicit statements of Frost's predicament, and one of the most moving of them. "Spring Pools," from the same volume, appears to treat the same subject, but less explicitly. In paraphrase, it is a warning to the summer woods not to drink up the pools of snow water and the flowers that grow from them—these flowery waters and these watery flowers—and organize them into something greater. It is a poem on the love for the small, the fleeting, and the elusive experience of the late Romantic; in this respect, and in respect to the extraordinary sensitivity of its execution, it reminds me strongly of a poem by Paul Verlaine: *"Le Piano que baise une main frêle."* Superficially considered, the poem by Verlaine deals with a subject which is very different and more obviously decadent; but decadence is a state of mind, not a matter of the landscape which happens to provide the symbols, and in spiritual quality the two poems are remarkably similar.

The symbolic lyrics which I have been discussing are all to be found in the volume called *West-Running Brook,* the fifth collection. There is one poem in the volume, the sonnet entitled "Acquainted with the Night," which surpasses any poem thus far mentioned and which seems to me one of the two or three best poems that Frost has written. Superficially, the poem deals with the feeling of loneliness which one has when walking late at night in a strange city; but symbolically it deals with the poet's loneliness in a strange and obscure world, and the clock which tells him that the time is neither wrong nor right is a symbol of the relativism which causes his melancholy. The understanding of his predicament appears to be greater in this poem than in most of the others; he knows, at least, that it is a predicament and realizes the state of mind to which it has brought him. In the seventh volume, *A Witness Tree,* there is an even more impressive piece entitled "The Most of It." This poem represents a momentary insight into the vast and brute indifference of nature, the nature toward which Frost has cherished so sentimental a feeling through so many poems. For a moment the poet appears to be appalled. The poem deals with a protagonist who seems to have cultivated solitude, like Frost, and who heard only the echo of his own voice in the wilderness but who longed for a personal reply from nature. The reply, when it came, was not the one he had wanted. One morning he saw a splash on the far side of the lake, and something swimming toward him, and then:

> Instead of proving human when it neared
> And some one else additional to him,
> As a great buck it powerfully appeared,

> Pushing the crumpled water up ahead,
> And landed pouring like a waterfall,
> And stumbled through the rocks with horny tread,
> And forced the underbrush—and that was all.

Frost's buck has much the same kind of symbolic grandeur as the apocryphal beast in "The Second Coming," by Yeats, and he has the advantage of greater reality; the style combines descriptive precision with great concentration of meaning and at the same time is wholly free from decoration, ineptitude, and other irrelevancy. The poem gives one some idea of how great a poet Frost might conceivably have been, had he been willing to use his mind instead of letting it wither. In this poem especially, and to some extent in "Acquainted with the Night," the poet confronts his condition fairly and sees it for what it is, but the insight is momentary: he neither proceeds from this point to further understanding nor even manages to retain the realization that he has achieved. Much else in *A Witness Tree* is similar to the earlier work, and the next and last two books, *A Masque of Reason* (which I have described in some detail) and *Steeple Bush,* are his feeblest and least serious efforts.

There are a few other poems in the later books, however, which are impressive, and they ought to be mentioned in justice to their author, although little would be gained from a detailed account of them. In *A Further Range* there is a moderately long lyric entitled "The Vindictives," which deals with the looting of the Inca empire by the Spaniards, and with the way in which the Incas in return sacked their own country and buried the gold.

> One Inca prince on the rack,
> And late in his last hour alive,
> Told them in what lake to dive
> To seek what they seemed so to want.
> They dived and nothing was found.
> He told them to dive till they drowned.
> The whole fierce conquering pack
> Hunted and tortured and raged.
> There were suns of story and vaunt
> They searched for into Brazil
> Their tongues hanging out unassuaged.

This is probably the only poem in Frost in which one can find anything resembling heroic action; the poem is motivated by a simple and honest

hatred of brutality and injustice so obvious that they cannot be overlooked. The hatred in question, however, can be justified only by
certain ideas, the ideas of Christian and classical philosophy, which,
although they are a part of Frost's background and influence him to this
extent, he has during all of his career neglected or explicitly maligned.
The poem is a little loose in construction and is occasionally careless
in style; but it has an honesty and a controlled violence which make
it very impressive. In *A Witness Tree* there are several other fine but
minor lyrics which stay in one's mind, especially "The Rabbit Hunter,"
"Never Again Would Birds' Song Be the Same," and "I Could Give All
to Time." "Come In" is a memorable lyric, but perhaps it contains too
much of Frost's professional and somewhat sentimental charm.

In *A Witness Tree* there is a narrative of considerable interest, "The
Discovery of the Madeiras." It retells a story from Hackluyt about a pair
of lovers who elope from England; the captain of their vessel, who had
been a slaver, tells the man a singularly brutal story about the murder
of a pair of Negroes who were lovers; the man repeats it to his lady,
and she withdraws to her cabin, becomes ill, and eventually dies. In
style the poem resembles "The Vindictives," but it has less force at
its best and is often undistinguished. It is written in eight-syllable lines
rhyming in couplets and has something of the effect of a modern and
sophisticated ballad. But the best of the old border ballads differ in
one important respect: they deal, commonly, with an important decision consciously made, and with the resultant action, which is frequently
violent but which is also important, either for good or for evil; Frost's
poem deals with the accidental impingement of a brutal fact upon a
morbid sensibility and the collapse of the sensibility. Frost's poem to
this extent is the product of a decadent state of mind. Frost runs up
against another difficulty in this poem which he encounters in all his
narratives: the virtual impossibility of writing a short and purely
realistic narrative which shall attain great power. The narrative, if it is to
be short, must be symbolical or allegorical, it must be packed with the
power of generalization; if it is to be purely realistic, it must be developed
and explored fully in its capacity as a particular history. The short story
writer in prose meets the same difficulty, but the short story is a longer
and freer form and so has a better chance of success; and furthermore it
makes a more modest claim upon our expectations, so that we are less
likely to trouble ourselves about its limits.

V

These remarks have been unfair to Frost in certain respects. I have
quoted most extensively from his didactic poems, and especially from

those in blank verse. Frost is at his worst in didactic writing, in spite of his fondness for it: his ideas are impossible and his style is exceptionally shoddy. Furthermore, although Frost is frequently very skillful in the handling of short rhymed forms, he is extremely inept in managing blank verse; in blank verse his theory of conversational style shows itself at its worst—the rhythms are undistinguished and are repetitious to the point of deadly monotony. But it is in these poems that Frost states his ideas most unmistakably, and it is necessary to understand the ideas to form an estimate of him at all. He is at his best, as regards style, in the short rhymed lyric, but his short lyrics are less explicit in stating their themes, and unless one comes to them with a clear concept of Frost's principal themes one may overlook the themes or mistake them. Frost is at his best in such poems as "The Most of It" and "Acquainted with the Night," in which he seems to be more or less aware of the untenability of his own position and to face his difficulty, or as "The Vindictives," in which as the result of a fortunate accident of some kind he is able simply to ignore his usual themes and write as if he had never heard of them. The bulk of his really memorable work, however, is to be found among the symbolic lyrics, of which "The Last Mowing" and "Spring Pools" are excellent examples, lyrics in which the descriptive element is beautifully handled, in which the feeling is communicated with a sufficient degree of success to make them unforgettable but with so great a degree of imprecision as to make them curiously unsatisfactory. For the feeling does not arise merely from the contemplation of the natural objects described: if it did so, it would be too strong and too mysteriously elusive for its origins; the feeling arises mainly from the concepts of which the natural objects are the symbolic vehicles, and those concepts, as I have shown, are unacceptable, and when one tries to project them clearly into terms of human action are unimaginable. Frost's instinctualism, his nostalgia for dream and chaos, are merely the symptoms of sentimental obscurantism when, as in Frost's work, they are dealt with lightly and whimsically, but if taken seriously, as in the work of Crane and Pound, they may lead to more serious difficulties. They do not lead toward intelligence, no matter how far the individual devotee may travel in their company; they lead away from intelligence. They lead away from the true comprehension of human experience which makes for great, or even for successful, poetry. The element of the unimaginable, and hence of the imprecise, which lurks in the theme of "The Last Mowing" will make it forever, and in spite of its real and extraordinary virtues, a very imperfectly successful poem; this poem simply will not stand comparison with such pieces, for example, as "Low Barometer," by Robert Bridges, as Howard Baker's poem on Psyche, or as J. V. Cun-

ningham's epigrams on Swift and on the calculus. "The Last Mowing"
will for some years be a more popular poem than these, however, for,
as I have said, Frost's confusion is similar to that of the public, and
most readers of poetry still regard poetry as a vague emotional indulgence:
they do not take poetry seriously and they dislike serious poetry.

Frost, then, may be described as a good poet in so far as he may be
said to exist, but a dangerous influence in so far as his existence is
incomplete. He is in no sense a great poet, but he is at times a distinguished and valuable poet. In order to evaluate his work and profit
by it, however, we must understand him far better than he understands
himself, and this fact indicates a very serious weakness in his talent.
If we do not so understand him, his poetry is bound to reinforce some
of the most dangerous tendencies of our time; his weakness is commonly
mistaken for wisdom, his vague and sentimental feeling for profound
emotion, as his reputation and the public honors accorded him plainly
testify. He is the nearest thing we have to a poet laureate, a national
poet; and this fact is evidence of the community of thought and feeling
between Frost and a very large part of the American literary public.
The principles which have saved some part of Frost's talent, the principles of Greek and Christian thought, are principles which are seldom
openly defended and of which the implications and ramifications are
understood by relatively few of our contemporaries, by Frost least of all;
they operate upon Frost at a distance, through social inheritance, and
he has done his best to adopt principles which are opposed to them.
The principles which have hampered Frost's development, the principles of Emersonian and Thoreauistic Romanticism, are the principles
which he has openly espoused, and they are widespread in our culture.
Until we understand these last and the dangers inherent in them and so
abandon them in favor of better, we are unlikely to produce many poets
greater than Frost, although a few poets may have intelligence enough
to work clear of such influences; and we are likely to deteriorate more
or less rapidly both as individuals and as a nation.

To the Laodiceans

by Randall Jarrell

Back in the days when "serious readers of modern poetry" were most patronizing to Frost's poems, one was often moved to argument, or to article-writing, or to saying under one's breath: *What is man that Thou art mindful of him?* In these days it's better—a little, not much: the lips are pursed that ought to be parted, and they still pay lip-service, or little more. But Frost's best poetry—and there is a great deal of it, at once wonderfully different and wonderfully alike—deserves the attention, submission, and astonished awe that real art always requires of us; to give it a couple of readings and a ribbon lettered First in the Old-Fashioned (or Before 1900) Class of Modern Poetry is worse, almost, than not to read it at all. Surely *we* [I don't know exactly whom this *we* includes, but perhaps I could say that it means "the friends of things in the spirit," even when the things are difficult, even when the things are in the flesh] are not going to be like the *Saturday Review* readers and writers who tell one how completely good Frost is, and in the next breath tell one how narrowly good, limitedly good, badly good Eliot is. Surely it is the excellence most unlike our own that we will be most eager to acknowledge, since it not only extends but completes us—and since only we, not the excellence, are harmed by our rejection of it.

Frost has limitations of a kind very noticeable to us, but they are no more important than those of other contemporary poets; and most of the limitations, less noticeable to us, that these poets share, Frost is free of. If it makes good sense (but a narrow and ungenerous, though essential, sense) to say about Frost, "As a poet he isn't in Rilke's class at all," it does *not* make such sense if you substitute for Rilke's name that of Eliot or Moore or Stevens or Auden, that of any living poet. We can already see, most vividly, how ridiculous posterity is going to find the people who thought Marianne Moore's poems "not poetry at all," *The Waste Land* a hoax, and so on; but is posterity going to find any less ridiculous the intellectuals who admitted Frost only as a second-class citizen of the Republic of Letters, a "bard" whom it would be absurd to compare with real modern poets like—oh, E. E. Cummings? Frost's daemonic gift of always getting on the buttered side of both God and Mammon; of doing and saying anything and everything that he pleases, and still getting the World to approve or tactfully ignore every bit of it; of not only allowing, but taking a hard pleasure in encouraging, fools and pedants to adore him as their own image magnified—all this has helped to keep us from seeing Frost for what he really is. And here one has no right to be humble and agreeable, and to concede beforehand that *what he really is* is only one's own "view" or "interpretation" of him: the regular ways of looking at Frost's poetry are grotesque simplifications, distortions, falsifications—coming to know his poetry well ought to be enough, in itself, to dispel any of them, and to make plain the necessity of finding some other way of talking about his work.

Any of us but Frost himself (and all the little Frostlings who sit round him wondering with a foolish face of praise, dealing out ten monosyllables to the homey line) can by now afford just to wonder at his qualities, not to sadden at his defects, and can gladly risk looking a little foolish in the process. The real complication, sophistication, and ambiguity of Frost's thought [what poet since Arnold has written so much about isolation, and said so much more about it than even Arnold? what other poet, long before we had begun to perfect the means of altogether doing away with humanity, had taken as an obsessive subject the wiping-out of man, his replacement by the nature out of which he arose?], the range and depth and height of his poems, have had justice done to them by neither his admirers nor his detractors—and, alas, aren't going to have justice done to them by me now. If one is talking about Frost's poetry to friends, or giving a course in it to students, one can go over thirty or forty of his best poems and feel sure about everything: one doesn't need, then, to praise or blame or generalize—the poems speak for themselves almost as well as poems can. But when one writes a little article about Frost, one feels lamentably sure of how lamentably short of his world the article is going to fall; one can never write about him without wishing that it were a whole book, a book in which one could talk about hundreds of poems and hundreds of other things, and fall short by one's essential and not accidental limitations.

I have sometimes written, and often talked, about Frost's willful, helpless, all too human mixture of virtues and vices, so I hope that this time

I will be allowed simply—in the nice, old-fashioned, looked-down-on phrase—to appreciate. And I want to appreciate more than his best poems, I want to exclaim over some of the unimportantly delightful and marvellously characteristic ones, and over some of the places where all of Frost and all of what is being described are married and indistinguishable in one line. But first let me get rid, in a few sentences, of that Skeleton on the Doorstep that is the joy of his enemies and the despair of his friends. Just as a star will have, sometimes, a dark companion, so Frost has a pigheaded one, a shadowy self that grows longer and darker as the sun gets lower. I am speaking of that other self that might be called the Grey Eminence of Robert Taft, or the Peter Pan of the National Association of Manufacturers, or any such thing—this public self incarnates all the institutionalized complacency that Frost once mocked at and fled from, and later pretended to become a part of and became a part of. This Yankee Editorialist side of Frost gets in the way of *everything*—of us, of the real Frost, of the real poems and their real subject-matter. And a poet so magically good at making the subtlest of points surely shouldn't evolve into one who regularly comes out and tells you the point after it's been made—and comes out and tells you in such trudging doctrinaire lines, a point like the end of a baseball bat. Frost says in a piece of homely doggerel that he has hoped wisdom could be not only Attic but Laconic, Boeotian even—"at least not systematic"; but how systematically Frostian the worst of his later poems are! His good poems are the best refutation of, the most damning comment on, his bad: his *Complete Poems* have the air of being able to educate any faithful reader into tearing out a third of the pages, reading a third, and practically wearing out the rest.

We begin to read Frost, always, with the taste of "Birches" in our mouth—a taste a little brassy, a little sugary; and to take it out I will use not such good and familiar poems as "Mending Wall" and "After Apple-Picking," or such a wonderful and familiar (and misunderstood) poem as "An Old Man's Winter Night," but four or five of Frost's best and least familiar poems. Let me begin with a poem that, at first glance, hardly seems a Frost poem at all, but reminds us more of another kind of unfamiliar poem that Housman wrote; this poem is called "Neither Out Far Nor In Deep":

> The people along the sand
> All turn and look one way.
> They turn their back on the land.
> They look at the sea all day.

> As long as it takes to pass
> A ship keeps raising its hull;
> The wetter ground like glass
> Reflects a standing gull.
>
> The land may vary more;
> But wherever the truth may be—
> The water comes ashore,
> And the people look at the sea.
>
> They cannot look out far.
> They cannot look in deep.
> But when was that ever a bar
> To any watch they keep?

First of all, of course, the poem is simply there, in indifferent unchanging actuality; but our thought about it, what we are made to make of it, is there too, made to be there. When we choose between land and sea, the human and the inhuman, the finite and the infinite, the sea *has* to be the infinite that floods in over us endlessly, the hypnotic monotony of the universe that is incommensurable with us—everything into which we look neither very far nor very deep, but look, look just the same. And yet Frost doesn't say so—it is the geometry of this very geometrical poem, its inescapable structure, that says so. There is the deepest tact and restraint in the symbolism; it is like Housman's

> Stars, I have seen them fall,
> But when they drop and die
> No star is lost at all
> From all the star-sown sky.
>
> The toil of all that be
> Helps not the primal fault:
> It rains into the sea
> And still the sea is salt.

But Frost's poem is flatter, greyer, and at once tenderer and more terrible, without even the consolations of rhetoric and exaggeration— there is no "primal fault" in Frost's poem, but only the faint Biblical memories of "any watch they keep." What we do know we don't care about; what we do care about we don't know: we can't look out very far, or in very deep; and when did that ever bother *us*? It would be hard to find anything more unpleasant to say about people than that last stanza; but Frost doesn't say it unpleasantly—he says it with flat ease, takes everything with something harder than contempt, more passive than acceptance. And isn't there something heroic about the whole business, too—something touching about our absurdity? If the fool persisted in his folly he would become a wise man, Blake said, and we have persisted. The tone of the last lines—or, rather, their careful suspension between several tones, as a piece of iron can be held in the air between powerful enough magnets—allows for this too. This recognition of the essential limitations of man, without denial or protest or rhetoric or palliation, is very rare and very valuable, and rather usual in Frost's best poetry. One is reminded of Empson's thoughtful and truthful comment on Gray's "Elegy": "Many people, without being communists, have been irritated by the complacence in the massive calm of the poem . . . And yet what is said is one of the permanent truths; it is only in degree that any improvement of society would prevent wastage of human powers; the waste even in a fortunate life, the isolation even of a life rich in intimacy, cannot but be felt deeply, and is the central feeling of tragedy."

Another of Frost's less familiar poems is called "Provide Provide":

> The witch that came (the withered hag)
> To wash the steps with pail and rag
> Was once the beauty Abishag,
>
> The picture pride of Hollywood.
> Too many fall from great and good
> For you to doubt the likelihood.
>
> Die early and avoid the fate.
> Or if predestined to die late,
> Make up your mind to die in state.
>
> Make the whole stock exchange your own!
> If need be occupy a throne,
> Where nobody can call *you* crone.
>
> Some have relied on what they knew;
> Others on being simply true.
> What worked for them might work for you.
>
> No memory of having starred
> Atones for later disregard
> Or keeps the end from being hard.

> Better to go down dignified
> With boughten friendship at your side
> Than none at all. Provide, provide!

For many readers this poem will need no comment at all, and for others it will need rather more than I could ever give. The poem is—to put it as crudely as possible—an immortal masterpiece; and if we murmur something about its crudities and provincialisms, History will smile tenderly at us and lay us in the corner beside those cultivated people from Oxford and Cambridge who thought Shakespeare a Hollywood scenario-writer. Since I can't write five or six pages about the poem, it might be better to say only that it is full of the deepest, and most touching, moral wisdom—and it is full, too, of the life we have to try to be wise about and moral in (the sixth stanza is almost unbearably actual). The Wisdom of this World and the wisdom that comes we know not whence exist together in the poem, not side by side but one inside the other; yet the whole poem exists for, lives around, the fifth stanza and its *others on being simply true*—was restraint ever more moving? One can quote about that line Rilke's *In the end the only defence is defence-lessness*, and need to say no more. But the rest of the poem is the more that we need to say, if we decide to say any more: it says, in the worldliest and homeliest of terms, that expediency won't work—the poem is, even in its form, a marvellous *reductio ad absurdum* of expediency—but since you *will* try it, since you *will* provide for the morrow, then provide hard for it, be really expedient, settle yourself for life in the second-best bed around which the heirs gather, the very best second-best bed. The poem is so particularly effective because it is the Wisdom of this World which demonstrates to us that the Wisdom of this World isn't enough. The poem puts, so to speak, the minimal case for morality, and then makes the minimal recommendation of it (*what worked for them might work for you*); but this has a beauty and conclusiveness that aren't minimal.

The most awful of Frost's smaller poems is one called "Design":

> I found a dimpled spider, fat and white,
> On a white heal-all, holding up a moth
> Like a white piece of rigid satin cloth—
> Assorted characters of death and blight
> Mixed ready to begin the morning right,
> Like the ingredients of a witch's broth—
> A snow-drop spider, a flower like froth,
> And dead wings carried like a paper kite.

> What had that flower to do with being white,
> The wayside blue and innocent heal-all?
> What brought the kindred spider to that height,
> Then steered the white moth thither in the night?
> What but design of darkness to appall?—
> If design govern in a thing so small.

This is the Argument from Design with a vengeance; is the terrible negative from which the eighteenth century's Kodak picture (with its *Having wonderful time. Wish you were here* on the margin) had to be printed. If a watch, then a watch-maker; if a diabolical machine, then a diabolical mechanic—Frost uses exactly the logic that has always been used. And this little albino catastrophe is too whitely catastrophic to be accidental, too impossibly unlikely ever to be a coincidence: accident, chance, statistics, natural selection are helpless to account for such designed terror and heartbreak, such an awful symbolic perversion of the innocent being of the world. Frost's details are so diabolically good that it seems criminal to leave some unremarked; but notice how *dimpled, fat,* and *white* (all but one; all but one) come from our regular description of any baby; notice how the *heal-all,* because of its name, is the one flower in all the world picked to be the altar for this Devil's Mass; notice how *holding up* the moth brings something ritual and hieratic, a ghostly, ghastly formality, to this priest and its sacrificial victim; notice how terrible to the fingers, how full of the stilling rigor of death, that *white piece of rigid satin cloth* is. And *assorted characters of death and blight* is, like so many things in this poem, sharply ambiguous: *a mixed bunch of actors* or *diverse representative signs.* The tone of the phrase *assorted characters of death and blight* is beautifully developed in the ironic Breakfast-Club-calisthenics, Radio-Kitchen heartiness of *mixed ready to begin the morning right* (which assures us, so unreassuringly, that this isn't any sort of Strindberg *Spook Sonata,* but hard fact), and concludes in the *ingredients* of the witch's broth, giving the soup a sort of cuddly shimmer that the cauldron in *Macbeth* never had; the *broth,* even, is brought to life—we realize that witch's broth *is* broth, to be supped with a long spoon. For sweet-sour, smiling awfulness *snow-drop spider* looks unsurpassable, until we come to the almost obscenely horrible (even the mouth-gestures are utilized) *a flower like froth;* this always used to seem to me the case of the absolutely inescapable effect, until a student of mine said that you could tell how beautiful the flower was because the poet compared it to froth; when I said to her, "But—but—but what does froth *remind* you of?" looking desperately into her blue eyes, she replied: "Fudge. It reminds me of making fudge."

And then, in the victim's own little line, how contradictory and awful everything is: *dead wings carried like a paper kite!* The *dead* and the *wings* work back and forth on each other heart-breakingly, and the contradictory pathos of the *carried* wings is exceeded by that of the matter-of-fact conversion into what has never lived, into a shouldered toy, of the ended life. *What had that flower to do with being white,/The wayside blue and innocent heal-all?* expresses as well as anything ever has the arbitrariness of our guilt, the fact that Original Sin is only Original Accident, so far as the creatures of this world are concerned. And *the wayside blue and innocent heal-all* is, down to the least sound, the last helpless, yearning, trailing-away sigh of too-precarious innocence, of a potentiality cancelled out almost before it began to exist. The *wayside* makes it universal, commonplace, and somehow dearer to us; the *blue* brings in all the associations of the normal negated color (the poem is likely to remind the reader of Melville's chapter on the Whiteness of the Whale, just as Frost may have been reminded); and the *innocent* is given a peculiar force and life by this context, just as the name *heal-all* comes to sad, ironic, literal life: it healed all, itself it could not heal. The *kindred* is very moving in its half-forgiving ambiguity; and the Biblical *thither in the night* and the conclusive *steered* (with its careful echoes of "To a Water-Fowl" and a thousand sermons) are very moving and very serious in their condemnation, their awful mystery. The partly ambiguous, summing-up *What but design of darkness to appall* comes as something taken for granted, a relief almost, in its mere statement and generalization, after the almost unbearable actuality and particularity of what has come before. And then this whole appalling categorical machinery of reasoning-out, of conviction, of condemnation—it reminds one of the machine in *The Penal Colony*—is suddenly made merely hypothetical, a possible contradicted shadow, by one off-hand last-minute qualification: one that dismisses it, but that dismisses it only for a possibility still more terrifying, a whole new random, statistical, astronomical abyss underlying the diabolical machinery of the poem. "In large things, macroscopic phenomena of some real importance," the poem says, "the classical mechanics of design probably *does* operate—though in reverse, so far as the old Argument from Design is concerned; but these little things, things of no real importance, microscopic phenomena like a flower or moth or man or planet or solar system [we have so indissolubly identified ourselves with the moth and flower and spider that we cannot treat our own nature and importance, which theirs symbolize, as fundamentally different from theirs], are governed by the purely statistical laws of quantum mechanics, of random distribution, are they not?" I have given this statement of "what the poem says"—it says much more—an exaggeratedly physical, scientific form because both a metaphorically and literally astronomical view of things is so common, and so unremarked-on, in Frost. This poem, I think most people will admit, makes Pascal's "eternal silence of those infinite spaces" seem the hush between the movements of a cantata.

Another impressive unfamiliar poem is "The Most of It," a poem which indicates as well as any I can think of Frost's stubborn truthfulness, his willingness to admit both the falseness in the cliché and the falseness in the contradition of the cliché; if the universe never gives us either a black or a white answer, but only a black-and-white one that is somehow not an answer at all, still its inhuman not-answer exceeds any answer that we human beings could have thought of or wished for:

> He thought he kept the universe alone;
> For all the voice in answer he could wake
> Was but the mocking echo of his own
> From some tree-hidden cliff across the lake.
> Some morning from the boulder-broken beach
> He would cry out on life, that what it wants
> Is not its own love back in copy speech,
> But counter-love, original response.
> And nothing ever came of what he cried
> Unless it was the embodiment that crashed
> In the cliff's talus on the other side,
> And then in the far distant water splashed,
> But after a time allowed for it to swim,
> Instead of proving human when it neared
> And someone else additional to him,
> As a great buck it powerfully appeared,
> Pushing the crumpled water up ahead,
> And landed pouring like a waterfall,
> And stumbled through the rocks with horny tread,
> And forced the underbrush—and that was all.

But one of the strangest and most characteristic, most dismaying and most gratifying, poems any poet has ever written is a poem called "Directive." It shows the coalescence of three of Frost's obsessive themes, those of isolation, of extinction, and of the final limitations of man—is Frost's last word about all three:

Back out of all this now too much for us,
Back in a time made simple by the loss
Of detail, burned, dissolved, and broken off
Like graveyard marble sculpture in the weather,
There is a house that is no more a house
Upon a farm that is no more a farm
And in a town that is no more a town.
The road there, if you'll let a guide direct you
Who only has at heart your getting lost,
May seem as if it should have been a quarry—
Great monolithic knees the former town
Long since gave up pretence of keeping covered.
And there's a story in a book about it:
Besides the wear of iron wagon wheels
The ledges show lines ruled southeast northwest,
The chisel work of an enormous Glacier
That braced his feet against the Arctic Pole.
You must not mind a certain coolness from him
Still said to haunt this side of Panther Mountain.
Nor need you mind the serial ordeal
Of being watched from forty cellar holes
As if by eye pairs out of forty firkins.
As for the wood's excitement over you
That sends light rustle rushes to their leaves,
Charge that to upstart inexperience.
Where were they all not twenty years ago?
They think too much of having shaded out
A few old pecker-fretted apple trees.
Make yourself up a cheering song of how
Someone's road home from work this once was,
Who may be just ahead of you on foot
Or creaking with a buggy load of grain.
The height of the adventure is the height
Of country where two village cultures faded
Into each other. Both of them are lost.
And if you're lost enough to find yourself
By now, pull in your ladder road behind you
And put a sign up CLOSED to all but me.
Then make yourself at home. The only field
Now left's no bigger than a harness gall.
First there's the children's house of make believe,
Some shattered dishes underneath a pine,

The playthings in the playhouse of the children.
Weep for what little things could make them glad.
Then for the house that is no more a house,
But only a belilaced cellar hole,
Now slowly closing like a dent in dough.
This was no playhouse but a house in earnest.
Your destination and your destiny's
A brook that was the water of the house,
Cold as a spring as yet so near its source,
Too lofty and original to rage.
(We know the valley streams that when aroused
Will leave their tatters hung on barb and thorn.)
I have kept hidden in the instep arch
Of an old cedar at the waterside
A broken drinking goblet like the Grail
Under a spell so the wrong ones can't find it,
So can't get saved, as Saint Mark says they mustn't.
(I stole the goblet from the children's playhouse.)
Here are your waters and your watering place.
Drink and be whole again beyond confusion.

There are weak places in the poem, but these are nothing beside so much longing, tenderness, and passive sadness, Frost's understanding that each life is pathetic because it wears away into the death that it at last half-welcomes—that even its salvation, far back at the cold root of things, is make-believe, drunk from a child's broken and stolen goblet, a plaything hidden among the ruins of the lost cultures. Here the waters of Lethe are the waters of childhood, and in their depths, with ambiguous grace, man's end is joined to his beginning. Is the poem consoling or heart-breaking? Very much of both; and its humor and acceptance and humanity, its familiarity and elevation, give it a composed matter-of-fact magnificence. Much of the strangeness of the poem is far under the surface, or else so much on the surface, in the subtlest of details (how many readers will connect the *serial ordeal* of the eye-pairs with the poem's Grail-parody?), that one slides under it unnoticing. But the first wonderful sentence; the six lines about the wood's excitement; the knowledge that produces the sentence beginning *make yourself up a cheering song;* the *both of them are lost;* incidental graces like the *eye-pairs out of forty firkins,* the *harness gall,* the *belilaced cellar hole* closing *like a dent in dough,* the plays on the word *lost;* the whole description of the children's playhouse, with the mocking (at whom does it mock?) and beautiful *weep for what little things could make them glad;* the grave, terrible *this was no playhouse but a house in earnest;* the four wonderful conclusive sentences—these, and the whole magical and helpless mastery of the poem, are things that many readers have noticed and will notice: the poem is hard to understand, but easy to love.

In another poem Frost worries about the bird that, waked in moonlight, "sang halfway through its little inborn tune," and then he realizes that the bird is as safe as ever, that any increase in danger must necessarily be an infinitesimal one, or else

> It could not have come down to us so far
> Through the interstices of things ajar
> On the long bead chain of repeated birth.

The thought, which would surely have made Darwin give a little gratified smile, might very well have pleased with its "interstices of things ajar" that earlier writer who said, "Absent thee from felicity awhile/ And in this harsh world draw thy breath in pain." For Frost is sometimes a marvellous rhetorician, a writer so completely master of his own rhetorical effects that he can alter both their degree and kind almost as he pleases. In "The Black Cottage" he is able to write the most touchingly and hauntingly prosaic of lines about the passing away of this world:

> He fell at Gettysburg or Fredericksburg.
> I ought to know—it makes a difference which:
> Fredericksburg wasn't Gettysburg, of course . . .

and he is also able to end the poem with the magnificence of

> "As I sit here, and oftentimes, I wish
> I could be monarch of a desert land
> I could devote and dedicate forever
> To the truths we keep coming back and back to.
> So desert it would have to be, so walled
> By mountain ranges half in summer snow,
> No one would covet it or think it worth
> The pains of conquering to force change on.
> Scattered oases where men dwelt, but mostly
> Sand dunes held loosely in tamarisk
> Blown over and over themselves in idleness.
> Sand grains should sugar in the natal dew
> The babe born to the desert, the sand storm

Retard mid-waste my cowering caravans—
There are bees in this wall." He struck the clapboards,
Fierce heads looked out; small bodies pivoted.
We rose to go. Sunset blazed on the windows.

One sees this extraordinary command in the composed, thoughtful, and traditional rhetoric of "The Gift Outright," one of the best of Frost's smaller poems, and perhaps the best "patriotic" poem ever written about our own country:

The land was ours before we were the land's.
She was our land more than a hundred years
Before we were her people. She was ours
In Massachusetts, in Virginia,
But we were England's, still colonials,
Possessing what we still were unpossessed by,
Possessed by what we now no more possessed.
Something we were withholding made us weak
Until we found it was ourselves
We were withholding from our land of living,
And forthwith found salvation in surrender.
Such as we were we gave ourselves outright
(The deed of gift was many deeds of war)
To the land vaguely realizing westward,
But still unstoried, artless, unenhanced,
Such as she was, such as she would become.

The third sentence is a little weakly and conventionally said; but the rest! And that *vaguely realizing westward!* The last three lines, both for tone and phrasing, are themselves realized with absolute finality, are good enough to survive all the repetitions that the generations of the future will give them.

We feel, here, that we understand why the lines are as good as they are; but sometimes there will be a sudden rise, an unlooked-for intensity and elevation of emotion, that have a conclusiveness and magnificence we are hardly able to explain. Frost ends a rather commonplace little poem about Time with a blaze of triumph, of calm and rapturous certainty, that is as transfiguring, almost, as the ending of "A Dialogue of Self and of Soul":

I could give all to Time except—except
What I myself have held. But why declare

The things forbidden that while the Customs slept
I have crossed to Safety with? For I am There,
And what I would not part with I have kept.

A man finishes an axe-helve, and Frost says:

But now he brushed the shavings from his knee
And stood the axe there on its horse's hoof,
Erect, but not without its waves, as when
The snake stood up for evil in the Garden . . .

It would be hard to find words good enough for *this*. Surely anybody must feel, as he finishes reading these lines, the thrill of authentic creation, the thrill of witnessing something that goes back farther than Homer and goes forward farther than any future we are able to imagine: here the thing in itself, and man's naked wit, and Style—the elevation and composed forbearance of the Grand Style, of the truly classical— coalesce in an instant of grace.

Frost calls one poem "The Old Barn at the Bottom of the Fogs," and starts out:

Where's this barn's house? It never had a house,
Or joined with sheds in ring-around a dooryard.
The hunter scuffling leaves goes by at dusk,
The gun reversed that he went out with shouldered.
The harvest moon and then the hunter's moon.
Well, the moon after that came one at last
To close this outpost barn and close the season.
The fur-thing, muff-thing, rocking in and out
Across the threshold in the twilight fled him . . .

How can you resist a poet who can begin a poem like this—even if the poem later comes to nothing at all? Nor is it any easier to resist the man who says "To a Moth Seen in Winter," "with false hope seeking the love of kind," "making a labor of flight for one so airy":

Nor will you find love either nor love you.
And what I pity in you is something human,
The old incurable untimeliness,
Only begetter of all things that are . . .

What an already-prepared-for, already-familiar-seeming ring the lines have, the ring of that underlying style that great poets so often have in common beneath their own styles! I think that Dante would have read with nothing but admiration for its calm universal precision the wonderful "Acquainted with the Night," a poem in Dante's own form and with some of Dante's own qualities:

> I have been one acquainted with the night.
> I have walked out in rain—and back in rain.
> I have outwalked the furthest city light.
>
> I have looked down the saddest city lane.
> I have passed by the watchman on his beat
> And dropped my eyes, unwilling to explain.
>
> I have stood still and stopped the sound of feet
> When far away an interrupted cry
> Came over houses from another street,
>
> But not to call me back or say goodbye;
> And further still at an unearthly height,
> One luminary clock against the sky
>
> Proclaimed the time was neither wrong nor right.
> I have been one acquainted with the night.

Is this a "classical" poem? If *it* isn't, what is? Yet doesn't the poem itself make the question seem ignominious, a question with a fatal lack of magnanimity, of true comprehension and concern? The things in themselves, the poem itself, abide neither our questions nor our categories; they are free. And our own freedom—the freedom to look and not to disregard, the freedom to side against oneself—is treated with delicate and tender imaginativeness in "Time Out":

> It took that pause to make him realize
> The mountain he was climbing had the slant
> As of a book held up before his eyes
> (And was a text albeit done in plant).
> Dwarf-cornel, gold-thread, and maianthemum,
> He followingly fingered as he read,
> The flowers fading on the seed to come;
> But the thing was the slope it gave his head:
> The same for reading as it was for thought,
> So different from the hard and level stare
> Of enemies defied and battles fought.
> It was the obstinately gentle air

That may be clamored at by cause and sect
But it will have its moment to reflect.

There is even more delicacy and tenderness and imagination in "Meet-ing and Passing," a backward-looking love-poem whose last two lines, by an understatement beyond statement, make tears of delight come into one's eyes—nothing else in English is so like one of those love-poems that, in 1913, Hardy wrote about a woman who had just died; and noth-ing else in English expresses better than that last couplet—which does not rhyme, but only repeats—the transfiguring, almost inexpressible reach-ing-out of the self to what has become closer and more personal than the self:

> As I went down the hill along the wall
> There was a gate I had leaned at for the view
> And had just turned from when I first saw you
> As you came up the hill. We met. But all
> We did that day was mingle great and small
> Footprints in summer dust as if we drew
> The figure of our being less than two
> But more than one as yet. Your parasol
>
> Pointed the decimal off with one deep thrust.
> And all the time we talked you seemed to see
> Something down there to smile at in the dust
> (Oh, it was without prejudice to me!)
> Afterward I went past what you had passed
> Before we met and you what I had passed.

And Frost (no poet has had even the range of his work more unforgive-ably underestimated by the influential critics of our time) is able once or twice to give sexual love, passion itself, as breath-takingly conclusive an embodiment. Here I am not speaking of the sinister, condemning, tender "The Subverted Flower," a flawed but extraordinary poem that at once embodies and states in almost abstract form his knowledge about part of love; I mean the wonderful conclusion of "The Pauper Witch of Grafton," where the testy, acrid mockery of the old pauper, of the "noted witch" always plagued by an adulterous generation for a sign, turns into something very different as she remembers the man who first exposed and then married her:

> I guess he found he got more out of me
> By having me a witch. Or something happened

To turn him round. He got to saying things
To undo what he'd done and make it right,
Like, "No, she ain't come back from kiting yet.
Last night was one of her nights out. She's kiting.
She thinks when the wind makes a night of it
She might as well herself." But he liked best
To let on he was plagued to death with me:
If anyone had seen me coming home
Over the ridgepole, 'stride of a broomstick,
As often as he had in the tail of the night,
He guessed they'd know what he had to put up with.
Well, I showed Arthur Amy signs enough
Off from the house as far as we could keep
And from barn smells you can't wash out of ploughed ground
With all the rain and snow of seven years;
And I don't mean just skulls of Roger's Rangers
On Moosilauke, but woman signs to man,
Only bewitched so I would last him longer.
Up where the trees grow short, the mosses tall,
I made him gather me wet snow berries
On slippery rocks beside a waterfall.
I made him do it for me in the dark.
And he liked everything I made him do.
I hope if he is where he sees me now
He's so far off he can't see what I've come to.
You *can* come down from everything to nothing.
All is, if I'd a-known when I was young
And full of it, that this would be the end,
It doesn't seem as if I'd had the courage
To make so free and kick up in folks' faces.
I might have, but it doesn't seem as if.

When I read the lines that begin *Up where the trees grow short, the mosses tall,* and that end *And he liked everything I made him do* (nobody but a good poet could have written the first line, and nobody but a great one could have forced the reader to say the last line as he is forced to say it), I sometimes murmur to myself, in a perverse voice, that there is more sexuality there than in several hothouses full of Dylan Thomas; and, of course, there is love, there. And in what poem can one find more of its distortion and frustration, its helpless derangement, than in the marvellous "A Servant to Servants"? But here I come to what makes the critic of Frost's poetry groan, and sadden, and almost despair:

several of his very best poems, the poems in which he is most magnificent, most characteristic, most nearly incomparable, are far too long to quote. If I could quote "Home Burial," "The Witch of Coös," and "A Servant to Servants," Pharisee and Philistine alike would tiptoe off hand in hand, their shamed eyes starry; anyone who knows these poems well will consider the mere mention of them enough to justify any praise, any extravagance—and anybody who doesn't know them doesn't know some of the summits of our poetry, and is so much to be pitied that it would be foolish to blame him too. I don't know what to do about these poems, here: may I just make a bargain with the reader to regard them as quoted in this article?

I have used rather an odd tone about them because I feel so much frustration at not being able to quote and go over them, as I so often have done with friends and classes; they *do* crown Frost's work, are unique in the poetry of our century and perhaps in any poetry. Even such lesser poems of the sort as "The Fear" and "The Black Cottage" would be enough to make another poet respected; and it is discouraging, while mentioning Frost's poems about love, not to be able to quote "To Earthward" and "The Lovely Shall Be Choosers," two very beautiful and very unusual poems. And this reminds me that I have not even mentioned "Desert Places," a poem almost better, at the same game, than Stevens' beautiful "The Snowman." This is the best place to say once more that such an article as this is not relatively but absolutely inadequate to a body of poetry as great as Frost's, both in quality and in quantity—can be, at best, only a kind of breathless signboard. Almost all that Frost has touched, from the greatest to the smallest things, he has transfigured.

Frost is so characteristic and delightful in slight things, often, that one feels a superstitious reluctance to dismiss them with *slight*. The little "In a Disused Graveyard" is, plainly, the slightest and least pretentious of fancies; but the justest of fancies, too—and how much there is underneath its last five lines, that changes their shape almost as the least white of a wave-top is changed by the green weight under it:

> The living come with grassy tread
> To read the gravestones on the hill;
> The graveyard draws the living still,
> But never any more the dead.
>
> The verses in it say and say:
> "The ones who living come today
> To read the stones and go away
> Tomorrow dead will come to stay."

So sure of death the marbles rhyme,
Yet can't help marking all the time
How no one dead will seem to come.
What is it men are shrinking from?

It would be easy to be clever
And tell the stones: Men hate to die
And have stopped dying now forever.
I think they would believe the lie.

Nothing could be slighter than these two lines called "The Span of Life":

The old dog barks backward without getting up.
I can remember when he was a pup.

Yet the sigh we give after we've read them isn't a slight one: this is age in one couplet. And another couplet, one called "An Answer," I can hardly resist using as a sort of shibboleth or Stanford-Binet Test of the imagination: if you cannot make out the sea-change this strange little joke, this associational matrix, has undergone somewhere down in Frost's head, so that it has become worthy of Prospero himself, all nacreous with lyric, tender, amused acceptance and understanding and regret—if you can't feel any of this, you *are* a Convention of Sociologists. Here it is, "An Answer":

But Islands of the Blessèd, bless you son,
I never came upon a blessèd one.

Frost's account of a battle, in "Range-Finding," is an unprecedentedly slight one. This battle, before it killed any of the soldiers—and Frost does not go on to them—cut a flower beside a ground bird's nest, yet the bird kept flying in and out with food; and a butterfly, dispossessed of the flower, came back and flutteringly clung to it. Besides them there was

a wheel of thread
And straining cables wet with silver dew.
A sudden passing bullet shook it dry.
The indwelling spider ran to greet the fly,
But finding nothing, sullenly withdrew.

That is all. An occasional lameness or tameness of statement mars the poem, gives it a queer rather attractive old-fashionedness, but does not destroy it. This is the minimal case, the final crystalline essence of Stendhal's treatment of Waterloo: a few fathoms down the sea is always calm, and a battle, among other things, at bottom is always, this; the spider can ask with Fabrizio, "Was that it? Was I really at Waterloo?"

I mustn't go on quoting slight things forever, yet there are many more that I would like to quote—or that the reader might like to reread, or read: "An Empty Threat," "The Telephone," "Moon Compasses," "The Hill Wife," "Dust of Snow," "The Oven Bird," "Gathering Leaves" (that saddest, most-carefully-unspecified symbol for our memories), "For Once, Then, Something," "The Runaway," "In Hardwood Groves," "Beech," "The Ingenuities of Debt," "The Investment," the "Books" part of "A Fountain, a Bottle, a Donkey's Ear and Some Books"— these, and poems like "The Pasture" and "Stopping by Woods on a Snowy Evening," that many readers will not need to reread, but will simply repeat. (Frost is, often, as automatically memorable as any savage chronicle rhymed and metred for remembrance: I was floating in a quarry with my chin on a log when I first discovered that I knew "Provide Provide" by heart, and there are six or eight more that I know without ever having memorized them.) Here is a poem titled "Atmosphere," and subtitled "Inscription for a Garden Wall":

> Winds blow the open grassy places bleak;
> But where this old wall burns a sunny cheek,
> They eddy over it too toppling weak
> To blow the earth or anything self-clear;
> Moisture and color and odor thicken here,
> The hours of daylight gather atmosphere.

Now this is more than slight, it's nothing; I admit it; yet, admit it, isn't it a nothing that Marvell himself could have been proud of? And after reading it, can you understand how *any* critic could have patronizingly pigeonholed the man who wrote it? Frost writes a poem about a barn that is left over after its farmhouse has burnt down (of the house only the chimney is left, to stand "like a pistil after the petals go"); the poem is called "The Need of Being Versed in Country Things," and it ends:

> The birds that came to it through the air
> At broken windows flew out and in,
> Their murmur more like the sigh we sigh
> From too much dwelling on what has been.
>
> Yet for them the lilac renewed its leaf,
> And the aged elm, though touched with fire;

And the dry pump flung up an awkward arm;
And the fence post carried a strand of wire.

For them there was really nothing sad.
But though they rejoiced in the nest they kept,
One had to be versed in country things
Not to believe the phoebes wept.

But here I am not only left helpless to say whether this is slight or not,
I don't even want to know: I am too sure of what I have even to want
to say what it is, so that I will say if you ask me, as St. Augustine did
about Time: "I know if you don't ask me."

I don't want to finish without saying how much *use* Frost's poems are
to one, almost in the way that Hardy's are, when one has read them for
many years—without saying how little they seem performances, no matter how brilliant or magical, how little things made primarily of words
(or of ink and paper, either), and how much things made out of lives
and the world that the lives inhabit. For how much this poetry *is* like
the world, "the world wherein we find our happiness or not at all,"
"the world which was ere I was born, the world which lasts when I am
dead," the world with its animals and plants and, most of all, its people:
people working, thinking about things, falling in love, taking naps; in
these poems men are not only the glory and jest and riddle of the
world, but also the habit of the world, its strange ordinariness, its ordinary strangeness, and they too trudge down the ruts along which the
planets move in their courses. Frost is that rare thing, a complete or
representative poet, and not one of the brilliant partial poets who do
justice, far more than justice, to a portion of reality, and leave the rest
of things forlorn. When you know Frost's poems you know surprisingly
well how the world seemed to one man, and what it was to seem that
way: the great *Gestalt* that each of us makes from himself and all that
isn't himself is very clear, very complicated, very contradictory in the
poetry. The grimness and awfulness and untouchable sadness of things,
both in the world and in the self, have justice done to them in the
poems, but no more justice than is done to the tenderness and love and
delight; and everything in between is represented somewhere too, some
things willingly and often and other things only as much—in Marianne
Moore's delicate phrase—"as one's natural reticence will allow." If some
of the poems come out of a cynical commonsense that is only wisdom's
backward shadow, others come out of wisdom itself—for it is, still, just
possible for that most old-fashioned of old-fashioned things, wisdom,
to maintain a marginal existence in our world. If we compare this wis-

dom with, say, that of the last of the Old Ones, Goethe, we are saddened and frightened at how much the poet's scope has narrowed, at how difficult and partial and idiosyncratic the application of his intelligence has become, at what terrible sacrifices he has had to make in order to avoid making others still more terrible. Yet how many poems, how many more lines, are immediately and supplely responsive with the unseparated unspecialized intelligence that is by now almost as natural to man—that being men have so laboriously created—as dreams and hunger and desire. To have the distance from the most awful and most nearly unbearable parts of the poems, to the most tender, subtle, and loving parts, a distance so great; to have this whole range of being treated with so much humor and sadness and composure, with such plain truth; to see that a man can still include, connect, and make humanly understandable or humanly unununderstandable so *much*—this is one of the freshest and oldest of joys, a joy strong enough to make us forget the limitations and excesses and baseness that these days seem unforgettable, a joy strong enough to make us say, with the Greek poet, that many things in this world are wonderful, but of all these the most wonderful is man.

Robert Frost and the Interrupted Dialogue

by Harold H. Watts

For some writers one needs to imitate Corneille, who—as jest has it—wrote his tragedies with an hourglass in his hand. An hourglass —or at least a calendar—is a useful adjunct for those whose gaze moves back and forth over Yeats's career or Donne's. It is not a very useful aid to persons who are considering the career of Robert Frost, of whom one is tempted to observe that he has not had a career but a state of being. His diction, his subject matter, his way of reading his subject matter— have not these been the same early and late? *Yes* is what one should answer when one observes the persistence of language and habits of working up what the poet takes from experience. *No*—but it is (as I shall indicate) a qualified *no*—if one has in mind what Frost reads into his poems.

The bulk of his poetry is a dialogue in which the two speakers are Robert Frost himself and the entity which we call nature or process. It is a dialogue in which Frost puts a variety of questions to the natural world that lies just beyond his doorstep and receives a variety of answers. They are answers that an ethically curious person like Frost can profit by. Whether he—and we—are meant to profit by them, whether the replies and the chance instructions that come to man from nature are fortuitous blows or carefully planted clues: this is not always important to Frost. That man may well find his relevancies in the irrelevancies of process is a possibility that does not often disturb Frost.

But one does not need to have a calendar at hand to observe that this peaceful dialogue between Frost and nature—this peaceful flow of New England information from snow-crust to sheet of paper—has of late decades been interrupted, has been intruded upon by another sort of

Harold H. Watts, "Robert Frost and the Interrupted Dialogue," *American Literature*, XXVII (March 1955), 69-87. Reprinted by permission of the author and Duke University Press.

dialogue. To see what this new dialogue is—to see how and why it inter-
rupts the first one—is useful for several reasons. We shall see more clearly
what are the sinews and the occasional soft tissues of the predominating
interchange, the man-process interchange. Further, when we understand
the element of the inevitable in the interruption that, from time to time,
takes place, we shall have a better general understanding of the way
in which a rather strict and doctrinaire view of man's place in the world
can empower a poet's account of that place, and at the same time lead
a poet to misrepresent just what that place is.

II

It is because of the interruption we study that Frost's account of man's
dialogue with nature has a chance of taking on a quality that it usually
lacks. In a poem like "West-Running Brook" nature is no longer the
active, creative process questioned by the human spectator who is almost
entirely passive. For in that poem man has the chance of making a good
deal of the riffle in the stream set up by a rock and opposing the "inevitable" downward flow of the brook. The riffle "sends up" water to the
stream's source; and man—just perhaps—has the ability to "send up"
something towards *his* source instead of reflecting, in his moral life, the
"inevitable" downward flow of the stream.

Are we back to sermons in stones, lessons in west-running brooks?
I think so, except that Frost is chary of following up such leads. But
these leads stand; they are not totally ignored. On the other hand, they
are not systematically worked out, and they do not yield the fruit that
they might bear, were their cultivator more curious. If man and nature
(process) have a common origin, then man and process are—if the
phrase be permitted—peers, however unlike. Frost, in first "mounting"
his dialogue, was willing to suppose that it was nature that always led,
always gave the clues, and that it was man who followed. But if what
nature speaks to us—its intimations of source and "sending up" rather
than drifting down—is what we already possess, are not we and process
aspects of a common creation? Is it not possible that the knowledge that
nature offers us glancingly and indifferently is knowledge that we already
possess in a different and perhaps more eminent way? If so, the very
conditions of the man-process dialogue are altered. Process should take its
turn at listening too. And, more importantly, man should try lending
his ear to some other speaker: to himself or to society and history, made
up of many such speakers as himself. Man should not hesitate to say to
process—say quite counter to Frost's usual vein of insight—"I too was

in Arcadia" or, less classically, "I too have been in the counsels of the Most High."

Frost recognizes this possibility which intrudes upon his habitual dialogue; it is his exploration of it that is casual and condescending. The poem "Riders" commences:

> The surest thing there is is we are riders,
> And though none too successful at it, guiders,
> Through everything presented, land and tide
> And now the very air, of what we ride. (p. 345) [1]

That is, we are—in Frost's sense of the word—"environmentalists" and move intelligently with the beast (process) which carries us, a beast that Frost calls, in this same poem, "our wildest mount—a headless horse." He asks:

> What is this talked-of mystery of birth
> But being mounted bareback on the earth?

If we are so mounted on the earth, on the "headless horse," on an entity that bears us forward without direction and intelligence, by what right can we think of ourselves as "guiders"? If nature, the "headless horse," is solely a succession of particular events or facts (as it is in much of Frost's verse) or—when generalized—is just the drift of process, and if we have no secret links with it because of a common creation, we cannot presume to guide. We cannot look to our source along with the riffle of water in "West-Running Brook." But at times Frost suggests that we should so presume.

It is this possibility of guiding as well as riding that leads to the interruption of the man-process dialogue that is normative in Frost. Yet one must confess that this vein is but one among the many aspects of the confrontation of man with nature, as Frost manages it. Frost may sometimes speak for man. He may lament the abandoned woodpile and the house taken over by nature (pp. 126 and 216), and he may shape a fable or myth in which the wind is taught song by man (p. 274). But the road that aspect of the dialogue would seem to point to is, in Frost's phrase, "a road not taken"—or, if taken, not taken with the seriousness with which Frost travels his preferred road. Frost cannot escape his

---

[1] All references are to pages of *The Complete Poems of Robert Frost* (New York: Holt, Rinehart & Winston, Inc., 1949).

favorite conversation; humanity keeps breaking in. He bears the interruption with as much grace as he can summon, but one must say at once that this grace is insufficient. Certainly, the conditions of Frost's profitable dialogue with nature were, for much of his poetry, "enabling." But one cannot but feel that these same conditions become "disenabling" when Frost turns to the chance that man is a "rider" who is also a "guider."

This is Frost's problem: to be responsive to the pressures of nature or process, man must live with the pressures that come from other men (modern society, traditional culture) reduced to a minimum. Thus, to have a flexible dialogue with process, man must have a fixed (and negative) response to whatever in society passes beyond the simple, "natural" social relations of the rural community. Frost must work to assert the discontinuity of natural process and human society. He must, with amused resignation, lift his gaze from the swamp orchids as the lineman passes holding up the wires that will bear the nonsense of Montreal to the fools of Boston (p. 158). He must scornfully toss a turtle's egg at the train that bears human beings from one artificial complexity to another (p. 349).

The conflict comes to this. In one direction—that of the man-process dialogue—there is a various and flexible accumulation of insight; in another direction—that of what we shall call the man-society dialogue—there is, when evasion is impossible, the cherishing of fixed, predetermined stereotypes rather than the continuation of sympathetic attention that we should hope to see. This is the division that keeps Frost from following up what his perceptions about the common origin of process and society point to. A poem like "West-Running Brook" may suggest that both process and society are "natural" since both are the work of some kind of *deus faber,* with both bearing equally the marks of his skill and the marks of his insufficiency. But Frost, by long habit, is committed to acceptance of but half of the truth just raised. Process is the vehicle of *all* the meaning that man has any chance of taking unto himself. Man's experience of man-in-society is a second-rate sort of experience. And so, by easy extension, is man's experience of God-in-society a poor substitute for whatever divine traces of purpose one can isolate in process.

Because of this emphasis, Frost is interdicted the easy glide from nature to society that, for example, many a Stoic—ancient or modern—has taken. One might say that Frost is a Stoic who asserts that "natural law" is published in one authentic volume instead of two. The ordinary Stoic may turn from his readings in the book of process to study the volume that tells him of human society, and all without any sense that he is canceling his study of the first volume; both volumes possess the same author. Frost would like to overlook the question as to whether the process-volume had an author. (There stands the book, and is that not more than enough?) But he knows—as one knows a slogan rather than a fact—who the author of the book about human society is. The author is man, who scarce has the authority to compose at all and who can be counted on to write badly or uninstructively.

Therefore, when Frost is forced to turn his attention from process to society, he feels that he is in the presence of material that is of little intrinsic interest and of even less authority over his own spirit. Indeed, he would like to do without this second volume; he would like to persist with his reading of process. Since he cannot, since the social pressures and the decay of political morality and the algae-growth of planned societies keep—like humanity itself—breaking in, he takes up themes that he neglected in his earlier poetry. But he takes them up with an air of having moved into another realm where problems must be faced and solved so differently that one cannot hope for a profit like the profit one gets when a question is put and "solved" in the process-man dialogue. Only nature is "natural," it would seem. Yet we can recall that *natural* was a word that a man like Montaigne used easily and casually; he did not suppose that human society was so hopelessly cut off from nonhuman nature that the two entities could not vie with each other in giving man abundant clues to his own nature. (The Christian, it is true, draws the line between process and society a little more deeply than did Montaigne. But he draws it nowhere near so deeply as Frost draws it. For the Christian, process is just as much God's creation as is man. The conditions of man's existence are more complicated than those faced by process, by natural creation. But considerable cross-reference persists; neither entity is regarded, as in Frost, as a second-class citizen.)

The point at which Frost might have moved on to society—and at the same time deepening his dialogue with process—was a touchy point. It was the point at which the metaphysical becomes more than a momentarily perceived turn of dialogue. Frost, one may judge, is determined to allow the metaphysical no more honor than that of being a momentarily perceived turn of dialogue. He is willing to note a fleeting perception of drift or—just as often—design in process; but he is studiedly incurious as to what one may make of such perceptions. For example, what the idea of God or design in nature at a minimum demands is the *pervasiveness* of the perceived design. Thus, structure cannot be thought of as in one place present and in another place absent—present in process, absent in human society and its history. But Frost is not willing to grant that man's efforts in society, in the accumulation of traditions, may have an instructive power equal to that of process. Is it not possible—one may ask, using the far-from-normative language of "West-Running Brook"—that both society and process display the same "sending-up"?

> Our life runs down in sending up the clock.
> The brook runs down in sending up our life.
> The sun runs down in sending up the brook.
> And there is something sending up the sun. (p. 329)

Should we not give serious, sustained, and flexible attention to what in society is a "throwing backward on itself"?

III

With Frost the question just asked leads to a sharp interruption in his preferred flow of question and answer. To turn from process to society must, in any case, amount to a change of question, a varying of one's basic attention. But it need not amount to a transformation of the quality of attention one gives. Frost does not bring to bear on our troubled human society the kind of attention he gives generously to process. Instead, he begins a *new* dialogue.

I should like to make clear in what territory this new dialogue is displayed. It appears only occasionally in the earlier poems, and I shall quote apposite passages without implying that they are characteristic. The dialogue appears with frequency in *A Witness Tree* and *Steeple Bush* and in the two plays which Frost calls "masques": *A Masque of Reason* and *A Masque of Mercy*. To be sure, in these collections are many poems in which the old dialogue persists, with the precise limitations of curiosity we have noted. I insist on no more than this: that whenever Frost turns to a consideration of man in society, he eschews the profits of his earlier conversation with nature. Nature or process is out of touch with the task of reckoning with man in society, man enduring the agonies that society involves him in.

So this second dialogue displays Frost at least as a less apt and flexible observer; he learns much less from human society than he did from process. Why? Because he is older? I think there is a more just explanation. Frost learns less because he has posited a discontinuity, because he has not followed up the perception embodied in "West-Running Brook": that process and society "aspire" to "send-up" to a common source. This insight is put to one side when Frost suggests that the beliefs that societies have lived by are not "natural" but "artificial." It is as though one should say, "God made nature, and man made the town"—the town or, more inclusively, the whole course of human history, the whole close-woven mesh of human values. If this is true (and one should, whatever his theology, deny it if one wishes to create a dialogue that ranges freely, with full cross-reference and instruction, between nature and town), then human history is a "mistake." (And process is "right," even when it contradicts itself, even when we cannot understand it.) Moreover, the efforts to project for a few more generations the structure of a certain society and its traditions are, though perhaps necessary, neither noble nor enlightening. Society—unlike process, which bears either the mark of God's shaping hand or just the note of the nonhuman—carries only the imprints fumblingly imposed by man.

Towards these latter marks—towards man's philosophical systems and man's social reforms—Frost displays two attitudes. (They are logically at odds, but, since Frost holds them alternately, there is no existential difficulty.) Frost shows skepticism for all human effort, or he may offer some human effort an as-if acceptance. The skepticism appears in the sort of poem that appears in *A Witness Tree* and *Steeple Bush;* the as-if acceptance appears chiefly in the two "masques." Neither attitude represents more than endurance of a necessary evil. (The dialogue with process was a pursuit—a very great pursuit—of a possible good.) It is as though Frost is saying of society, this necessary evil, "Well, if you must hanker to find a place for man, for yourself even, in society, these are some of the old accounts." The dialogue with process was a various account of firsthand contact; what we have to note now is Frost's sorting of hearsay about man and his purely human fate. It is a sorting forced upon Frost by the urgencies of his time. But it is one that takes him away from the proper study of mankind: nature or process.

This break need not have taken place had Frost been willing to let process speak to him fully of metaphysics as well as of "practical" human problems. Metaphysics of some sort—and I do not mean anything authoritative, ambitious, and systematic—could have annealed the far too clean break between natural process and social development that Frost early made. Some degree of philosophic insight could have suggested that society, like process, was capable of conversation various and soaring, depressing or frustrating—and pointed.

But Frost states his view of such philosophic aid in "The Bear." After praising the "uncaged process of the bear," Frost notes:

> The universe seems cramped to you and me.
> Man acts more like the poor bear in a cage
> That all day fights a nervous inward rage,
> His mood rejecting all his mind suggests. (p. 347)

He is caged because he is no longer free to ignore the philosophical and social entities that speak up to him, that speak to man stammeringly and in useless stereotypes as soon as man leaves the illuminating hillside. The counsels of the hillside are, as we have seen, various enough. But they are not, for Frost at least, at cross-purposes. It is as though Frost finds that the sheer variety of counsel, of negation and affirmation, that comes from process is one of its greatest gifts; this variety is a stimulus to continued attention from man. The case is altered when man turns to nature that is social and historical. (To us it must seem that nature that is human also offers the attentive man a various dialogue, full of counsel wide-ranging and stimulating.) What reception does the skeptical New England poet give to the "caged bear" as he sways behind the bars of philosophy, tradition, and accumulated historical event?

> He sits back on his fundamental butt
> With lifted snout and eyes (if any) shut,
> (He almost looks religious but he's not) ,
> And back and forth he sways from cheek to cheek,
> At one extreme agreeing with one Greek,
> At the other agreeing with another Greek
> Which may be thought, but only so to speak.
> A baggy figure, equally pathetic
> When sedentary and when peripatetic. (pp. 347 f.)

Recall that man was not "equally pathetic" when he moved from one extreme of the man-process dialogue to another, from process as drift to process as purpose. For the wide range of possibilities that process "speaks" of do not cease to be stimulus, education, and discipline, whatever their logical confusion. In contrast, the wide range of possibilities that specifically human nature has created or informed—social forms and traditional culture, the systems of thought that interpret these—are another sort of stimulus. They are a stimulus to skepticism, they are at best a negative education, and they are a discipline if the cultivation of contempt is a discipline.

Concluding remarks on the two "masques" will temper these observations but will not reverse them. The "masques"—whatever they do signify—do not signify that Frost, at a late date, has decided that the dialogue with society can be regarded as more than a necessary—and almost evil—interruption of the man-process dialogue from which the poet and his readers draw real profit. The "masques" do not indicate that Frost is at last following up and consolidating the metaphysical flashes that process sends out. The "masque" must, in the "Frost story," stand for a sad acceptance of traditional stereotypes rather than for some kind of insight that, if not new, is felt as new. Novelty of this sort occurs only in the poems on which Frost's reputation rests: the conversations with process that he has had, against his will, to interrupt.

What Frost observed of the factory in "A Lone Striker," he may well be considered to observe of all institutions, of all organized and consciously directed culture and fairly coherent systems of thought.

> The factory was very fine;
> He wished it all the modern speed.
> Yet, after all, 'twas not divine,
> That is to say, 'twas not a church. (p. 356)

"He" is the tardy worker, but here we must let the pronoun stand for Frost. (And "church" means no traditional social institution but that which can mediate real significance. So Frost might as well say, " 'Twas not nature.") As Frost, speaking for himself and for the worker, says of the machines in the factory:

> Man's ingenuity was good.
> He saw it plainly where he stood,
> Yet found it easy to resist. (p. 356)

It is easy to resist provided there is a forest one knows. It is a sound preference that puts contemplation of process ahead of work at a spinning machine. At least, Frost says of this defense that leads the worker along a woodland path:

> Nor was this just a way of talking
> To save him the expense of doing.
> With him it boded action, deed. (p. 356)

"Deed," we have suggested, is putting the right questions to process and gathering in the carelessly provided answers. This is true unless we think of man as "guider" as well as "rider" of nature. But such a turn of the dialogue has metaphysical overtones that Frost resists as much as he can.

So the factory (and all the the factory implies) is "not divine," "not a church." The worker, in consequence, "never would assume that he'd/Be any institution's need." Nor, to reverse the last phrase, would he be quick to assume that any institution would be his need. In fact, he is loth to brood long on either possibility—of being "rider," of being "guider"; it is best not to ask what one is as one gallops along on the "headless horse" that is society or human history. With this entity, one must resist setting up any relation at all. What a man must work for—and this is from the little mute drama that concludes *Steeple Bush,* "From Plane to Plane"—is something quite different.

> A man has got to keep his extrication.
> The important thing is not to get bogged down
> In what he has to do to earn a living. (p. 580)

Whenever one catches Frost in a dialogue with society, one must perceive that much of his effort goes to keep himself from getting "bogged down." What he strives to create is not a just apprehension of what he faces; his greatest labor goes to keeping open a safe avenue of retreat to that other and more important conversation.

Nothing so well creates and keeps clear such an avenue as a ready, pervasive skepticism. Skepticism is defensible; social experience is a tissue of contradictions out of which it can be quickly fashioned. But one must observe that the dialogue Frost esteems (that with process) also abounds in contradictions. Yet Frost is eager to cherish whatever process tells him, whether it negates or affirms the human, whether—on a more general level—process announces drift or design. Frost at least reverses field when he has to listen to what human nature tells him, when he has to observe the confusion and ambiguity which *its* counsels display. For he decides that *this* multiplicity of counsel is a sanction to skepticism rather than an invitation to the sharpest attention imaginable. Instead of listening to and watching human society as sharply as possible (it would seem to us to deserve at least as much attention as the new apple tree or the dried-up brook), we are to listen to society, to watch it, with only a careless and detached indulgence. This attitude is sufficient to reveal to us the contradictions and ambiguities that will sanction amused tolerance. This attitude does not urge us farther, to see the drive or drift of human history that makes it, to many men at least, as absorbing as natural process, as full of confused instruction as the passage of winter into spring.

Frost's poems in this category are witty and urbane, as a person will find when he reads through *A Witness Tree* and *Steeple Bush.*

But they are both slight and journalistic in tone. Why should they not be? "Birches" and "Tree at My Window" are the products of loving attention; the poems we now speak of are the off-hand records of attention grudgingly given. "Grudgingly" is not too strong a word. Frost contrasts the truly firm roundness of the physical globe with the inferior globe that is human society.

> The world's one globe, human society
> Another softer globe that slightly flattened
> Rests on the world, and clinging slowly rolls. (p. 427)

In the presence of the globe called human society, he faces a set of possibilities that he derogates in advance. His skepticism may be sufficiently informed (it is almost impossible not to be informed about the matters we now treat), but it is also defensive. The avenue of retreat to the better dialogue must be kept clear; and Frost can retreat along it if human agony and complexity press too close.

Here one should perhaps say, in a phrase from radio, "Correction." Human agony and complexity of an individual and isolated and human sort are indeed treated with great sympathy and some deftness. But this latter agony is always one that, though thoroughly human, is susceptible of being regarded as close to natural process. Birth and death and the process-conditioned tensions between couples isolated on run-down farms: these are the human themes that Frost can take up. And they are not contemptible. But they are all concerned with sustaining a dignified human stance in the face of natural process. Frost is not very curious about the onerous task of maintaining a dignified stance in the midst of societies and customs that man himself has made and is making. Here Frost's low estimate of this portion of experience intervenes, and he gives us no companion piece to match his pictures of man facing up to snowstorm and drouth.

When we call to mind the complexity of life in society, we know that this life finds expression not only in actual events, in the social structures and the desperate expedients which society and history present. It also finds expression in the fairly systematic glosses which philosophy has provided to accompany and light up (if that is at all possible) the actual events. Frost judges that such glosses are unclear and so rather useless. It is true that, even in Frost's accounts, the counsels of process are not clear either. But they are able to give Frost—or rural man—a basis for "deeds" as purely human material does not. And "deeds" include not just the contemplation of process but also what we would call acts: sowing and harvesting, displaying courage in storm, rendering service to other persons along the road, the perception of their simple points of view. But all of this we may call—in distinction to what we treat now—process piety. (A cheerful epigram sums up this piety:

> We dance round in a ring and suppose,
> But the Secret sits in the middle and knows. [p. 495])

IV

There is, in Frost, no societal piety. We have already shown this by our glances at his stereotypes for factory and city. (The city, for example, is simply in a state of unconscious war with the waters over which it has been built. From the brook rise thoughts that keep "This new-built city from both work and sleep" [p. 285].) We must note here Frost's estimate of that barely tolerable efflorescence of city life and factory: national government. Frost would intensify Lord Acton's apothegm and say that that government is best which governs not at all, which makes no demands on our attention. Frost holds against the United States government of the thirties and forties not only its interference in human affairs. He resents its pervasive propaganda for this interference. It was a propaganda which forced the minds of Americans not to agreement with the measures (such agreement was for Frost unthinkable); it forced American minds to a *consideration* of these measures, to tedious and time-consuming rejection of these measures by the discovery of apt alternates.

It must be said that Frost discovers no apt alternate unless laissez faire be an alternate. (Does Frost have clue for this from Adam Smith or from process?) Frost presents us, in "The Roadside Stand," the pathetic hopes of country folk who set up their stands to snare the nickels and dimes of passing city folk. Such country folk are in graver danger than comes from financial disappointment.

> . . . greedy good-doers, beneficent beasts of prey,
> Swarm over their lives enforcing benefits
> That are calculated to soothe them out of their wits,
> And by teaching them how to sleep the sleep all day,
> Destroy their sleeping at night the ancient way. (pp. 370 f.)

"The ancient way" is, being translated, simply the old country "laws" of supply and demand untouched by the energetic hands of "greedy good-doers." The same skepticism is found in the rather early "New

Hampshire"; it unfolds itself fully in the later "political pastoral" entitled "Build Soil." It persists, with due allowance for changed conditions, in the several mentions of "one world" and international co-operation in *Steeple Bush*. (See, for examples, passages on the following pages in the *Complete Poems*: 542, 547, 557, and 566.)

The accents vary, but the point is the same. The immediate pressures of nature put healthful limits on the social imagination or fancy that must deploy itself in the country. One cannot "plan" winter or seedtime; and one can appeal to this limitation to justify one's lack of sympathy with attempts to reshape the social and economic structure of a great nation. The view that a nation should be more than a reflection of natural process—that its emergent shape should bear the marks not of spontaneous and unthinking process but of human choice operating among a variety of possibilities—is antipathetic to Frost. But this indifference to the social operation of human choice is more limiting than Frost supposes. Laissez faire, it should be clear, is not more "natural" than a planned society since both resultant social structures record human choices made in considerable despite of process. But to Frost, any such evidence would but serve as further sanction for skepticism of all conscious choice; the evidence could not become an invitation for us to sharpen our analyses of the choices that both precede and accompany our social activity.

Frost's skepticism toward history, political and cultural, displays similar marks. To plan a society or to profit from the events that have overtaken other societies—both acts fall into the same condemnation. He quotes a wise saw from a wall in ancient Ctesiphon:

> But judging by what little of it stands,
> Not even the ingenuities of debt
> Could save it from its losses being met. (p. 570)

Ctesiphon failed; what can we learn from Ctesiphon? Occasionally this skepticism is tempered by a natural piety toward men who have existed.

> How often is the case
> I thus pay men a debt
> For having left a place
> And still do not forget
> To pay them some sweet share
> For having once been there. (p. 577)

But this piety, is should be noted, extends only to the fact that men did exist, did strive, did drive their chariots along a certain path that

Frost now walks along. But this piety does not extend to the products of the efforts of earlier man. It does not ask us to assess the value of the precise objects earlier men made, the precise wisdom that they drew from strife and existence. The cave man and Pericles and the neighbor down the New Hampshire roadside are peers; and the cave man and the neighbor have the edge on Pericles since their existence has vague, undifferentiated meaning; whereas the existence of Pericles amounted to an assertion of *this* human good and not that. Frost does not need to feel repugnance for the existence of the cave man; what he was and did is not overprecise—was, we can suppose, chiefly an acceptance of the general range of possibilities that process imposes. In contrast, Pericles or any other great figure falls into attitudes that demand us to consider a precise human context and compare it with other precise human contexts. This is what Frost is unwilling to do. Alexander cancels Pericles, and Jesus cancels Alexander—and all are canceled by Machiavelli. The "great action" in which they are involved does not bear a distinct or important burden of meaning for us.

We might ask—as Frost does not—whether the type of person he does choose to revere and admire is not in part a product of such "great actions," which amount to the continuing display of human possibilities in the context of many cultures. Has not all this made —at least in large part—the neighbors whom Frost admires rather than just their close proximity to process, at a safe distance from city lights and hard pavements? What, indeed, are the roots of New England character? Some of the roots, certainly, extend back into time and across the Atlantic; not all the roots find their nourishment in the rocky soil of New Hampshire and the burned-over swamps.

V

In *Steeple Bush* Frost takes up—long enough to effect a skeptical twist of the wrist—some of the themes that seem to us closely connected with history and social forms. What is faith, what is the self, what is eternity, what is human knowledge? Plainly, there is no answer single or simple. Because this is so, we need not—in Frost's opinion—commit ourselves to the sort of serious, sober, and finally passionate consideration of the multiple answers that, if we follow Frost, must indeed mark our study of the various things that nature or process says. Frost contents himself with twitting the classic answers to these socially conditioned questions.

Two poems serve to illustrate this working out of his skeptical defense against involvement in a man-society discourse. They are "A Steeple on the House" and "A Wish to Comply." One concerns the certainties of religion, the other the certainties of science. Thus, to the questions about eternity that man has woven in with the questions about the good society and the meaning of history, Frost makes reply like a man who carelessly lifts up a handful of sand, which he then lets run through his fingers.

> What if it should turn out eternity
> Was but the steeple on our house of life . . . ? (p. 540)

No one ever really uses the belfry of a church; and the most we need concede to the belfry and to what is popularly associated with it is this:

> A spire and belfry coming on the roof
> Means that a soul is coming on the flesh.

This echoes the earlier remark about the soft globe that humanity superimposes on the hard globe that is the earth in process, the earth natural. As indicated, science comes off no better than conventional religion. The poet chronicles his partly dutiful efforts to see the "Millikan mote," but

> I rather suspect
> All I saw was the lid
> Going over my eye.
> I honestly think
> All I saw was a wink. (p. 553)

The poet stares at the steeple less long than he does at a growing birch, and he dismisses the mote with mild jocosity. So much for religion, so much for exact science: thus Frost's protective skepticism.

Two "dramas"—*A Masque of Reason* and *A Masque of Mercy*—expand the skeptical observations we have sampled. Do they leave skepticism behind? We have earlier said that they do amount to a kind of acceptance of what man has said about virtues that are distinctly not process-virtues but social virtues: virtues that man has hammered out throughout centuries of experience that is historical. And both little plays take historical experience as points of departure; both concede that the sections of experience refracted in these plays (*reflected* is distinctly not the word) are important sections. *A Masque of*

Reason involves Job in a conversation with God on the value of the important test that, many centuries ago, Job underwent. *A Masque of Mercy*—though the setting is a modern bookshop—does involve at least Jonah and St. Paul. The sober point of each play—a point that is not binding since Frost must keep his avenue of escape open—is some observation, of general import, about social, nonprocess experience. Frost concedes that Job had his trial but wishes to suggest that the point of the trial as most men take it—that Job's story is an account of man's apprenticeship to faith—is not the only one. Frost shows that the Job-experience freed God from the need to be reasonable, from having to provide men with their just deserts. A similar irony, arrived at by turning the accepted versions inside out, appears in *A Masque of Mercy*. Jonah was sent to inflict justice on a godless people; what Frost's Jonah is really distressed by is his suspicion, confirmed by Frost's Paul, that God's angry prophet cannot trust God to remain unmerciful.

In both plays the central points are sophisticated, as if to assert at every turn that the drama proceeds on an as-if basis. The presentation is, for example, faced, though not too successfully (Frost has left behind him the world that harbored *Home Burial*). In fact, Frost shows for a hesitant Jean Giraudoux, that is, the Giraudoux of *Amphitryon 38*. Job's wife is a mild feminist, she poses God, Job, and Satan for a picture; and Jonah and Paul are often distracted in their conversation by the owner of the bookshop into which they have stumbled. (The owner of the bookshop is married to a sluttish woman called Jesse Bel.) Particularly in *A Masque of Mercy* does the variety of persons allow Frost to view more freely, more sympathetically and yet without commitment, some slightly shaded stereotypes uttered concerning human problems. But when, after a quite theological debate, the Keeper (of the shop) speaks,

> My failure is no different from Jonah's.
> We both have lacked the courage in the heart
> To overcome the fear within the soul
> And go ahead to any accomplishment. (p. 642)

Fear, significantly, is not the child of the unknown in these two plays; it is the offspring of the mind, which looks for and dreads the undeviating workings of justice; and courage, conveniently said to be of the heart, is more closely allied with process than with society and its often overexplicit "rational" explanations of how the human universe works.

When Frost concludes the second "masque" by causing the Keeper to say: "Nothing can make injustice just but mercy"—it is open to question whether this wells up from Frost's experience as deep and pure as: "Something there is that doesn't love a wall." That is, each reader must decide how fully these exercises come to being a recantation of Frost's usual skeptical interest in human values, how nearly they are the continuation, in a new context, of the sympathy both friendly and reverent that Frost has for process. Some will conclude that the plays reflect a grudging recognition of what men have been saying for centuries, a grudging recognition of the ambiguities in which man-in-society is immersed and of the need one has of coming to grips with these persistent uncertainties.

Whether the interest be perfunctory and only a short step away from Frost's usual amused survey of the specifically human scene or, in contrast, tardy and yet sincere, the fact is that the job is not very well performed. The poet gives signs of being inattentive to the human dialogue of which he is now giving his hasty account. He is inattentive because he has for many years divided each person's awareness into two parts. One part (man's experience of process) is richly rewarding. The other part (the one we have just surveyed) is abounding in confusions that need be neither seriously studied nor heroically endured, provided one has kept open his New England farmhouse. Frost is first-rate when he deals with problems, with experiences, that he is persuaded are first-rate. He is, in some of his later work, hasty and even colorless and abstract when he deals with what he has persuaded himself is the inferior half of the discontinuity he has set up—when he feels that the really important dialogue has been cut across by what is little more than chatter or, as he himself would say, "talk talk."

Yet, as already pointed out, his own poetry contains clues pointing to a different sort of attention. Thus, in "Lucretius versus the Lake Poets," he ridicules an academic debate during which the theory has been advanced that nature is no more than "pretty scenery." Frost remarks:

> For I thought Epicurus and Lucretius
> By Nature meant the Whole Goddam Machinery. (p. 558)

If one is to take a phrase like this seriously, one is not free to dismiss part of life as pretty scenery and part (the social part) as almost empty dialogue. True, society and man and ideas are rich sources of obscurity. But they are also part of the "Whole Goddam Machinery"; they are cogs that really do mesh with the parts that Frost singles out for his respectful study. Yet Frost's most deeply held belief amounts to no less than this: that there is a part of the "machinery" that is real and instructive to man and a part that is not. His choice commits him to a humanism that is sensitive and, in its own way, compassionate. But it is also a humanism which seeks to put the poet and his talents only obliquely in the service of a mankind in which the poet has a distinctly limited and ironical trust. The limitation and irony are not well-founded unless one grants Frost's assumption: that a part of the machine that is the universe really works and that another part— society, thought, history—grinds emptily, century after century.

"A Momentary Stay Against Confusion"

by John T. Napier

It is now several years since I opened a small volume of poems, *New Hampshire,* bought as gift for a girl I was seeking to impress. A great deal has happened in the world and to me during those years. Another world war. The loosing of bonds in the atomic nucleus. New instruments that greatly extend our capabilities for seeing and hearing. And yet the perspective of things has not so altered that I am unable to enjoy the poems encountered then for the first time. The choice would be no different if some reversal of time could bring it to be made again.

The lyrics of Robert Frost, as he thinks poems should do, keep their freshness as "metal keeps its fragrance." They belong in the company of songs made by Herrick, Ben Jonson, and Yeats. But if the reader has not already put them to test, I must in the main leave this to his future pleasure. What is to concern me here is a different matter, a side of Frost that may not have been anticipated by the audience for his early poems. To be sure, even in a lyric such as "Rose Pogonias" are signs the poet may show "how there may be a better wildness of logic than of inconsequence." Yet, to have foretold the course of his demonstration would have required a clairvoyance modestly avoided by Frost. The matter I believe is one of some consequence to American poetry or perhaps simply for poetry—with no restriction as to national boundary. In working over the course I have chosen, many inviting paths will be neglected because of the great range in the poems Frost has made. His affinities with Horace and his admiration for Herrick have been mentioned already by others. These relations call for leisurely illumination by scholars. More to my point are certain failures of understanding which may possibly affect the work of our younger poets.

John T. Napier, "A Momentary Stay Against Confusion," *The Virginia Quarterly Review,* XXXIII (Summer 1957), 378-94. Reprinted by permission of the author and *The Virginia Quarterly Review.*

And these failures, if the situation can be saved, should not be left to later correction by the universities.

By comparison with Eliot or Yeats or Pound, Frost has said little about his philosophy of the poem. His infrequent remarks include two short prefatory essays, "The Constant Symbol" and "The Figure a Poem Makes," which contain the gist of his ideas on making poems. These sparely-worded comments, together with an essay, "Poetry and School," are worth more attention than has been given them so far. Quotation from them has been such as to make one think the quoters see them as miscellanies full of wise saws and modern instances. They are on the contrary significant definitions of the poet's intention.

In "The Figure a Poem Makes," Frost says:

> I tell how there may be a better wildness of logic than of inconsequence. But the logic is backward, in retrospect, after the act. It must be more felt than seen ahead like prophecy. It must be a revelation, or a series of revelations, as much for the poet as for the reader. For it to be that there must have been the greatest freedom of the material to move about in it and to establish relations in it regardless of time and space, previous relation, and everything but affinity.

This statement comes after teasing but effective thrusts at the modern poet's tendency to abstract—for sound, for wildness, or for whatever other pure essence may be appealing at the moment. The point of consequence to Frost, however, is that the poem is a revelation, a discovery in some respects similar to Kekulé's dream of the benzene nucleus or Poincaré's sudden realization of the fuchsian functions at the moment of putting his foot on an omnibus step. This idea is hardly welcome to those critic-poets of the present day who would believe that, given a sufficient knowledge of techniques and the required degree of persistence, a poem can surely be made.

Nevertheless, Frost only affirms, more briefly than Hadamard and other students of the creative process have done, that enlightenments are involved over which the creative thinker has no conscious control. Einstein has said of great advances in scientific theory that they occur in the manner of quantum jumps, being discontinuities rather than logical progressions. The Gestalt psychologist, Wertheimer, interested himself in the flexible restructuring that accompanies creative thought, a matter of suddenly grasping a new pattern. While extended effort (as in the case of the fuchsian functions) may be required to elaborate the sudden insight, the integral character of the new pattern is not attained by the process of elaboration.

The first part of Frost's statement—that there may be a better wildness of logic than of inconsequence—will furnish the text of much to follow; we may, however, linger a bit over his ideas of poetic process. These ideas link him with Wordsworth. Where Wordsworth spoke of "emotion recollected in tranquility," the unconscious stage of preparation is spoken of by Frost as if we were giants hurling experience ahead of ourselves for such a time as we "may want to strike a line of purpose across it for somewhere."

Examination of Frost's ideas on the poetic process shows him at odds with the majority of recent poets. His belief in the importance of normal gestation and birth for a poem over against its being coddled into life after a protracted Caesarean operation sets off his mode of creation clearly from that favored by many poets since Poe. The author of "The Raven," infatuated with his Eldorado of rationalizing the creative process, began the school of the self-conscious artist. At some stage in his work, such a poet conceives of an effect he would achieve and proceeds by deliberate, often elaborate, techniques to achieve it. Poe's method found acceptance among the French, who seem born with a penchant for the philosophy of technique; and from Baudelaire to Valéry there is a continuously evolving body of precepts for poetic midwifery. The mature fruits of the seed cast abroad by Poe were returned to American poets through the efforts of Pound and Eliot, especially those of Pound.

Interestingly enough, the two American poets accepted the French adaptation of Poe's method only in the company of a profound change in the philosophy of poetry. I wish to label this change briefly the failure of rationality. Eliot emphasizes Baudelaire's rôle in the revolt against rationalism—or, from a more sympathetic viewpoint, the revolt against scientific and industrial materialism. From Baudelaire on, the growth of antirationalism in poetry has taken various strange bypaths in search of more profound spiritual insights; the common quality of poems made by all these schools, however, is the avoidance of rational structure. Paradoxically, it may seem that, as the poem has become more irrational in structure, the technical theory of the poem has become more rational, more precise and exacting. Poets like Mallarmé allowed the rationalization of the creative method to absorb disproportionate quantities of their energy.

Frost then confronts us with atypical attitudes toward the making of poems. One cannot imagine his submitting a poem of his to the sort of editing Pound performed on *The Waste Land* for Eliot. His poems are at the same time atypical in their characteristic logical structure. In the judgment of some critics and poets, he has simply fallen behind, but this judgment is deceptively easy to make. Rather than reach the conclusion too easily that Frost is primarily a fine lyric poet, limited by a conservative aesthetic and—as Yvor Winters would have it—a disability for dealing with other than minor themes, it may be worthwhile to make further inquiry as to his intention. But in order to do this, there is first a need to look at a rather general concept of the poem as a symbol.

II

The viewpoint to be explored in the present inquiry is that of Susanne Langer. In *Feeling and Form* she defines the poem as a unitary symbol which creates the illusion of virtual experience. This definition says that the poem, like the sonata, has no equivalent meaning and that no accumulation of program notes can replace experiencing the peculiar illusion it offers. We can read the most accurate account of the ingredients contained in a plum pudding and have not even the faintest notion of its taste. The experiencing of a poem is unique in the same way that diving into a clear pool is unique, known only to one who has had the experience. But the definition puts no restrictions on the nature of the verbal materials or kinds of experience to be comprised in the illusion of the poem. As to the so-called didactic poem, Mrs. Langer says:

> . . . all this analysis [of Herrick's "Delight in Disorder"] is not intended as an exercise in the New Criticism, but merely to show that all poetry is a creation of illusory events, even when it looks like a statement of opinions, philosophical or political or aesthetic. The occurrence of a thought is an event in the thinker's personal history, and has as distinct a qualitative character as an adventure, a sight, or a human contact; it is not a proposition, but the entertainment of one, which necessarily involves vital tensions, feelings, the imminence of other thoughts, and the echoes of past thinking. Poetic reflections, therefore, are not essentially trains of logical reasoning, though they may incorporate fragments, at least, of discursive argument. Essentially they create the *semblance* of reasoning; of the seriousness, strain and progress, the sense of growing knowledge, growing clearness, conviction and acceptance—the whole experience of philosophical thinking.

One has only to consider the quality of Donne's work to realize the value of this viewpoint.

Despite recent interest in Donne, there is really little poetry of our time that aims to create the semblance of reasoning. Donne's spiritual intensity attracts the modern poet, but not his semblance of rational thought. The following lines from "Altarwise by Owl-Light" are given as more typical of the experience provided us by the modern poem than, say, Frost's "The Lesson for Today":

> Then, penny-eyed, that gentleman of wounds,
> Old cock from nowheres and the heaven's egg,
> With bones unbuttoned to the half-way winds,
> Hatched from the windy salvage on one leg,
> Scraped at my cradle in a walking word
> That night of time under the Christward shelter,
> I am the long world's gentleman, he said,
> And share my bed with Capricorn and Cancer.

Here is a vague semblance of events in the order of some time sequence, but scarcely the semblance of reasoning. The rationale in a modern poem, if one exists at all, is likely to be a dream-world logic rather than any sequential reasoning tied to the world of our waking hours. The disappointment of poets with materialism, supported by science and its instrument, rational thought, has led our poets generally to avoid exhibiting the semblance of reasoning in their poetry; although reasoning is perhaps the most characteristic experience of our everyday world.

Recalling the poetry of Donne, Pope, or even Wordsworth, with his transcendent experiences, we have no trouble in seeing that good poems have been written creating the semblance of reasoning. This small poem by Donne, "A Jeat Ring Sent," may serve as reminder of what the experience is like:

> Thou art not so black, as my heart,
>   Nor halfe so brittle, as her heart, thou art;
> What would'st thou say? shall both our properties
>   by thee bee spoke,
>   Nothing more endlesse, nothing sooner broke?
> Marriage rings are not of this stuffe;
>   Oh, why should ought lesse precious, or lesse tough
> Figure our loves? Except in thy name thou have
>   bid it say,
>   I'm cheap, and nought but fashion, fling me'away.
> Yet stay with mee since thou art come,
>   Circle this fingers top, which did'st her thombe.
> Be justly proud, and gladly safe, that thou dost
>   dwell with me,
>   She that, Oh, broke her faith, would soon breake thee.

Logical progression in this poem has apparently much in common with one of Euclid's theorems. Syllogism is the basic relation between parts of it; but. as Frost would say, the logic is backward, reminiscing, and the conclusion must have been a revelation to the poet, as to the reader, when arrived at.

One point, at least, is clear in considering such a poem as this: that for the poem to present a semblance of reasoning, the words used in it must continue to perform their denotative as well as their connotative function. Otherwise the logical structure used to create the semblance of reasoning falls apart. Looking back for a moment at Dylan Thomas's lines, we realize his words do not consistently stand in a denotative relation to things; they do so only partially or they lean wholly on connotation.

Langer's view of the poem as a symbol creating the illusion of virtual experience does not in any way prejudge against the poem presenting experience out of the rational order. Neither, however, does it prejudge in favor of such poems. What she does say is that ideas are not easily handled in poetry: there is a temptation for the poet to be led into discourse. But she says the good poet is able to avoid this danger and that his only care is to see that his material, whatever it may be, is completely transformed in the symbol he creates.

III

With these points of reference established, it is feasible to consider the fact that many of Frost's poems do present the semblance of reasoning as the preferred virtual experience. The poet has stated his preference in "The Constant Symbol":

> There are many other things I have found myself saying about poetry, but the chiefest of these is that it is metaphor, saying one thing and meaning another, saying one thing in terms of another, the pleasure of ulteriority. Poetry is simply made of metaphor. So also is philosophy—and science, too, for that matter, if it will take the soft impeachment from a friend. Every poem is a new metaphor inside or it is nothing. And there is a sense in which all poems are the same old metaphor always.

The metaphor spoken of by Frost is often an extended sort of metaphor, as it is in "The Silken Tent," and it may be extended to the point of involving those dangerous subjects for poetry—ideas—as does the metaphor that becomes "The White-Tailed Hornet." Finally, however, one must come to the question of what Frost is trying to do with his extended metaphor in creating the semblance of reasoning. Is there any significant purpose beyond the creation of good poems of the traditional kind?

Frost has ties with tradition; but they are ties with the English tradition of Wordsworth and the American tradition of Emerson. His kind of humanism is different from the latter-day humanism of Babbitt and Eliot, an antiscientific variety once described as "a very porcupine hunched up against our familiar world." Wordsworth set out as his object in *Lyrical Ballads* "to choose incidents and situations from common life . . . and, at the same time, to throw over them a certain coloring of imagination, whereby ordinary things should be presented to the mind in an unusual aspect. . . ." Against this we may put a line from one of Frost's early poems: "The fact is the sweetest dream that labor knows."

This aspect of Frost's intention is fairly well accepted; there is another part of his purpose linking him also with Wordsworth, however, that is not so well recognized. Wordsworth predicted:

> If the labours of Men of science should ever create any material revolution, direct or indirect, in our condition, and in the impressions which we habitually receive, the Poet will sleep then no more than at present; he will be ready to follow the steps of the Man of science, *not only in those general indirect effects, but he will be at his side, carrying sensation into the midst of the objects of the science itself* [italics added].

While modern poetry in general has ignored this promise, Frost has worked toward its fulfillment in some degree. He has been too much aware of both the enlargement and the limitations in modern science to overextend himself by attempting another grand-scale *De Rerum Natura*—if he were of that turn. But he has done what seems more basic to closing the present gap between poet and scientist: he has demonstrated with careful logic certain points of congruency in their tasks. Frost calls the white-tailed hornet a poet going about his job of making comparisons. No less are metaphor and analogy tools of the scientist, as Frost remarks in the passage already cited. The problem for the poet is to find how much the metaphor can carry; for the scientist, what may be discarded, and how soon, without endangering his prospects of a worthwhile clarification.

The problem of figurative thinking as a tool for scientific discovery and of the implication of its use, as this use relates to the validity of scientific knowledge, is discussed by Mary B. Hesse in "Science and the Human Imagination." After noting a recent growth in efforts by the logicians of science to impose "semantic" rules on analogies "so as to do away with the ambiguities of the model itself," she has this to say about the handling of heuristic analogies:

> . . . it is exactly this vague 'surplus meaning' which gives the clues for further development. It is easy to see now for instance what semantic rules are

required for Maxwell's theory of radiation. Here the model of waves in material aether implied too much—the analogy of wave motion was necessary, but not the implication of a material in which the waves travelled. But this could not possibly have been known until various calculations and observations had been made on the basis of simple extensions of the original wave model. In other words explicit semantic rules, like all types of formalization, 'freeze' a theory at the stage at which it is formalized. Surely the heuristic function of analogies must be regarded as an essential part of scientific theories.

The poetry that presents a semblance of reasoning, then, and science are alike in the respect that "there must have been the fullest freedom of the material to move about in it and to establish relations in it," though perhaps not "regardless of time and space" in the scientific analogy. The closeness of reasoning in Miss Hesse's own statement, however, points to the requirement that a poem aiming to present a semblance of modern scientific reasoning or its effects on our everyday perception of things, in its final shape as a symbol, will need to be carefully wrought to create an adequate illusion.

Beginning with *West-Running Brook,* though he does not forsake the lyric, Frost commits himself to exploring the implications of scientific thought for the feeling man who must live with it. "The Bear" gives evidence of deepening insight and is earnest for a group of such interesting explorations in *A Further Range,* subtitled *Taken Doubly*:

> Or if he rests from scientific tread,
> 'Tis only to sit back and sway his head
> Through ninety odd degrees of arc, it seems,
> Between two metaphysical extremes.
> He sits back on his fundamental butt
> With lifted snout and eyes (if any) shut,
> (He almost looks religious but he's not),
> And back and forth he sways from cheek to cheek
> At one extreme agreeing with one Greek,
> At other agreeing with another Greek. . . .

The close texture of logic in this, however, has not dissipated the lyric feeling, for there are these opening lines:

> The bear puts both arms around the tree above her
> And draws it down as if it were a lover.
> And its choke cherries lips to kiss good-by,
> Then lets it snap back upright in the sky.

Poets and semanticists alike have shown concern over how man nowadays employs the metaphor in his social affairs. One of the semanticists recently commented that our use of metaphors in all kinds of writing and talk furnishes a key to our changing attitudes. He mentioned, for example, the Nazi scientists' fond hope of finding out the laws of society by observation of ant colonies. He further remarked our fascination with the metaphor of the machine, even though we should know better, having built into our machines the characteristics we find similar to our own. Finally, this writer expressed his anxiety because our metaphors no longer point beyond human achievement but look to the lower animals and even to insects for comparisons.

After reading the essay, it occurred to me that Frost had treated the same anxiety in "The White-Tailed Hornet *or, The Revision of Theories*":

> 'Those are just nailheads. Those are fastened down.'
> Then disconcerted and not unannoyed,
> He stooped and struck a little huckleberry
> The way a player curls around a football.
> 'Wrong shape, wrong color, and wrong scent,' I said.
> The huckleberry rolled him on his head.

The poem concludes with impeccable logic, after observing the hornet's further betrayal by his faulty instinct and after likening this to our betrayal of ourselves by downward comparisons, that "Nothing but fallibility was left us,/ And this day's work made even that seem doubtful." It would be a mistake, if Langer is correct, to saddle the poet with the finality of the judgment. To do so with Frost would be to forget the probability of irony and fall into a pit already occupied by other critics.

IV

"The White-Tailed Hornet" shows what Frost has been able to do toward creating a semblance of reasoning well-made enough to compare with, or perhaps lend lessons to, the reasoning of semanticists; and we are by his demonstration prepared to follow somewhat more carefully those poems that carry "sensation into the midst of the objects of the science itself." His care for the implications of scientific knowledge appears even in *A Boy's Will*. The poem "Stars" suggests an indifference in scientific fact to our human needs:

> And yet with neither love nor hate,
> Those stars like some snow-white

> Minerva's snow-white marble eyes
> Without the gift of sight.

Later, in "Bond and Free," the poet cannot restrain his curiosity but wonders whether all does not come with searching to Love who is content to wait:

> Thought cleaves the interstellar gloom
> And sits in Sirius' disc all night,
> Till day makes him retrace his flight,
> With smell of burning on every plume
> Back past the Sun to an earthly room.
>
> His gains in heaven are what they are.
> Yet some say Love by being thrall
> And simply staying possesses all
> In several beauty that Thought fares far
> To find fused in another star.

In neither of these poems has the poet succeeded in finding a point of tangency with ordinary human experience. The first poem must equate the modern blindness of the stars with the marble eyes of the Roman goddess of wisdom; the second has echoes of Icarus and Prometheus.

By the time of *New Hampshire,* Frost has begun to find the ordinary a matrix for the extraordinary. A poet-farmer, having picked up and loaded a meteorite with other stones on his sled, ". . . dragged it through the plowed ground at a pace/ But faintly reminiscent of the race/ Of jostling rock in interstellar space." The wonder and otherworldliness are not entirely gone in this translation of a star:

> Though not, I say, a star of death and sin,
> It yet has poles, and only needs a spin
> To show its worldly nature and begin
>
> To chafe and shuffle in my calloused palm
> And run off in strange tangents with my arm
> As fish do with the line in first alarm.
>
> Such as it is, it promises the prize
> Of the one world complete in any size
> That I am like to compass, fool or wise.

The strangeness is there but perhaps also a hint that this heavy substance from somewhere light-years away may after all have a kinship with our planet home.

The same volume contains "The Star-Splitter," a poem giving Donne no quarter by way of structure or the skill with which exact ideas are expressed in idiomatic language. Burning one's ancestral home for the insurance money needed to buy a telescope and then going to work as an assistant railroad clerk in order to have leisure for using it does typify the lot of modern man. But, as the poem says of McLaughlin, we each must ". . . satisfy a life-long curiosity/ About our place among the infinities." The ending is one which if taken literally as the poet's own viewpoint might lead critics to charge purblind conservatism:

> Do we know any better where we are,
> And how it stands between the night tonight
> And a man with a smoky lantern chimney?
> How different from the way it ever stood?

One thing is wrong with such an easy conclusion: the speaker in this poem—with his idea that the telescope splits a star into quicksilver parts —is naïve in a way not shared by Frost except in his rôle as a poet.

One of Frost's finest astronomical lyrics occurs in *New Hampshire*. "I Will Sing You One-O" is doubly fine for acclimating the short line of Herrick to the conditions of modern thought. The steeples, pealing out together at the hour of one:

> . . . spoke for the clock
> With whose vast wheels
> Theirs interlock.
> In that grave word
> Uttered alone
> The utmost star
> Trembled and stirred,
> Though set so far
> Its whirling frenzies
> Appear like standing
> In one self station.

The resonance of this poem with modern scientific thought can be felt in considering a statement by Sir James Jeans that "We cannot move a finger without disturbing all the stars."

West-Running Brook shows Frost continuing to watch the skies, but with an uneasiness that reflects our growing, always-to-be-incomplete, knowledge of the universe and our realization of the staggering immensity of space:

> What is this talked-of mystery of birth
> But being mounted bareback on the earth?

After a lull in *A Further Range,* except for "Lost in Heaven" and the lovely "Moon Compasses," comes the harvest of *A Witness Tree,* including "All Revelation," "Our Hold on the Planet," "A Loose Mountain (Telescopic)," and "The Lesson for Today." A resolution of the space-anxiety, hinting at maturer wisdom, is achieved in the last poem mentioned:

> Space ails us moderns: we are sick with space.
> Its contemplation makes us out as small
> As a brief epidemic of microbes
> That in a good glass may be seen to crawl
> The patina of this the least of globes.
> But have we there the advantage after all?
> You were belittled into vilest worms
> God hardly tolerated with his feet;
> . . . .
> The cloister and the observatory saint
> Take comfort in about the same complaint.
> So science and religion really meet.

These lines, included in a session of comparing ills between the modern and the medieval poet, are taken by Yvor Winters as directed mainly at critics. Such an interpretation seems to miss the larger pattern in Frost's poetry through this period and especially the import of the poem's last line: "I had a lover's quarrel with the world."

If we venture into the too-common practice of giving poets credit for unqualified endorsement of attitudes exhibited in their poems, we should be called upon to recognize in Frost a hard-won optimism. "Our Hold on the Planet" appears to state the careful balancing of probabilities, a continuing growth of wisdom:

> Take nature altogether since time began,
> Including human nature, in peace and war,
> And it must be a little more in favor of man,
> Say a fraction of one per cent at the very least,
> Or the number living wouldn't be steadily more,
> Our hold on the planet wouldn't have so increased.

Through all his pondering on the infinitesimalizing magnitudes of space, Frost has kept his gift for song as man his hold on the planet:

> It gently threw us a glittering shower down.
> And when we had taken that into the roots of grain,
> It threw us another and then another still. . . .

The poet reached something through his questioning that resembles the viewpoint expressed by Sir Charles Sherrington in *Man on His Nature*:

> One thing we can discern about Nature as a factor in this question, an element in this situation; at least it is a harmony. Now that for us the magical has been exorcised from it we can feel the vast unbroken harmony it is. Where tragedy and where comedy and where both it is at least a harmony all its own. That we should have attained that knowledge, that it should be given us to apprehend that, that we can follow it as that, can hear it, trace it, retrace it in part and even forecast it as such, is an inexpressibly estimable good. We are privileged in this. It is, so far as we can detect, uniquely the possession of ourselves—it is *the* human possession . . . The mind which began by being one thing has truly—as so often in evolution—gone on to being another thing. Even should mind in the cataclysm of Nature be doomed to disappear and man's mind with it, man will have had his compensation: to have glimpsed a coherent world and himself an item in it. To have heard for a moment a harmony wherein he is a note.

Frost, with a more acute ear for the odd and humorous noises man can make, depicts the situation thus in "Etherealizing":

> A theory if you hold it hard enough
> And long enough gets rated as a creed:
> Such as that flesh is something we can slough
> So that the mind can be entirely freed.
> Then when the arms and legs have atrophied,
> And brain is all that's left of mortal stuff,
> We can lie on the beach with the seaweed
> And take our daily tide baths smooth and rough.
> There once we lay as blobs of jellyfish
> At evolution's opposite extreme.
> But now as blobs of brain we'll lie and dream,
> With only one vestigial creature wish:
> Oh, may the tide be soon enough at high
> To keep our abstract verse from being dry.

A young American poet who would go farther along the road Frost has taken—making poems that present the semblance of reasoning in such a way that "sensation is carried into the midst of the objects of the science"—has no easy road to take. The journey will demand an education, however obtained, broader than the specialized curricula followed by many of today's poet-critics. Knowing the musical phrases of the Provençal poets or the sayings of Confucius seems to scant the job, estimable as such knowledge is.

It is in fact easy to miss the evidence of Frost's deep interest in the growth of human knowledge. One poem, "A Wish to Comply," at first appeared remote from any such interest except for a reference to "Millikan's mote." Until I was reminded of Frost's genius for understatement, it would hardly have occurred to me, a confessed amateur, that what he had christened as lackadaisical "motes" were in reality the highly energetic cosmic particles. And the poem turns on his skepticism as to what he can see in one of Wilson's cloud chambers—a sort of essay in miniature on Frost's uncertainty principle.

The last of the star poems in *Steeple Bush* gives us a poet looking yet to the stars for guidance; the wisdom is beyond that of a younger man who saw in the stars only the blind eyes of a Minerva in marble. To his calling upon it, the star replies only in the terms of man's knowledge, saying "I burn," but Frost observes it:

> . . . steadfast as Keats' Eremite,
> Not even stooping from its sphere,
> It asks a little of us here.
> It asks of us a certain height,
> So when at times the mob is swayed
> To carry praise or blame too far,
> We may choose something like a star
> To stay our minds on and be staid.

The growth of Frost's work tells us that we may yet have poetry made in the semblance of reasoning. It tells us how this poetry may move at least with some understanding in realms most poets have deserted. And we may go to Frost once more to learn "how a poem can have wildness and at the same time a subject that shall be fulfilled":

It should be of the pleasure of a poem itself to tell how it can. The figure a poem makes. It begins in delight and ends in wisdom. The figure is the same as for love. No one can really hold that the ecstasy should be static and stand still in one place. It begins in delight, it inclines to the impulse, it assumes direction with the first line laid down, it runs a course of lucky events, and ends in a clarification of life—not necessarily a great clarification, such as sects and cults are founded on, but in a momentary stay against confusion.

So, it seems, has his own work as a poet been begun in delight and has grown to wisdom.

Robert Frost and His Use of Barriers:
Man vs. Nature Toward God

by Marion Montgomery

I

The casual reader of Frost's poetry is likely to think of Frost as a nature poet in the tradition of Wordsworth. In a sense, nature is his subject, but to Frost it is never an impulse from a vernal wood. His best poetry is concerned with the drama of man in nature, whereas Wordsworth is generally best when emotionally displaying the panorama of the natural world. "I guess I'm not a nature poet," Frost said in a television interview in the fall of 1952. "I have only written two poems without a human being in them." Just what, then, is Frost's conception of the natural world to which Wordsworth was so religiously devoted and what, according to Frost, is man's relation to it?

As a starting point, we may recall the epitaph Frost proposes for himself in "The Lesson for Today": "I had a lover's quarrel with the world." This lover's quarrel is Frost's poetic subject, and throughout his poetry there are evidences of this view of man's existence in the natural world. His attitude toward nature is one of armed and amicable truce and mutual respect interspersed with crossings of the boundaries separating the two principles, individual man and forces of the world. But *boundaries* are insisted upon. In "Two Look at Two," the man and woman do feel that there is an affinity between themselves and the buck and doe that stare back at them. The experience is one which Wordsworth would appreciate. After the deer have fled

> Still they stood,
> A great wave from it going over them,
> As if earth in one unlooked-for favor
> Had made them certain earth returned their love.

Marion Montgomery, "Robert Frost and His Use of Barriers: Man vs. Nature Toward God," *The South Atlantic Quarterly*, LVII (Summer 1958), 339-353. Reprinted by permission of *The South Atlantic Quarterly*.

And there are other such instances. Reginald Cook recounts a conversation with Frost in which "he recalled how once he had come upon some cliff brake at the cliff's edge, and how once in a kitchen in his Franconia farm house, while he was looking westward into a sunset, the window was suddenly darkened by an owl that banked as it turned in its flight, and he felt as if he had been 'spoken to—favored.'" The poem "Dust of Snow" was originally called "A Favor" because, according to Frost, it had come to him as one of "nature's favors." However, even in these moments of favor we shall always find the barriers which cannot be crossed. Nature's favors are restricted: the humor of "Dust of Snow" does not obscure the fact that the crow's actions are accidental and unintended; there is a windowpane between the poet and the owl; and in the poem "Two Look at Two" there is a man-made fence, an important part of the poem, standing between the human and natural world. Man is never completely certain that the earth, the natural world, returns his love.

From the publication of *A Boy's Will* down to the present time Frost has indicated a realization that nature, *natura naturata,* not only will, but sometimes seems intended to, hurt those who love it. The immediate natural world even seems to be moving toward chaos, intending to take man along with it if he isn't careful. But man has an advantage:

> We may doubt the just proportion of good and ill.
> There is much in nature against us. But we forget:
> Take nature altogether since time began,
> Including human nature, in peace and war,
> And it must be a little more in favor of man.
> ("Our Hold on the Planet")

To sustain such injuries as nature inflicts "It's well to have all kinds of feeling, for it's all kinds of a world." And Frost expresses his all kinds of feeling toward the natural world. Wordsworth would never, even in his latest view of the natural world, have written

> I have wished a bird would fly away,
> And not sing by my house all day;
> Have clapped my hands at him from the door
> When it seemed as if I could bear no more.
> ("A Minor Bird")

Frost knows, too, that "In Time of Cloudburst" the much-needed rain has come to "exact for present gain/ A little future harm." But Frost also knows that, despite man's disadvantages, "The way of understanding is partly mirth" ("Not Quite Social"). So at times he writes of the natural world in a cavalier fashion which Wordsworth would consider heretical. "You know Orion always comes up sideways," he says in "The Star-Splitter," and he pokes fun at the seasons in "Two Tramps in Mud Time." It is no spirit of nature which sends Frost's rain or wind; he never sees in the natural world the pervading spirit which Wordsworth saw. It may be that a mountain "had the slant/ As of a book held up before his eyes/ (And was a text albeit done in plant)" ("Time Out"). But the mountain is not a personality as it is for Wordsworth in *The Prelude* and in other poems. Frost makes his attitude toward nature clear when he says in "New Hampshire" that "I wouldn't be a prude afraid of nature," and again rather flatly, "Nothing not built with hands of course is sacred."

Frost at times speaks directly to objects in nature, as Wordsworth did. But what is high seriousness in Wordsworth is fancy or humor in Frost. Frost goes on at length in a Polonius-to-Laertes speech to his orchard, which he is leaving for the winter. Watch out for the rabbits and deer and grouse; they will eat you. And if the sun gets too hot before the proper season, you won't be bearing next summer. The final word is "Goodby and Keep Cold." In another poem and in a more serious vein, he speaks to "The Tree at My Window," which he watches tossed about by the winds, and compares its state to his own, deciding that

> That day she put our heads together,
> Fate had her imagination about her,
> Your head so much concerned with outer,
> Mine with inner, weather.

In these instances of direct address, however, we never suppose that Frost feels the kind of brotherhood for natural objects that Wordsworth expresses through much of his poetry. Always, to Frost, man differs essentially from other features and objects. His trees, though he speaks to them, do not take on grave countenances. The weather that buffets them is "outer" and bears them to the withered bracken. They trail their leaves before them like girls drying their hair in the sun. But this is motion of natural objects and not emotion, human simile but not human feeling. In "A Considerable Speck" Frost says, after examining the microscopic creature, "Plainly with an intelligence I dealt." And in "Departmental" he seems to be interpreting the ants in human terms. But we make a mistake if we suppose that he would ascribe mind to the "miscroscopic item" in the first poem or human behavior to the actions of the ants in the second. The truth is that in each of these poems

Frost is preparing the way obliquely for direct statement. In "A Considerable Speck" we have the final "No one can know how glad I am to find/ On any sheet the least display of mind." And "Departmental" ends with the comment on the ants, "How thoroughly departmental." In the more direct poem, "The Bear," we find "The world has room to make a bear feel free;/ The universe seems cramped to you and me." Whenever Frost talks directly to or directly of natural objects or creatures, we feel that he is really looking at man out of the corner of his eye and speaking to him out of the corner of his mouth. In all these poems Frost is describing the animal and vegetable natures in man, not reading man's nature into the animal and vegetable worlds, as Wordsworth was inclined to do.

II

If Frost feels, as he seems to, that the natural world is impersonal, unfeeling, and at best animal creation, what does he think of its creator? In his early poetry he, like the people he refers to in "The Strong Are Saying Nothing," holds his silence. He does not choose to make any sweeping statements about God any more than he does about nature or man. This has occasioned the belief among some critics that Frost is at best agnostic. But perhaps Frost feels that Heaven "gives its glimpses only to those/ Not in position to look too close ("A Passing Glimpse"). He tells us of the time when "For Once, Then, Something" is almost seen: he stares into the crystal well, but when he almost sees a white stone or truth or whatever it is, a drop of water from a fern falls and shatters the surface. Sometimes the boundaries are mysteriously drawn by something other than man, and in those instances where the understanding fails, Frost "frankly calls himself superstitious," says his friend Sidney Cox, "by which he means that he accepts no explanation of mystery." He would not, for example, have us discount entirely the possibility that witches exist. Of his "Witch of Coös" he warns that she is "A veritable witch in a county in upper New Hampshire. There's a difference between a trance-medium and a witch. Saul's witch of Endor was a trance-medium, but this is a witch. Do not approach this witch with condescension." If his method is humorous, he still intends some seriousness.

Frost's hesitancy in speaking dogmatically on the subject of the supernatural is due more to his acceptance of man's limitations and the acceptance of mystery in existence than to agnosticism. Man's understanding of the natural world comes slowly. "The most exciting movement in nature is not progress, advance, but expansion and contraction, the opening and shutting of the eye, the hand, the heart, the mind."

Man lives in the natural world and thereby develops his mind so that he may perhaps reach beyond the boundary separating the natural and supernatural. "We throw our arms wide with a gesture of religion to the universe; we close them around a person. We explore and adventure for awhile and then draw in to consolidate our gains. The breathless swing is between subject matter and form." He is quite ready to believe that which is appealing *if* it is also reasonable. Then he will express opinion. At the same time he is not willing to discard completely the appealing if it fails to be reasonable, knowing the fallibility of reason. He rather reserves judgment. Experience comes early, understanding later.

In his later years Frost, feeling more sure of what he thought was true, has spoken more freely of his views of God, as of man and the natural world. An indication of his broadening scope appeared in his book *A Further Range,* published in 1936, and finally, he has come to devote two of his latest works, *A Masque of Reason* (1945) and *A Masque of Mercy* (1947), to the question of man's relation to God. In *A Masque of Reason* Frost attempts to justify God's ways to man, which justification is that none is necessary. In this work Frost presents God in a rather familiar fashion, and this presentation of a somewhat undignified God has occasioned difficulty for many readers. The reviewers in *Poetry* and the New York *Times* consider the masque an indication of Frost's cynicism and of his rejection of the Christian God because, they argue, the masque convicts God of cruel injustice to man. If this is Frost's view, if God has put man in a hopeless and unjust position, then Frost's view of the individuality of man, of his ability to overcome evil and assert his dignity through courage, a view apparent in much of his poetry, is at odds with his view of God's relationship to man.

But Frost's presentation of a cavalier God is a deliberate device which points up the theme of the masque. We have already said that whenever Frost speaks of or to nature he is showing us nature in man. In this picture of God given in *A Masque of Reason* he is showing us not lack of reason or justice in God, but rather man's stubbornness and lack of understanding. It is like man, especially in our day, to see God "pitching throne with a ply-wood chair." It is like man to exclaim with Job's wife, "It's God. I'd know him by Blake's picture anywhere." As it has been the human error to read man into nature, so is it the human error to read man into God: and Frost's poem, satirical in its shrewd observation on this human fallibility, is concerned with this problem. Is man's reason sufficient to overcome the wall between himself and God? Job and Job's wife are after a rational explanation of man's predicament which will clarify everything and bridge the gap between the finite mind and the infinite. The theme of the poem, then, is that understanding is dependent not only upon reason, but upon faith as well, a faith which helps the finite mind accept the mystery its reason will not completely explain. When God attempts to help Job by telling him that what his trial has done is to establish the principle "There's no connection man can reason out/ Between his just deserts and what he gets," Job is unsatisfied. Job's wife, the ardent feminist, tries to taunt God into explaining by insisting that "Of course, in the abstract high singular/ There isn't any universal reason." The couple refuses to accept God's statement that "My forte is truth,/ Or metaphysics, long the world's reproach/ For standing still in one place true forever." They insist on a reason so that they can make progress in the world. God leaves them pondering his statement that "I was just showing off to the Devil, Job," an explanation they are more likely to accept than any other.

How, then, does man fit into this impersonal world which God says in *A Masque of Reason* He and the devil groped out together? To Frost, the mindless world, despite its laws and patterns of cause and effect, lacks completeness. "There Are Roughly Zones," the title of a poem says, but understanding man is created so that he may try to make the world complete. Man's hands and mind bring order to himself to the world around him. Having all kinds of feelings for this all kinds of a world, he is able to bring order to the natural world "by making a garden and building a wall. That garden is art." And the man who erects the wall and makes the garden is in the world for that purpose, not that he may expect to bring permanent order but that he may work out his own salvation. Frost's consistency in this view from early to latest publication is shown by the two masques and by a poem from his first publication, *A Boy's Will*. "The Trial by Existence," which appeared in *A Boy's Will*, suggests that it is futile to attempt a complete explanation of why there are so many difficulties to prevent man's taking in and building his garden in the world. Man's real virtue, it argues, is to dare, to seek to build the wall which allows the garden to flourish for a time. Frost concludes that it is not important in the final reckoning whether or not one has actually succeeded in erecting a great or small wall or in raising a great or small garden; man is not measured by his works. Lewellyn Jones, commenting on "The Trial by Existence," says the conclusion reached is "a recognition that suffering is always in terms of what we are, not an alien something hitting us by chance from without but somehow or other implicit in our very constitution."

When the bravest is slain, the poem says, he will awake in paradise to discover that the greatest reward of daring the struggle is still to dare. In a poem written much later than "Trial by Existence" Frost says again, "Let me be the one/ To do what is done" ("Build-Soil" 1936). The virtue is in the doing, not in what is done. "Trial by Existence" invites a close comparison with Wordsworth's "Intimations Ode," and Frost seems to have had Wordsworth's poem in mind when writing it. Frost's poem shows the souls in Heaven before they come to earth. Each soul wishes to come to earth so that it may pit itself

> Heroic in its nakedness,
>   Against the uttermost of earth.
> The tale of earth's unhonored things
>   Sounds nobler there than 'neath the sun. . . .

And so God allows the soul its earthly journey, but He makes one condition: Frost's God, unlike Wordsworth's, decrees that no soul shall have any memory of its other state and that none may remember that it chose its earthward journey. For this knowledge would be such comfort to the soul on earth and such a crutch to it in times of trial that its trial would be less heroic, if not invalid. God says to the soul ready to descend to earth:

> '. . . the pure fate to which you go
>   Admits no memory of choice,
> Or the woe were no earthly woe
>   To which you give the assenting voice.'

The soul is allowed a final moment of decision. This bargain struck in Heaven is the reason why we have no memory that tells us we chose the woe of the world. Only thus is man rid of pride. The significance of this idea to what we have said above is apparent, and it is consistent to find Frost's God saying, thirty-five years later, that "There's no connection man can reason out/Between his just deserts and what he gets." "The Trial by Existence" is allegorical, and through it Frost argues that there is no possibility that man will be able to lay aside his varying opinion of himself and come to rest in an official verdict straight from God, as Job of the masque hopes to do. Man may badger, as Job does, and he may say confidentially to God:

> The front of being answerable to no one
> I'm with you in maintaining to the public.
> But, Lord, we showed them what?

Such attempts by man bring only limited responses, and God's most comforting words to Job are that together He and Job have found out

> . . . the discipline man needed most
> Was to learn his submission to unreason;
> And that for man's own sake as well as mine,
> So he won't find it hard to take his orders
> From his inferiors in intelligence
> In peace and war—especially in war.

So, Frost concludes, that is the way things stand between man and God. Man, like Job, continually repeats, "The artist in me cries out for design," and design man tries to discover. The barrier between creator and created is maintained. God will not let man see completely into the life of things. To this barrier are added the limitations imposed on man by his reason, or mind, and his desire, or heart. Yet reason and desire arouse the complementary faith which helps man accept his situation and grow from that point of acceptance. For here is true understanding in man, the recognition through reason, and acceptance through faith, of man's limitations and of the belief in God as "that which man is sure cares, and will save him, no matter how many times or how completely he has failed," as Frost said in 1916.

III

Frost considers this would be a pretty desperate and meaningless situation but for man's own ability to erect and destroy barriers. We find, in "Triple Bronze," that the powers that be provided man with his hide for inner defense, and that man himself makes a wall "Of wood or granite or lime" which crime cannot breach. Finally, "a number of us agree/ On a national boundary," and the barriers of skin and home and country are defenses between "too much and me." This concern with barriers is the predominant theme in Frost's poetry. The barriers fall into several categories. First of all there is the great natural barrier, the void between man and the stars, a barrier which man continually, and sometimes foolishly, tries to bridge in his attempt to escape his limited haunt. The very stars, because of their remoteness, reduce man if he confuses distance and size with his own nature. Writing to a poet of an earlier age, an age in which man felt compelled to revolt from religion because God's remoteness seemed to reduce man, Frost compares that age with our own: "We both are the belittled human race,/ One compared with God and one with space" ("The Lesson for Today").

But the remoteness of the stars is also something which man may lean his mind on and be stayed. What is more disturbing to man than the barrier of space is the barrier between man and the immediate natural world, for it is in this realm of desert places that most of man's "gardening" takes place. This is where the "breathless swing between subject matter and form" becomes most apparent. And it is the struggle in this sphere which reveals what men are. In "Brown's Descent," the old farmer maintains his fight against the physical world, grimly and determinedly. Though he slides all the way down the mountain on the icy snow, he never gives up his struggle against gravity; and he wins, too. For finally, bowing to natural laws, he goes around the mountain and re-establishes himself on top. Nature's laws are inexorable, but man is armed against them: he can make allowances. There are those souls, of course, who are content to have a barrier stand as a continual challenge which they never quite accept; such is the old teamster of "The Mountain" who lives and works in the shade of the mountain he always intends to climb but never does. And there are those who accept the challenge and go down in defeat; the deserted village of the "Census-Taker" with its gaunt and empty buildings is evidence of such failure. The woman in "A Servant to Servants" has lost out to the wilderness by losing her sanity. Her days are spent alone, caring for the house while the men are away, and the emptiness of the world has overcome her. There are others on the border-line of tragic failure. The "Hill Wife," though not out of her mind, still has a fear of her house once she has left it deserted and has to return to it. When she comes back she has to reconquer it:

> They learned to rattle the lock and key
> To give whatever might chance to be
> Warning and time to be off in flight.

Courage is needed to reclaim the house. The preacher in the long poem "Snow" insists on going into the heart of the blizzard when he could remain overnight with his neighbors with no inconvenience to them or himself. But he must go and conquer the blizzard. Wherever there is failure, wherever the natural world has won out, there are always the young who follow to restore where their fathers failed. In "Generations of Men" the boy and girl meet for the first time at the ruins of an old homeplace, sit on the edge of the cellar, and talk about families and the decayed place. In the end they are in love, or about to fall in love, and have made a pact to return and rebuild the old homeplace.

This war between man and the natural world did not exist for Wordsworth so positively as it does for Frost. Wordsworth in his early poetry tended to deny all barriers in his effort to become one with the great moving spirit of things, the soul of the world. He wanted to achieve the "abstract high singular" that Job's wife disparages in Frost's masque, to concern himself with the general idea rather than with the physical world. His approach was transcendental in that he denied the existence of barriers. For Frost there can be no such simplification of the problem of spirit and matter. Despite the necessity of maintaining one's garden against nature and of advancing it, there are certain limits which man cannot overstep, and one of them is the nature of physical existence. Frost has made no Platonic crosscuts to separate form and matter as Wordsworth did between 1798 and 1805. Existence is form plus matter to Frost, and any conflict in the world is conflict between such existences —form-and-matter man against form-and-matter world.

IV

There is a fourth category of barriers in Frost's poetry—those between man and man. To Frost these barriers serve as framework for mutual understanding and respect. It is because of barriers that we understand each other, and, far from striving to tear them down as is the modern tendency, Frost insists on recognizing them. He even builds them wherever they seem necessary. The conflict caused by friction of personal barriers, "human nature in peace and war," is the subject of his most dramatic poetry.

The most distinct illustration of this barrier between man and man as a subject in Frost's poetry occurs in the well-known "Mending Wall." When the two neighbors meet in the spring to set the wall between them again, the narrator attempts to draw the neighbor out. Why do we go to all this trouble to repair walls? What are walls for anyhow? The only answer he is able to get is that "Good fences make good neighbors." The reader might suppose from this poem that Frost does not particularly hold with the need for fences, but note that it is the narrator who "lets his neighbor know" when time comes to do the work. The narrator questions the necessity of the wall in an effort to make the neighbor think and come out of the darkness of mind he is walking in. Both men know that good fences make good neighbors, but only one of them knows why or that the wall is more than a barrier between neighbors. Something in the world doesn't like a wall between a man and the world or between a man and his neighbor. Something wants all walls down so that individual identity may be destroyed. The wise person knows that a wall is a point of reference, a touchstone of sanity, and that it must be not only maintained but respected as well. Frost complains in "Trespass" of the person who went poking about his property without permission, until there

> came his little acknowledgement:
> He asked for a drink at the kitchen door,
> An errand he may have had to invent,
> But it made my property mine once more.

Man's tendency, once he has brought what he understands as form to the semichaos of his world, is to try also to impose the form he understands on the mind of his fellow-men—to insist that they see as he sees. Since each man is an individual intended to discover his individuality by revealing or restoring order through his peculiar art—whether that art be the splitting of birch logs, the making of ax-helves, or the writing of poems about these activities—one thing he must remember: each man reveals form which is indwelling in the material with which he works. There are roughly zones which limit man's gardening, his restoration of order in his own image. The wood which the ax-helve is made from has its grain, and the artist reveals form within the limitations of that grain. If he does his job well, the ax-helve will bend in use without breaking. All the helve-maker may boast of is his ability to reveal the form he has discovered in a particular piece of wood; his understanding of the form and his dexterity in revealing it mark his accomplishment. But when man imposes what he thinks should be the form of an ax-helve on a piece of wood whose grain will not allow the form, the first solid whack will split the finished helve. By showing the difference between a good and a bad helve, the French Canadian in "The Ax-Helve" argues against one man's imposing what he finds himself to be upon another man. The Canadian, it finally appears, is arguing that his children ought not to be forced to go to public schools where they will have themselves ground down to a form which is not in their nature.

V

Frost's view of man's nature, then, is consistent throughout his poetry. Each man is, in a sense, a stranger in this world, and so he remains. His is not to question why he is alone or why the world seems to be against him. He is to begin the breathless opening and closing of the mind, the hand, the heart, the eye upon the world, growing as he does so. As he grows he understands himself more, and as he understands himself he also understands more of the world and of his fellows. With understanding comes love which makes him respect the chaos of the world with which he is in conflict, the material with which he works. The same love makes him respect and accept differences between men also. He respects others' individual differences and expects that others will respect his. And he knows that those differences are not to be overcome by the "tenderer-than-thou/ Collectivistic regimenting love/ With which the modern world is being swept" ("A Considerable Speck"). That would be to reduce man to a numerical and animal problem, to make him no more than the other creatures who share the world of nature with him. "Our worship, humor, conscientiousness" have long since gone to the dogs under the table, he says in "The White-Tailed Hornet," because we have insisted on instituting downward comparisons. The result, Frost feels, has been to destroy man's proper place in the world. Scientific man has made so bold as to demonstrate the infallibility of natural laws and then has proceeded to measure himself against them. As long as there was man's fallibility, as long as he could bow to natural law, there was some distinction in being man. Frost observes in this poem, however, that even the hornet is fallible—it can't tell the difference between a nail-head and a fly, and when it does strike at a fly it misses. It serves man right, Frost says, to be denied even the distinction of fallibility since he so willingly turned from measuring himself against the angels and God to measure himself against the "dogs under the table."

In arguing man's distinction, Frost will not go to the two extremes offered by the philosophy of Plato on the one hand or the science of Democritus on the other. He will not accept pure spirit or idea as an explanation of man and a way out of the universe, nor will he accept the scientist's materialism measured with microscope and telescope as an alternate. Unhappy man tries both like a bear in a cage:

> He sits back on his fundamental butt
> With lifted snout and eyes (if any) shut,
> (He almost looks religious but he's not),
> And back and forth he sways from cheek to cheek,
> At one extreme agreeing with one Greek,
> At the other agreeing with another Greek.
> ("The Bear")

Frost's latest comments on man's position are made in *A Masque of Mercy*. My Brother's Keeper, the cynical, modern materialist, is one who avows at first that he had rather "be lost in the woods Than found in church." But though Keeper laughs at Jonah, who claims that God's justice is being withheld and that God has thus let him, his Old Testament Prophet, down, Keeper finally comes to see that

> My failure is no different from Jonah's.
> We both have lacked the courage in the heart

> To overcome the fear within the soul
> And go ahead to any accomplishment.
> Courage is what it takes and takes the more of
> Because the deeper fear is so eternal.

That deeper fear is that life is to no avail, that there is no reason to existence in the abstract high singular. The fear is that God's decision lastly on a man's deeds will be that the man, after all, is not acceptable. Once more Frost affirms that what is most important is the courage and not the accomplishment, the attempting and not successful completion:

> I can see that the uncertainty
> In which we act is a severity,
> A cruelty, amounting to injustice
> That nothing but God's mercy can assuage.

Thus speaks Keeper after his change of heart. And Paul, St. Paul, the spirit of the New Testament, finally convinces Keeper that man is saved only by God's mercy, which man receives for having labored under injustice, his inability to overcome completely the barriers imposed upon him and the temporal nature of those barriers which man himself may erect. This is the only way to man's salvation, for if he had not labored thus his limitations would not allow that salvation. To Frost, God is still "that which man is sure cares, and will save him, no matter how many times or how completely he has failed." Heaven, Paul argues in so many words, is like Silas's home—something man hasn't to deserve. Justice, Frost says, is only to the deserving, but mercy is for the undeserving. And those who demand justice because of the limitations imposed upon them will receive justice; those who with courage in the heart move toward understanding through faith and reason may expect God's mercy.

A Speech on Robert Frost:
A Cultural Episode

by Lionel Trilling

On March 26th [1959] Henry Holt and Company, the publishers of Robert Frost, gave Mr. Frost a dinner at the Waldorf-Astoria in celebration of his eighty-fifth birthday. I was the speaker at the dinner. I am publishing what I said about Mr. Frost not because I think it to be especially interesting in itself but because it made the occasion for a disturbance of some magnitude and I should like to answer the question that has often been put to me: What did I say that could so nearly have approached a scandal?

Some of the substance of my speech was made public by J. Donald Adams in his column in *The New York Times Book Review* of April 12th. Mr. Adams wrote from a copy of my manuscript which, with my permission, had been made available to him by Henry Holt and Company, and he reported with sufficient accuracy those parts of the speech to which he took exception. It should be said of Mr. Adams's reply to me that it took exception only to the critical judgment I had expressed. Mr. Adams did not question my taste or tact except in one small and perhaps facetious instance—he thought it "unfortunate . . . in view of Frost's shock of white hair," that I should have "identified the poet with the Bald Eagle." (But every American worthy of the name knows that the Bald Eagle is not bald at all and that in maturity it is distinguished by its shock of white hair.) Nevertheless the reply of Mr. Adams created the impression with some people that, so far from my having paid tribute to a venerable man at a celebration of his life and achievement, I had actually offered him an affront. I gather that the chief cause of the presumed offense was my having spoken of Mr. Frost as "a terrifying poet."

Certainly what I had said as reported by Mr. Adams offered an affront to some part of American opinion. It was a very deep affront if I can

Lionel Trilling, "A Speech on Robert Frost: A Cultural Episode," *Partisan Review*, XXVI (Summer 1959), 445-52. Reprinted by permission of the author.

judge by the letters, published in the *Book Review* of April 26th, which
applauded Mr. Adams for his reply to me. There were nine such letters
and all of them sounded a note of bitterness, or of personal grievance,
or of triumph over my having been so thoroughly taken down by Mr.
Adams. I must confess to being surprised by the low personal and intellectual tone of these letters. My estimate of the present state of American
culture had not prepared me for it. "Trilling doesn't have the good sense
to know when he is out of his field or his depth or whatever it is."
"Frost might have had the Nobel Prize if so many New York critics hadn't
gone whoring after European gods." "This Trilling fella had it coming
to him for some time." "I hope Robert Frost was having a nice plate
of buckwheat cakes and Vermont maple syrup as he read Mr. Adams's
remarks. He couldn't have done better unless he had taken the so-called
professor out to the woodshed." "I am a Freudian psychoanalyst, but
I couldn't agree with Mr. Adams more. Imagine calling Frost a 'terrifying
poet.' Professor Trilling never got lost in the Freudian wood. He is just
enmeshed in a Trilling world." (In his column Mr. Adams had urged me
"to come out of the Freudian wood . . . and face the facts of life." It
will be seen that I make no mention of Freud in my speech, but I do
speak of D. H. Lawrence, and Mr. Adams said that Lawrence was a genius
but hadn't understood "the American experience" because, like me, he
was "lost in the Freudian wood." Lawrence, of course, hated Freud and
took every occasion to denounce him.)

The personal and intellectual quality of the letters is especially interesting because of the professions of the people who wrote them: in
addition to the "Freudian psychoanalyst," the writers included the editor
of *The Atlantic Monthly,* the publisher of *The Saturday Review,* two
fairly well-known poets, a member of the Federal Trade Commission, a
well-known and quite literate writer of fiction and biography, a very
distinguished literary scholar. Only one of the writers, Mr. Weeks of *The
Atlantic Monthly,* knew at first hand, what I had said, having been
present at the dinner. He expressed himself as finding my remarks "ill-
judged and condescending for an occasion which was intended to be
appreciative," and went on to say that "it would have been more appropriate had the introduction been entrusted to W. H. Auden, particularly in view of England's early acceptance of Frost's work, in which
case we should have been spared the long Freudian self-analysis which
few could have come to hear." All the other writers knew what I had
said only from Mr. Adams's reply to it. That the literary scholar was
among their number made a circumstance to which I couldn't fail to
respond with some unhappiness, for I had first been Professor Emery
Neff's student when I was an undergraduate at Columbia College and

I had worked in his field and under his direction as a graduate student; I have always thought of Mr. Neff as the teacher from whom I had learned the methods and attitudes of the scholar; that he should so far have abrogated the rule and spirit of scholarship as to write in support of Mr. Adams's rebuke (as he chose to call it) without having seen the text of what I had said disturbed me deeply in a way I shall not now attempt to describe.

I have no doubt that the episode will yield cultural conclusions to whoever wants to draw them.

Because I am publishing the speech as a document, I give it exactly as I spoke it, not even mitigating the donnish humor of the opening paragraphs.

*   *   *

Mr. Rigg, Ladies and Gentlemen
(and I shall address Mr. Frost presently):

I am sure that anyone standing in my place tonight, charged with the happy office of greeting Mr. Frost on his birthday, on his massive, his Sophoclean birthday, would be bound to feel, as I do indeed feel, a considerable measure of diffidence.

For our occasion, although it isn't solemn, is surely momentous. We all of us know that we celebrate something that lies beyond even Mr. Frost's achievement as a poet. No person here tonight, no matter how high his regard for Mr. Frost as a poet may be, is under any illusion that Mr. Frost, at this point in his career, exists in the consciousness of Americans as only a poet. Just what he does exist as may perhaps be best understood by the archaeologists of a few milleniums hence. They will observe, those ardent students of our culture, how, at the time of the vernal equinox, feasts were held to celebrate the birth of this personage, and how, at a later time in the spring, at that ceremony which the ancient North Americans, with their infallible instinct for beauty, called by the lovely name of *Commencement*, it was customary to do him honor by a rite in which it was pretended that he was a scholar, a man of immense learning—a doctor—and no American university was thought to be worthy of the name until it had duly performed this rite, which was quaintly called *conferring a degree*. The time of year at which these ritual observances took place makes it plain to the archaeologists that they are almost certainly not dealing with an historical individual but rather with a solar myth, a fertility figure. They go on to expound the subtle process of myth which is to be observed in the fact that this vernal spirit was called *Frost*, a name which seems to contradict his nature and function. In their effort to explain this anomaly, they take note of evidence which suggests that the early North Americans believed that there were once two brothers, Robert Frost and Jack Frost, of whom one, Jack, remained unregenerate and hostile to mankind, while the other brother became its friend. But of course the archaeologists understand that this is a mere folk-explanation which explains nothing. They say, cogently enough, that mythical figures often embody contradictory principles, that just as Apollo was both destroyer and preserver, so Robert Frost was at one and the same time both ice and sun, and they point to a dark saying attributed to him: "Like a piece of ice on a hot stove, the poem must ride on its own melting."

Thus the ultimate myth. It tells us much about the nature of Robert Frost and I am glad to be able to communicate it to you.

But there is also the myth that is nearer at hand. We do not need to wait upon the archaeologists of the future to understand that Robert Frost exists not only in a human way but also in a mythical way. We know him, and have known him so for many years, as nothing less than a national fact. We have come to think of him as virtually a symbol of America, as something not unlike an articulate, an actually poetic, Bald Eagle. When we undertake to honor him, we do indeed honor him as a poet, but also as a tutelary genius of the nation and as a justification of our national soul.

This mythical existence of Robert Frost determines the nature of our occasion and makes it momentous. It substantiates my statement that anyone who speaks publicly about Mr. Frost tonight must do so under the constraints of an extreme diffidence.

Yet I must be more weighed down by diffidence than many others who might speak here. I must almost entertain a doubt of the appropriateness of my speaking here at all. For I cannot help knowing that the manifest America of Robert Frost's poems is not the America that has its place in my own mind. The manifest America of Mr. Frost's poems is rural, and, if I may say so, it is rural in a highly moralized way, in an aggressively moralized way. It thus represents an ideal that is common to many Americans, perhaps especially to Americans of the literary kind, who thus express their distaste for the life of the city and for all that the city implies of excessive complexity, of uncertainty, of anxiety, and of the demand that is made upon intellect to deal with whatever are the causes of complexity, uncertainty, anxiety.

I do not share this ideal. It is true that the image of the old America has a great power over me—that old America with which the America of Mr. Frost's poems seems to be continuous. And I think I know from experience—there are few Americans who do not—how intense can be the pleasure in the hills and the snow, in the meadows and woods and swamps that make the landscape of Mr. Frost's manifest America; and know, too, how great a part this pleasure can play in a man's moral being. But these natural things that give me pleasure constitute my notion of the earthly paradise, they are not the ruling elements of my imagination of actual life. Those elements are urban—I speak here tonight incongruously as a man of the city. I teach in an urban university. The magazine I most enjoy writing for is *Partisan Review,* to which, as I know, there is often imputed an excess of city intellectuality, even to the point of its being thought scarcely American at all.

Of course I have imagination enough to hate the city. And of course I have sensibility enough to be bored and exasperated by the intellectual life that is peculiar to the city, not only as that is lived by others but by myself. But to the essential work that is done by the critical intellect (I use the term in its widest sense), that work which, wherever it is carried on, must sooner or later relate itself to the metropolis or must seek, wherever it is carried on, to create around itself the intensity and variety that traditionally characterize the intellectual life of the metropolis— to that work I give a partisan devotion. I know all that can be charged against the restless, combative, abstract urban intellect: I know perhaps more than is known by its avowed antagonists. I also know that when it flags, something goes out of the nation's spirit, and that if it were to cease, the state of the nation would be much the worse.

It is a fact which I had best confess as simply as possible that for a long time I was alienated from Mr. Frost's great canon of work by what I saw in it, that either itself seemed to denigrate the work of the critical intellect or that gave to its admirers the ground for making the denigration. It was but recently that my resistance, at the behest of better understanding, yielded to admiration—it is probable that there is no one here tonight who has not admired Mr. Frost's poetry for a longer time than I have.

This will begin to explain why I am so especially diffident standing in this place. I have yet more to confess. I have to say that my Frost— *my Frost:* what airs we give ourselves when once we believe that we have come into possession of a poet!—I have to say that my Frost is not the Frost I seem to perceive existing in the minds of so many of his admirers. He is not the Frost who confounds the characteristically modern practice of poetry by his notable democratic simplicity of utterance: on the contrary. He is not the Frost who controverts the bitter modern astonishment at the nature of human life: the opposite is so. He is not the Frost who reassures us by his affirmation of old virtues, simplicities, pieties, and ways of feeling: anything but. I will not go so far as to say that my Frost is not essentially an American poet at all: I believe that he is quite as American as everyone thinks he is, but not in the way that everyone thinks he is.

In the matter of the Americanism of American literature one of my chief guides is that very remarkable critic, D. H. Lawrence. Here are the opening sentences of Lawrence's great outrageous book about classic American literature. "We like to think of the old fashioned American classics as children's books. Just childishness on our part. The old American art speech contains an alien quality which belongs to the American continent and to nowhere else." And this unique alien quality, Lawrence goes on to say, the world has missed. "It is hard to hear a new voice," he says, "as hard as to listen to an unknown language. . . . Why? Out of fear. The world fears a new experience more than it fears anything. It can pigeonhole any idea. But it can't pigeonhole a real new experience. It can only dodge. The world is a great dodger, and the Americans the greatest. Because they dodge their own very selves." I should like to pick up a few more of Lawrence's sentences, feeling the freer to do so because they have an affinity to Mr. Frost's prose manner and substance: "An artist is usually a damned liar, but his art, if it be art, will tell you the truth of his day. And that is all that matters. Away with eternal truth. Truth lives from day to day. . . . The old American artists were hopeless liars. . . . Never trust the artist. Trust the tale. The proper function of the critic is to save the tale from the artist who created it. . . . Now listen to me, don't listen to him. He'll tell you the lie you expect, which is partly your fault for expecting it."

Now in point of fact Robert Frost is *not* a liar. I would not hesitate to say that he was if I thought he was. But no, he is not. In certain of his poems—I shall mention one or two in a moment—he makes it per-fectly plain what he is doing; and if we are not aware of what he is doing in other of his poems, where he is not quite so plain, that is not his fault but our own. It is not from him that the tale needs to be saved.

I conceive that Robert Frost is doing in his poems what Lawrence says the great writers of the classic American tradition did. That enter-prise of theirs was of an ultimate radicalism. It consisted, Lawrence says, of two things: a disintegration and sloughing off of the old conscious-ness, by which Lawrence means the old European consciousness, and the forming of a new consciousness underneath.

So radical a work, I need scarcely say, is not carried out by reassurance, nor by the affirmation of old virtues and pieties. It is carried out by the representation of the terrible actualities of life in a new way. I think of Robert Frost as a terrifying poet. Call him, if it makes things any easier, a tragic poet, but it might be useful every now and then to come out from under the shelter of that literary word. The universe that he conceives is a terrifying universe. Read the poem called "Design" and see if you sleep the better for it. Read "Neither Out Far nor In Deep," which often seems to me the most perfect poem of our time, and see if you are warmed by anything in it except the energy with which emptiness is perceived.

But the *people*, it will be objected, the *people* who inhabit this possibly terrifying universe! About them there is nothing that can terrify; surely the people in Mr. Frost's poems can only reassure us by their integrity and solidity. Perhaps so. But I cannot make the disjunction. It may well be that ultimately they reassure us in some sense, but first they terrify us, or should. We must not be misled about them by the curious tenderness with which they are represented, a tenderness which extends to a recognition of the tenderness which they themselves can often give. But when ever have people been so isolated, so lightning-blasted, so tried down and calcined by life, so reduced, each in his own way, to some last irreducible core of being. Talk of the disintegration and sloughing off of the old consciousness! The people of Robert Frost's poems have done that with a vengeance. Lawrence says that what the Americans refused to accept was "the post-Renaissance humanism of Europe," "the old European spontaneity," "the flowing easy humor of Europe" and that seems to me a good way to describe the people who inhabit Robert Frost's America. In the interests of what great other thing these people have made this rejection we cannot know for certain. But we can guess that it was in the interest of truth, of some truth of the self. This is what they all affirm by their humor (which is so *not* "the easy flowing humor of Europe"), by their irony, by their separateness and isolateness. They affirm *this* of themselves: that they are what they are, that this is their truth, and that if the truth be bare, as truth often is, it is far better than a lie. For me the process by which they arrive at that truth is always terrifying. The manifest America of Mr. Frost's poems may be pastoral; the actual America is tragic.

And what new consciousness is forming underneath? That I do not know, possibly because I have not been long enough habituated to the voice that makes the relatively new experience I am having. I am still preoccupied with the terrifying process of the disintegration and sloughing off of the old consciousness.

Mr. Frost:

I hope that you will not think it graceless of me that on your birthday I have undertaken to say that a great many of your admirers have not understood clearly what you have been doing in your life in poetry. I know that you will not say which of us is in the right of the matter. You will behave like the Secret whose conduct you have described:

> We dance around in a ring and suppose.
> But the Secret sits in the middle and knows.

And I hope that you will not think it graceless of me that on your birthday I have made you out to be a poet who terrifies. When I began to speak I called your birthday Sophoclean and that word has, I think, controlled everything I have said about you. Like you, Sophocles lived to a great age, writing well; and like you, Sophocles was the poet his people loved most. Surely they loved him in some part because he praised their common country. But I think that they loved him chiefly because he made plain to them the terrible things of human life: they felt, perhaps, that only a poet who could make plain the terrible things could possibly give them comfort.

A Momentary Stay Against Confusion

by George W. Nitchie

. . . there is perfectly competent work in all Frost's books. If there were not, the vulnerable work would not matter; one could dismiss Frost as simply a second- or third-rate poet who had the luck to produce one good book, or as a poet who got started too late and then ran dry. But such dismissal will not do. No third-rate poet or dried-up poet, no matter how lucky, could produce a sequence like "Stars" (from *A Boy's Will*), "A Servant to Servants" (from *North of Boston*), "Snow" (from *Mountain Interval*), "An Empty Threat" (from *New Hampshire*), "Acquainted With the Night" (from *West-Running Brook*), "Neither Out Far Nor In Deep" (from *A Further Range*), "The Most of It" (from *A Witness Tree*), and "Directive" (from *Steeple Bush*), a sequence that extends over a period of at least thirty-four years, with Frost in his seventies at its close. The important question is not whether Frost is a good and important poet, but rather why a good and important poet should, with increasing persistence, take refuge in the arch, the cute, the complacent, the trivial, gradually abandoning areas of proven strength (the dramatic poems of *North of Boston, Mountain Interval,* and *New Hampshire*), and not really following up promising new departures ("The Subverted Flower," "The Discovery of the Madeiras," "Directive"). As Louise Bogan has said:

Frost's later work never completely realized the tragic power that *North of Boston* promised. In *West-Running Brook* (1928) he began to play with the role of self-conscious homespun philosopher. He began to give reasons for his innate, countryman's conservatism, and not only reasons, but arguments which were half apologies. His own native shrewdness began to get the upper hand. . . . he reinforced his stoicism, which in itself had a certain dignity,

"A Momentary Stay Against Confusion." From *Human Values in the Poetry of Robert Frost: A Study of a Poet's Convictions* (Durham, N. C.: Duke University Press, 1960), pp. 202-223. Reprinted by permission of Duke University Press; abridged by permission of the author.

with an active insistence upon burrowing under and digging safely in. We see in this attitude the ancient conservatism of the man who depends upon the earth for his living;[1] but Frost's later work seems to base its skepticism less upon intelligent common sense than upon unthinking timidity. The appeal Frost made to large numbers of people began to be attached to a series of refusals rather than to a set of affirmations.[2]

And the question to be answered is, Why?

Obviously, no answer to such a question can be more than tentative. Lionel Trilling has written of Wordsworth:

> . . . given the fact of the great power, the desire to explain its relative deterioration will no doubt always be irresistible. But we must be aware, in any attempt to make this explanation, that an account of why Wordsworth ceased to write great poetry must at the same time be an account of how he once did write great poetry. And this latter account, in our present state of knowledge, we cannot begin to furnish.[3]

Now, Frost's importance is not comparable to Wordsworth's; Wordsworth, after all, with Milton, Spenser, Chaucer, is one of the handful of poets who have not simply worked within a tradition but have been instrumental in shaping and giving direction to their tradition, and it would be rash indeed to attribute such weight to Frost, at least in our time. Even the cultists do not deny that Eliot has been the more powerfully influential poet; they merely deplore the fact and appeal to the judgment of history. But Trilling's warning is as applicable to Frost as it is to Wordsworth. The problem of why Frost has written unsatisfactory poems is inextricably involved with the problem of how he has written excellent poems; and if the latter problem were soluble, there would be no occasion for speculative criticism.

Insofar as art is important, however, the problem of unsatisfactory art is also important, however speculative and provisional one's examination of the problem may be. And I think that the most rewarding approach to that problem with respect to Frost is by way of comparison between Frost and some of his principal contemporaries. In a number of ways, Yeats is a particularly useful figure here. Both men have

---

[1] Frost's self-created role, again; his dependence upon the earth for his living lasted only five years, more than fifty years ago.

[2] Louise Bogan, *Achievement in American Poetry, 1900-1950* (Chicago: Henry Regnery Co., 1951), pp. 49-50.

[3] Lionel Trilling, *The Liberal Imagination: Essays on Literature and Society* (New York: Doubleday & Company, Inc. 1950), p. 153.

written a substantial quantity of poetry; Yeats's *Collected Poems* (most of the plays omitted) runs to over four hundred pages, Frost's *Complete Poems* (including the masques) to over six hundred. Both men began writing in the eighties or nineties of the last century, and their earliest work exhibits a comparable degree of vague, nostalgic yearning. Both were in their seventies at the time their most recent books were published, and both had been writing and publishing quite steadily from the time of their first books. (Yeats, of course, died in 1939; Frost continues to write. *Complete Poems* contains three poems evidently completed since the publication of *Steeple Bush* and *A Masque of Mercy,* and his privately printed Christmas poems keep appearing.) To a degree, they exhibit similar crotchets and prejudices. Both are fond of making cryptically oracular pronouncements—compare Yeats's "Lapis Lazuli" with Frost's concluding remarks on Robinson.[4] Both are scornful toward efforts at social reform—compare Yeats's "On a House Shaken by the Land Agitation" with Frost's "A Roadside Stand," or Yeats's treatment of Constance Markievicz in "Easter 1916" with Frost's "To a Thinker" or "The Lost Follower." Both profess a distrust of excessive intellection—compare Yeats's

> I would be ignorant as the dawn,

from "The Dawn," or

> An intellectual hatred is the worst,
> So let her think opinions are accursed,

from "A Prayer for My Daughter," with Frost's "The Bear" or with Thyatira's skepticism in *A Masque of Reason.* Both create more or less eccentric roles for themselves—Frost as the canny Yankee, Yeats as the fisherman of "The Tower," as the wild old wicked man of *Last Poems,* as one of "the indomitable Irishry" of "Under Ben Bulben."[5]

As a matter of fact, Yeats has evidently been a curiously attractive figure to Frost. Frost produced two of Yeats's plays at Pinkerton Academy in 1910. And in the two masques, Frost indicates that Yeats is on his mind. In *A Masque of Reason,* Thyatira, preparing to take a group snapshot of God, Job, and Satan, says:

[4] Frost's introduction to Edwin Arlington Robinson's *King Jasper* (Toronto: The Macmillan Company, 1935), p. xv.

[5] *The Collected Poems of W. B. Yeats* (New York: The Macmillan Company, 1951), pp. 144, 187, 343.

> There, that's just the right arrangement.
> Now someone can light up the Burning Bush
> And turn the gold enameled artificial birds on.
> I recognize them. Greek artificers
> Devised them for Alexius Comnenus.
> They won't show in the picture.

But "Sailing to Byzantium" does. And in *A Masque of Mercy,* Paul explains Keeper and Bel to Jonah:

> Don't you be made feel small by all this posing.
> Both of them caught it from Bel's favorite poet
> Who in his favorite pose as poet thinker
> (His was the doctrine of the Seven Poses)
> Once charged the Nazarene with having brought
> A darkness out of Asia that had crossed
> Old Attic grace and Spartan discipline
> With violence. The Greeks were hardly strangers
> To the idea of violence. It flourished
> Persisting from old Chaos in their myth
> To embroil the very gods about their spheres
> Of influence. It's been a commonplace
> Ever since Alexander Greeced the world.
> 'Twere nothing new if that were all Christ brought.
> Christ came to introduce a break with logic
> That made all other outrage seem as child's play:
> The Mercy on the Sin against the Sermon.

No other contemporary poet gets such sustained attention from Frost, even though Edward Thomas and Ridgely Torrence have poems addressed to them. To be sure, he is being snide at Yeats's expense, yet it is not easy to see why Yeats should have been so singled out. In *A Masque of Reason* the allusion is irrelevant, dragged in, and in *A Masque of Mercy,* though a connection is made, it is not clear what the quarrel is about. Paul conveniently forgets, in his closing lines, that it was precisely

> In pity for man's darkening thought

that Yeats's Christ came in "To Songs from a Play," and he says nothing about the arrogant idealism with which Yeats's poem closes, an idealism that would surely have been anathema to the historical Paul:

> Whatever flames upon the night
> Man's own resinous heart has fed.[6]

The whole situation strongly suggests, to one reader at least, a reluctant but powerful attraction toward Yeats's poetry and perhaps toward Yeats's general position as well.[7]

It would be possible to explain the situation simply as one craftsman's interest in another sufficiently like himself to make attraction possible but sufficiently different to prevent that attraction from ever approaching identification, to make possible an amused irritation at this other one's foibles. And perhaps that is the most that can safely be suggested. But at the risk of abandoning safety, I think something more funda-

---

[6] Yeats, *Collected Poems*, pp. 210-11.

[7] To carry this matter further, in Yeats's *Collected Poems*, "Two Songs from a Play" is followed imediately by "Fragments":

> "Locke sank into a swoon;
> The Garden died;
> God took the spinning-jenny
> Out of his side." (Yeats, p. 211.)

The author of "The Egg and the Machine" would hardly quarrel with the sentiment here expressed.

> "Where got I that truth?
> Out of a medium's mouth,
> Out of nothing it came,
> Out of the forest loam,
> Out of dark night where lay
> The crowns of Nineveh." (Yeats, p. 211.)

Or, as Frost put it, "trust my instinct—I'm a bard." Also, Jonah's conduct toward the end of *A Masque of Mercy* has an at least formal resemblance to the conduct of Yeats's antithetical man in pursuit of his Mask. The "irresistible impossibility" that Paul compels Jonah to see and follow—

> "Yes, Pilgrim now instead of runaway,
> Your fugitive escape become a quest"—

sets up remote echoes of Yeats's man of the second quarter who, in "The Phases of the Moon,"

> "follows whatever whim's most difficult

> Among whims not impossible." (Yeats, p. 161.)

Keeper, be it noted, simply turns away from that irresistible impossibility; but it is Jonah who is saved—presumably—at the end and Keeper who confesses his lack of courage, concerned more with finding himself than with finding an image. And the myth Frost constructs in "The Trial by Existence," like Yeats's myth in *A Vision*, involves a doctrine of successive reincarnations, though Frost's poem, included in *A Boy's Will*, antedates the privately printed version of *A vision* by at least twelve years.

mental is involved—at least that Yeats's particular achievement illuminates to a degree Frost's relative incompleteness. . . . Frost is unable or unwilling to indicate what the reality is that his characters confront, and the result is a degree of inconclusiveness; we are never quite sure what Jonah's death means, whether his commitment of himself implies an apprehension of reality or a self-destructive surrender to an impulsive whim—or whether surrender to whim *is* a means of apprehending reality.

Now, precisely one of the things that *A Vision* provided Yeats was an elaborately articulated theory of reality and a means of apprehending it—twenty-six such means, in fact; Frost was too moderate in attributing only seven poses to Yeats. And those poems that are now almost universally accepted as Yeats's finest were written after the theory had been worked out. That theory is more or less incredible; in R. P. Blackmur's temperate phrasing, it presents "a view of life most readers cannot share, and which, furthermore, most readers feel as repugnant, or sterile, or simply inconsequential." [8] But its incredibility does not matter much except in ultimate terms. For one thing, incredibility of one sort or another is a common characteristic of statements about the nature of reality. Yeats's spheres and gyres are intrinsically neither more nor less difficult to believe in than the Christian doctrine of the Incarnation; and, as Alfred North Whitehead has written of "the characteristic scientific philosophy which closed the seventeenth century,"

> it has held its own as the guiding principle of scientific studies ever since. It is still reigning. Every university in the world organizes itself in accordance with it. No alternative system of organizing the pursuit of scientific truth has been suggested. It is not only reigning, but it is without a rival.
>   And yet—it is quite unbelievable.[9]

And for another thing, while such incredibility may be disadvantageous as the basis for a totally adequate philosophy, it is not necessarily disadvantageous as the basis for a poet's strategy, especially when the poet translates his private, eccentric symbols into more generally accessible ones. We lose nothing by knowing that the "widening gyre" [10] of "The Second Coming" is explained in a good deal of detail in *A Vision,* but the sense of accelerating and disruptive centrifugal forces wrenching a culture apart is conveyed clearly enough without such

[8] R. P. Blackmur, *Form and Value in Modern Poetry* (Garden City, N.Y.: Doubleday & Company, Inc. 1957), p. 35.
[9] Alfred North Whitehead, *Science and the Modern World* (New York: The Macmillan Company, 1948), p. 56.
[10] Yeats, *Collected Poems,* p. 184.

knowledge. At its best, the system described in *A Vision* served to give shape and precision to Yeats's thinking and to the images he made. Of his own belief in that system, Yeats wrote:

> . . . some will ask whether I believe in the actual existence of my circuits of sun and moon. . . . To such a question I can but answer that if sometimes, overwhelmed by miracle as all men must be when in the midst of it, I have taken such periods literally, my reason has soon recovered; and now that the system stands out clearly in my imagination I regard them as stylistic arrangements of experience comparable to the cubes in the drawing of Wyndham Lewis and the ovoids in the sculpture of Brancusi. They have helped me to hold in a single thought reality and justice.[11]

This admission is a curiously complicated thing. On the one hand, it means that to Yeats the "truth" of *A Vision* is really on a par with Frost's "as ifs"; it is a "momentary stay against confusion," [12] a useful hypothesis that enables one to get by, "to hold in a single thought reality and justice," even though reality and justice may not strictly speaking belong in the same thought. On the other hand, it means that Yeats has done vastly more with his "as ifs" than has Frost, that he has compelled them to take their places in an elaborate closed system. Frost wrote, "The play's the thing. Play's the thing. All virtue in 'as if!'" [13] And yet, of all contemporary poets, it is not Frost but Yeats who has most completely and seriously acted on that premise, who has compelled his "momentary stay against confusion" to take on the status and the elaboration of a "clarification of life." [14] Frost tells us, of his own experience of writing poems,

> the impressions most useful to my purpose have always been those I was unaware of and so made no note of at the time when taken, and the conclusion is come to that like giants we are always hurling experience ahead of us to pave the future with against the day when we may want to strike a line of purpose across it for somewhere.[15]

Precisely. But Yeats took extraordinary pains to see to it that the future would be paved in the direction he wished to take. Frost has by and large trusted his luck. Poets and scholars, he writes,

[11] Quoted by Louis MacNeice, *The Poetry of W. B. Yeats* (Toronto: Oxford University Press, 1941), p. 129.

[12] *Complete Poems of Robert Frost 1949* (New York: Holt, Rinehart and Winston, Inc., 1949), p. vi.

[13] Frost, introduction to Edwin Arlington Robinson, *King Jasper*, p. xv.

[14] Frost, *Complete Poems*, p. vi.

[15] *Ibid.*, p. vii.

differ most importantly in the way their knowledge is come by. Scholars get theirs with conscientious thoroughness along projected lines of logic; poets theirs cavalierly and as it happens in and out of books. They stick to nothing deliberately, but let what will stick to them like burrs where they walk in the fields.[16]

Poetry, that is, is a chancy thing, a matter of the right man and the right burr crossing orbits at the right moment. And, of course, it is. But even the most casual collector of burrs may find it valuable to systematize his collection.

Yeats achieved such a systematization in the crazy symbolic machinery of *A Vision*. In 1928, three years after the first edition of *A Vision*, Yeats published *The Tower*—first *A Vision*, then such poems as "Sailing to Byzantium," "The Tower," "Nineteen Hundred and Nineteen," "Two Songs from a Play," "Leda and the Swan," and "Among School Children." In 1928 Yeats was sixty-three. But in 1939, at sixty-four Frost published the essay "The Figure a Poem Makes" as preface to his second *Collected Poems*. In that essay, Frost maintained that the poet is essentially an accidental collector of impressions and of knowledge; that the making of a poem is largely a matter of trusting to luck; that a poem's logic is "backward, in retrospect, after the act";[17] and that the reality a poet touches is chaos, "the vast chaos of all I have lived through." [18] From his contacts with that reality the poet may produce, if he is lucky, "a clarification of life—not necessarily a great clarification, such as sects and cults are founded on, but . . . a momentary stay against confusion." [19] And the implication is, I think, that whatever order a poem may express is a fortuitous thing—verbal rather than substantial, something to be enjoyed and admired for its originality, to derive comfort from, but not really to be trusted, not really real. The work is play, but not really for mortal stakes. Yeats committed himself to his laborious play, developed a coherent if absurd theory of reality, and wrote great poems. Frost has not made that mortal commitment; we can never really accept or reject his vision of reality, because it is never quite clear, never quite coherent, never quite there. Once more, the meaning of Jonah's death, of Job's revelation, slips away from us.

Yet these cryptic events are the central events of the poems in which they occur; they exemplify that "clarification of life" that Frost tells us poetry should provide. And we are compelled to conclude that in Frost's terms life cannot really be clarified, cannot be subjected to the order-

---

[16] *Ibid.*, pp. vii-viii.
[17] *Ibid.*, p. vii.
[18] *Ibid.*, p. vii.
[19] *Ibid.*, p. vi.

engendering discipline Yeats achieved; we are compelled to conclude that our momentary stays against confusion are not really stays, that death is merely baffling, and that all ends in jocular snapshot-taking. There is a sense in which, compared with Yeats, Frost is not really serious about his poetry and the convictions it embodies, and that unseriousness is not simply a matter of habitual irony and whimsical jocularity; rather it is a matter of refusing to recognize certain kinds of difficulty[20]—the difficulty of sticking to things deliberately rather than collecting them like burrs, the difficulty of making "stylistic arrangements of experience" out of one's perceptions of order, the difficulty of holding reality and justice in a single thought. As we have seen, "Directive" deals with psychic entrapment; but we have also seen that the entrapment in "Directive," compared with that in "Lycidas," is not really difficult to avoid. Common sense confronts sentimentality and wins, and though we applaud the outcome, we recognize that Milton's sense of the difficult and of man's capacity for dealing with the difficult is more compelling than Frost's. Both Milton and Yeats were tempted to conceive of life and reality as chaos, and the fact that neither surrendered to chaos is not unrelated to the seriousness with which, confronting emotional and intellectual difficulty, they clarified life and demonstrated man's capacity for arranging his experience.

Frost, of course, does not really conceive of life as chaos either; in however rudimentary a sense, any poem is an assertion of order and meaning. Yet the later Frost is more aware of human limitations than of human potentiality; he is more aware of how little man can do than of how much he can do in his confrontation of difficulty. And the result is a degree of narrowness, of incompleteness, even of falsification, in that vision of man and the world that Frost offers us in his more recent books. Keeper's failure, once more, that failure of

> the courage in the heart
> To overcome the fear within the soul
> And go ahead to any accomplishment,

is also Frost's; and that failure helps to explain, perhaps Frost's irritated awareness of Yeats in the masques, and almost certainly the degree to which Frost's later work exploits, in Louise Bogan's phrase, "a series of refusals rather than . . . a set of affirmations." [21] It has interfered with the clarity of his convictions; we are not sure what precisely is the nature of the wholeness achieved in "Directive," of the insight Jonah

[20] cf. below, p. 221.
[21] Bogan, *Achievement in American Poetry*, p. 50.

manages in *A Masque of Mercy*. It has compromised those convictions' seriousness; Frost's Mrs. Someone, of "An Importer," his Harrison, of "A Case for Jefferson," or the theorizers of "Etherealizing" are straw men compared with Yeats's Black and Tans in "Nineteen Hundred and Nineteen," or the sisters in "In Memory of Eva Gore-Booth and Con Markievicz." It has limited Frost's originality, the originality he prized in "The Figure a Poem Makes"; even at a purely literal level, it is more original to make good poetry out of absurd doctrine than out of isolated insights, to achieve a stylistic arrangement of experience than to let what will stick to one like burrs to trousers.

As Frost suffers by comparison with Yeats, so does he suffer by comparison with Eliot, and for broadly similar reasons. Like Yeats's cycles of sun and moon, Eliot's Anglo-Catholicism provides him with a hierarchy of values, a theory of reality, and a set of meaningful symbols—in brief, with a myth—that enables him to make large-scale, coherent, consistent propositions about man and the world he lives in. We need not agree with those propositions; we may be convinced that Celia Coplestone is dreadfully wrong in taking the road to martyrdom, or that Edward and Lavinia Chamberlayne are simply victims of hocus-pocus. But we are convinced that beneath or behind Eliot's writing there is a deliberate, sustained, and difficult effort, intellectual or emotional or whatever, to comprehend "the vast chaos of all [we] have lived through," [22] rendering that chaos deeply relevant to man's condition. "Theme alone," writes Frost, "can steady us down." [23] But Frost rarely convinces us that for him the need for theme operates in a context larger than that of the single poem, that there is any real necessity for themes of wider extension that those provided by luck, by bent, by the bardic instinct. Again, we may detect a sense in which Frost is not really serious about his convictions, a sense in which he is finally unwilling really to follow his thought to a sustaining conclusion. He leaves himself outs—the drumlin woodchuck's "strategic retreat"—and the result is that the tragic potential of *North of Boston* is never realized or even repeated in the later books. Eliot accepts the purposive universe of traditional Christianity, and in that acceptance finds his themes—salvation and damnation, purgatorial and infernal suffering, making perfect the will, accepting the past and thereby altering its meaning. His conclusions are sometimes not unlike Frost's. Like the woman in "The Discovery of the Madeiras," Prufrock cannot really bring himself to act, to commit himself to his own insight, and both are lost. Like the speaker of "Directive," the speaker of "Burnt Norton" knows that the

[22] Frost, *Complete Poems,* p. vii.
[23] *Ibid.*, p. vi.

past, though real, is past, that one may not merely surrender to the past save at the cost of aimless self-indulgence. Like Jonah or the speaker of "The Road Not Taken," Julia Shuttlethwaite knows that

> Everyone makes a choice, of one kind or another,
> And then must take the consequences.[24]

Harcourt-Reilly's lesson to Edward Chamberlayne—

> Let me free your mind from one impediment:
> You must try to detach yourself from what you
>   still feel
> As your responsibility—[25]

is the lesson mastered by the speaker of "The Thatch," that surrender to sentimental feelings of guilt and pity is self-destruction. While Keeper learns of his own failure of the courage to "go ahead to any accomplishment," Peter Quilpe is told by Lavinia that

> You've only just begun.
> I mean, this only brings you to the point
> At which you *must* begin.[26]

And as we have seen, Eliot's Harcourt-Reilly and Frost's Paul are curiously like each other.

But such incidental similarity does not really mean much. At least, its meaning is sharply limited by the absence in Frost of anything comparable to Eliot's sustained theme of sin and redemption, and to the use Eliot makes of that theme, that conviction, as a statement of the human condition and a measure of human worth. I have said that Frost gives us neither heroes nor villains. More important, at least in comparing him with Eliot, he gives us neither good people nor evil people, neither saints nor sinners. His people are attractive or admirable, pitiable or unpleasant or even contemptible, and to Frost such qualities are evidently sufficient. But Celia Coplestone, like the speaker of "Ash Wednesday," has both a sense of sin and a capacity for sainthood; possessing these characteristics, she is a much more complex image of man than are Frost's people, perhaps excepting Jonah. Whatever her merits as an

[24] Thomas Stearns Eliot, *The Cocktail Party* (New York: Harcourt, Brace and Co., 1950), p. 187.
[25] *Ibid.*, p. 185.
[26] *Ibid.*, p. 178.

effectively drawn dramatic character, she is in the tradition of Spenser's nameless protagonist, of Milton's Samson, and of Browning's Caponsacchi —ethically and teleologically meaningful figures, who choose, not the necessary or the expedient or the admirable, but the best. Again, as with Yeats, one need not accept Eliot's values or his doctrine in order to recognize that they enable him to deal with man in a larger, traditionally richer, more broadly meaningful context than Frost permits himself. There is no "best" in Frost, only the more or less rewarding. The word appears, to be sure; in Paul's last speech, it appears very emphatically:

> Our sacrifice, the best we have to offer,
> And not our worst nor second best, our best,
> Our very best, our lives laid down like Jonah's,
> Our lives laid down in war and peace. . . .

But its meaning floats away from one, refusing to attach itself to anything more graspable than a willingness to die in pursuit of—something, a shining gate we almost think we see, but that may not really be there. Eliot's world, his sense of the valuable and the real, may offend one. It may strike one as hieratic, or prim, or unhealthy, or simply repellent; but at least, like Yeats's, it is *there,* a determining and informing feature of his thought, contributing to his major poems a degree of solidity and commitment that Frost never really achieves.

There is little to be gained, I think, from pursuing such comparisons further, and it is quite true that the comparisons have been, in a way, both irrelevant to poetry and unfair to Frost. On the one hand, poetry is not necessarily required to provide us with a fully developed sense of man's potentialities and of the world he inhabits. We do not demand a consistent philosophy of Shakespeare, nor do we ask that

> Western wind, when will thou blow?
> The small rain down can rain!—
> Christ, if my love were in my arms
> And I in my bed again!

convince us of its moral and intellectual adequacy as a guide to life. The same thing is true of Frost's "Home Burial" or "The Fear," of "Moon Compasses" or "Devotion" or "The Pasture." Yet Shakespeare at least assures us that man is capable of tragic stature. And *A Masque of Mercy* is not precisely either a play or a pure lyric; like Pope's "An Essay on Man," though less didactic, it is a suasive poem, as are many of Frost's later poems, especially. Frost's role involves the advocacy of certain convictions about man and the world. There is a vatic element in his poetry, as there is in Eliot's; that element is a proper object of critical concern, and, as I have indicated in the preface, my concern is not primarily with aesthetics but with convictions.

On the other hand, the comparisons have been narrowly *ad hoc;* the critical questions they involve, though broad and important, are not the only important critical questions, even within the limits of my approach. One may legitimately wish that Eliot had more of the early Frost's sympathetic respect for humanity. Eliot writes of hollow men, men with no sustaining religious belief, and though he knows they are hollow, he does not always know that they may really be men, capable of dignity and stature and joy; Frost does, as he has demonstrated in "The Self-Seeker," "The Lovely Shall Be Choosers," "The Pauper Witch of Grafton," "West-Running Brook," and "Two Look at Two." As Stephen Spender has written:

> Eliot seems to think, quite rightly, that what makes people living is their beliefs. But to him it seems impossible to accept any belief that is not a religious belief; one either rejects all belief . . . or else one accepts a religious belief in salvation and damnation.[27]

Even in *A Masque of Mercy,* Frost's sense of human worth is less rigorously exclusive than Eliot's. And if Frost's attitude toward New England is anachronistic and hence of limited value, Yeats's attitude toward the Ireland of "Hard-riding country gentlemen"[28] does not escape the same limitation.

And yet I think such comparisons are legitimate, as long as one recognizes that they do not tell all about anything. One of the tests any significant poet must submit to is that of comparison with his contemporaries. And that comparison may legitimately be concerned with more than craftsmanship and verse technique. Yeats, Eliot, Auden, Stevens—men whose bare talent for writing verse, if there is such a thing, may well be no greater than Frost's—have done more than Frost has done; and that "more" has been persistently involved with those difficult questions of the ultimately real and valuable that Frost has persistently ducked. Twenty-five years ago, Frederic I. Carpenter wrote:

[27] Stephen Spender, *The Destructive Element: A Study of Modern Writers and Beliefs* (London: Jonathan Cape, Ltd., 1935), pp. 146-47.
[28] Yeats, *Collected Poems,* p. 343.

. . . the fault of Mr. Frost lies merely in this—that he is a poet, only. His criticism of life is merely poetic. He has not the cosmic imagination which creates its own world. . . .[29]

"Cosmic" and "creates" may be the wrong words for Eliot and Auden, but the point is a sound one. Frost's world is fragmentary and meaningless—fragmentary *because* meaningless, except as an alien entanglement that our wills must confront. It is, once more, "the vast chaos of all I have lived through," [30] within which a poem may exist but only as "a momentary stay against confusion." [31] One thinks of Oscar Wilde's impressions, of the Imagists' reverential fragments, and if the conjunction of Frost and Wilde is startling, that is partly because Frost has been less consistent than Wilde in abiding by his professed principles; the shining gate may be there, after all; the sphere of art and the sphere of morality, or of metaphysics, may not be absolutely distinct and separate. But Frost will not commit himself. And without such commitment, Frost offers us no tragic acceptance—only the drumlin woodchuck's canny adjustment.

It would be absurd to blame Frost for not being something that he is not, a man with a wholly coherent message. (The two masques look as though they have such a message, but, as we have seen, the message is more equivocal than it looks.) Yet Frost's apparent inability to find or invent a myth that would permit the development of sustained and sustaining themes, themes with a tragic potential, has had, I think, two unfortunate consequences for his art. On the one hand, there is the thinning out of his later writings, after *North of Boston*—the scattering of effects, the accelerating tendency to editorialize, to play the Yankee character, to destroy straw men, to be querulous or cranky or arch—the gestures of one who is not sure where he stands and who finds it increasingly difficult to make adequate compensation for the fundamental uncertainty. On the other hand, and complementary to that uncertainty, there is the tendency to value Frost as the author of certain good poems rather than as one who offers a body of work, an embodied vision of man. That latter point is surely a requisite, though it is not the only requisite, for a poet to whom one can confidently attribute the highest status as a recorder of enduring human values. Frost never gives one the clear sense of having mastered, even wrongly, any large-scale aggregation of human phenomena; his clarifications of life are seldom more

[29] Frederic I. Carpenter, "The Collected Poems of Robert Frost," *New England Quarterly*, V (January 1932), 159-60.

[30] Frost, *Complete Poems*, p. vii.

[31] *Ibid.*, p. vi.

than momentary stays against confusion. They rarely have the authority of Yeats's

> Whatever flames upon the night
> Man's own resinous heart has fed,[32]

of Eliot's

> The hint half guessed, the gift half understood, is
>   Incarnation.
> Here the impossible union
> Of spheres of existence is actual,[33]

of Auden's

> We must love one another or die,[34]

of Stevens'

> The prologues are over. It is question, now,
> Of final belief. So, say that final belief
> Must be in a fiction. It is time to choose.[35]

Set Frost's

> You ask if I see yonder shining gate
> And I reply I almost think I do

against such statements as these, and the uncertainty of Frost's affirmations, his fundamental indecisiveness, is clear.

What, then, is Frost's importance?—for his importance is real. I think there are two answers. In the first place, Frost is important

[32] Yeats, *Collected Poems*, p. 211.

[33] Thomas Stearns Eliot, *Four Quartets* (New York: Harcourt, Brace and Co., 1934), p. 27.

[34] Wystan Hugh Auden, "September 1, 1939," in *New Poems 1940: An Anthology of British and American Verse*, ed. Oscar Williams (New York: Yardstick Press, 1941), p. 28. The stanza containing this line does not appear in the version of the poem printed in Auden's *Collected Poetry*.

[35] *The Collected Poems of Wallace Stevens* (New York: Alfred A. Knopf, Inc., 1954), p. 250.

because he has demonstrated, by his performance in *North of Boston* and in a substantial scattering of poems since then, how much a poet can accomplish by a sympathetic identification with officially unimportant people, by absorption in a locale, by the ability to hear and retain and reconstruct the sound of speech, and by fidelity to a limited concept of experience. (Ezra Pound wrote of *North of Boston*: "Mr. Frost's people are distinctly real. Their speech is real; he has known them. I don't want much to meet them, but I know that they exist, and what is more, that they exist as he has portrayed them.")[36] Such characteristics alone cannot produce major poetry, although they may define a point from which major poetry starts. In this respect, Frost stands—and I think will continue to stand—as proof that poetry of less than absolute first rank need not mean incompetent poetry, or derivative poetry, or trivial poetry, or merely slick poetry. That demonstration, if obvious, cannot be made too often, and Frost has made it very well indeed.

And in the second place, Frost is important as a kind of American culture hero, as an index of certain persistent American characteristics. Discussing V. L. Parrington, Lionel Trilling has aptly characterized this aspect of Frost. Parrington's "best virtue was real and important. . . . He knew what so many literary historians do not know, that emotions and ideas are the sparks that fly when the mind meets difficulties." [37] Like Parrington, and like the perhaps mythical representative American, Frost "admires will in the degree that he suspects mind." [38] Like Parrington, Frost "still stands at the center of American thought about American culture because . . . he expresses the chronic American belief that there exists an opposition between reality and mind and that one must enlist oneself in the party of reality." [39] It does not of course follow that Frost is really a kind of New England Babbitt; and even if he were, it is worth remembering that Babbitt is ultimately an object, not of hatred nor even of contempt, but of love, and that Christopher Newman is in many respects Babbitt's brother. Frost is more articulate than any Babbitt, more self-aware, more sensitive to those whose organizations and circumstances are different from his own. Above all, he is more intelligent, more aware, in Denis Brogan's words, that "man does not live by bread alone, even pre-sliced bread, and [that] the material optimism bred by American experience has not been accompanied by an equally incontestable spiritual self-confidence." [40] Like Brogan, Frost knows that "life in

[36] Ezra Pound, "Modern Georgics," p. 129.
[37] Trilling, *The Liberal Imagination,* p. 4.
[38] *Ibid.,* p. 5.
[39] *Ibid.,* p. 10.
[40] Denis W. Brogan, *The American Character* (New York: Alfred A. Knopf, Inc., 1944), p. 65.

Gopher Prairie, in Zenith, in New York, even in Paris, [is] hard to live." [41]
And yet, like Trilling's Parrington, Frost has "after all but a limited sense of what constitutes a difficulty." [42] Distrusting intelligence, emphasizing will, he offers us a world in which those difficulties that cannot be resolved by an exercise of the will simply cannot be resolved, and had better be left alone. And in this respect, Frost's limitation is a limitation of the American literary tradition; in this respect, criticism of Frost is criticism of that tradition. Richard Chase writes:

> . . . one of the peculiarities of American literature is that on the whole it has been aware of only one philosophical question—namely, necessity vs. free will. This is a considerable limitation, to be accounted for by the Calvinist heritage and our American social disposition—which has so sharply set the individual off against society, and by failing to provide those mediating ideas and agencies natural to an aristocratic order, has produced a habit of mind favorable to the philosophical preoccupation of which I speak.[43]

The one difficulty that Frost really recognizes is that of maintaining the will in a world of largely alien necessity. Salvation, happiness, as Jonah learns, is a matter of devoting all one's energies, all one's will, to the pursuit of

> An irresistible impossibility.
> A lofty beauty no one can live up to
> Yet no one turn from trying to live up to.

Jonah's conversion, in 1947, brings one back to the myth of "The Trial by Existence," of 1913. In both poems, what really matters is not the exercise of intelligence; what matters is the joyfully, arduously willed acceptance of a world we never made, a world we can neither alter nor understand. It is Frost's strength that, within the narrow and comfortless limits that world provides, he has not gone merely sour, has not betrayed himself into gestures of despair. It is Frost's weakness that he has never transcended that world, has never found or developed a more variously meaningful discipline within which his own very considerable intelligence can move, enabling him to realize a coherent vision of man. "All I would keep for myself," writes Frost, "is the freedom of my material—the condition of body and mind now and then to summons aptly from the

[41] *Ibid.*, p. 73.
[42] Trilling, *The Liberal Imagination*, p. 4.
[43] Richard Chase, *Walt Whitman Reconsidered* (New York: William Morrow & Co., Inc., 1955), pp. 103-4.

vast chaos of all I have lived through." [44] And that is not enough—aptness alone is not enough—for consistently major art. It is his too frequent satisfaction with the merely apt—ultimately it may be only his too frequent satisfaction with the merely apt—that has kept Frost from an unequivocal greatness.

And yet aptness is important. When all else has been said, one of the final tests of a poet's excellence is his sense of what is relevant to his purpose, of what does or does not apply to a given situation in a given poem. In this respect, as in others, Frost's work is uneven. And yet in his best poems, his touch is sure. In "The Death of the Hired Man," "Home Burial," "A Servant to Servants," or "The Fear," there is nothing that does not belong, nothing that needs to be added. In such poems, the last lines are reliable touchstones. "Home Burial" concludes with one final exchange between husband and wife; the wife speaks first:

> '*You*—oh, you think the talk is all. I must go—
> Somewhere out of this house. How can I make you—'
>
> 'If—you—do!' She was opening the door wider.
> 'Where do you mean to go? First tell me that.
> I'll follow and bring you back by force. I *will!*—'

In a sense, the whole poem is there, epitomized in the door that is neither open nor shut. The wife cannot really leave; the husband cannot make her really stay. The talk *is* all, in the sense that neither husband nor wife is capable of conclusive action, of liberating either himself or the other. Not quite capable of tragic self-realization, they have only will, with no object for it to work on but one another: " 'How can I make you—' "; " 'I'll follow and bring you back by force' "; and the unshut, unopen door. This, at least, is the aptness of great poetry.

[44] Frost, *Complete Poems*, p. vii.

Frost as Modern Poet

by John F. Lynen

The present chapter is frankly speculative. My intent is to offer a few remarks on the development of Frost's art and its relation to poetry in the twentieth century. The effort to define a poet's thought is apt to be a perilous enterprise, but in the case of Frost the attempt needs to be made, for many of the misunderstandings about his poems result from the difficulty of locating his place in contemporary literature. One objective of this chapter will therefore be to point out his modernity; and this subsumes the other, which is to define some of the problems with which his poetry deals.

Such an exploration may best begin with the similarity we have noted between the nature poems and the pastorals. The duality of vision they manifest is a dominant characteristic of Frost's thought, and its origin can be most clearly discerned in his concept of nature. For Frost, nature is really an image of the whole world of circumstances within which man finds himself. It represents what one might call "the human situation." "Bereft" and "Once by the Pacific" illustrate the point well, but it is clearest in "The Star-Splitter," where the hero is led by his discouragement at the difficulties of his work to buy a telescope so that he may contemplate the stars which had seemed to ridicule his "hugger-mugger farming." The relationship between man and nature represents the whole problem raised by the opposition of mind and matter, of man's actual experience with its feelings, purposes, and intuitions of value and a scientific scheme of reality in which everything is reducible to matter and process. Frost's persistent concern with the remoteness of nature manifests his desire to accept the scientific scheme. Such acceptance would seem to be dictated by common sense—as Falstaff says, "Is not the truth the

"Frost as Modern Poet." From *The Pastoral Art of Robert Frost* by John F. Lynen. Copyright 1960 by Yale University Press. Reprinted by permission of Yale University Press.

truth?" But poetry is concerned with the very elements of experience which the scientific scheme excludes, and the poet who wishes to be loyal to scientific truth is faced with a difficult problem. If the "real" world is the world as science describes it, are feelings, purposes, and values "unreal"? Or is the actual lived experience in which they are infused a mere illusion? The unique form of Frost's nature poetry represents his way of resolving the problem, and it is, I suggest, an essentially modern solution.

A passage from Whitehead's *Science and the Modern World* will prove relevant. In surveying the history of science, Whitehead contends that beginning with the scientists of the Renaissance there developed a scheme of reality which has dominated Western thought to the present century:

> There persists . . . throughout the whole period the fixed scientific cosmology which presupposes the ultimate fact of an irreducible brute matter, or material, spread throughout space in a flux of configurations. In itself such a material is senseless, valueless, purposeless. It just does what it does do, following a fixed routine imposed by external relations which do not spring from the nature of its being.[1]

This sums up rather well the tacit assumptions underlying such a poem as "The Most of It," and Whitehead's historical perspective makes it clear that the problem at the center of Frost's nature poems is hardly new. He explains that while from the beginning there were continual attempts to modify this scheme of reality, such efforts could not succeed, because even those most opposed to it shared the tacit assumptions upon which the system rested. They were, so to speak, imprisoned by the concepts of science. So long as one assumes the irreducible brute matter Whitehead describes in the passage I have quoted, so long as one assumes the kind of space and the kind of time it postulates, one cannot break out of the Newtonian universe. Whitehead's purpose, of course, is to show how the new physics which began with Einstein alters basic concepts so as to make possible a more satisfactory world view. But such revision could hardly have affected Frost's basic conception of nature, which had already taken its characteristic form by 1914, five years before the general relativity theory was confirmed by experiment and a good many more before people other than specialists could begin to grasp what the discoveries meant.

The problem which science posed for Frost and the other poets who came to maturity in the period 1910-20 was the same as that which

[1] Alfred Whitehead, *Science and the Modern World* (New York: New American Library of World Literature, 1958), p. 18.

had confronted the Romantics and Victorians. How was the poet to portray human experience with its sensations, its emotions, its knowledge of good and evil, indeed, its very awareness of consciousness itself and yet at the same time recognize the validity of the scientific scheme, where everything is reduced to "the hurrying of material, endlessly, meaninglessly?" [2] For Frost's generation the question was harder and more urgent because by the turn of the century many of the more likely answers had been tried and proved inadequate. But the question had been there for a very long time—even in Pope, who appears to embrace science with a good deal of enthusiasm, there is a conflict between natural law and the hierarchy of values. The God of "An Essay on Man" may be wise in refusing to alter the fixed laws of nature for any human considerations, but Pope's witty effects develop largely from the sense that physics contradicts other aspects of the divine plan. "And now a bubble burst, and now a world" has more than a little shock value.

After this, the antiscientific bias of the Romantics is hardly surprising. The philosophic background of Romantic nature is far too complex a matter to be considered here, but the general intent of the Romantics is clear. They sought to solve the problem by asserting the unity of man and nature. Whether this involved seeing man as a part of nature, intuiting the common spirit infused in both, or seeing both as parts of a larger reality, the result was a humanizing of nature and a stressing of the emotional values in the landscape. In the course of the nineteenth century, this solution came to seem less and less adequate. Not that the Victorian poets merely copied the Romantics in their treatment of nature. Their nature poetry has its own distinctive qualities, but it is, I think, founded upon Romantic premises. It is possible that a poetic mode had simply worn out, but more likely, the gradual loss of faith in Romantic nature was caused by the increasing authority of science and its intrusion into new areas. In Wordsworth and Coleridge the portrayal of nature is combined with a good deal of philosophic speculation, which interprets and justifies it, but in the Victorians this intellectual framework is absent. Tennyson's argument in *In Memoriam* is not related to the *technique* of nature description he uses, whereas Wordsworth's argument in *The Prelude* is concerned with the very things which the descriptive technique demonstrates. Arnold often finds himself in the position of openly rejecting the premises from which his methods of describing nature are derived! One cannot help feeling that by mid-century the progress of science had swept away the intellectual foundations of Romantic nature poetry. I do not mean that it had refuted the abstract theories the Romantics favored—Hartleyan psychology, philos-

[2] *Ibid.*, p. 56.

ophical idealism, Neoplatonism, and the rest—but that it had killed their fundamental belief in nature as a divine creation embodying the spiritual and moral law. When Tennyson speaks of "Nature, red in tooth and claw" (*In Memoriam* LVI), we see how much, since the beginning of the century, the concept of nature had been narrowed to fit the scientific scheme. The Romantics would never have had such a thought; they did not confront a nature so emptied of moral and spiritual content. By the end of the nineteenth century the Romantic vision of nature had ceased to seem valid as a way of reconciling scientific fact with the perceptions of the imagination.

• Modern poetry may be said to have begun as a fresh attempt to solve the problem posed by science. Imagism, for example, represents an attempt to confront the physical facts of reality in the most direct way. The Imagists tended to advocate an abandonment of overtly stated ideas and sentiments, because these stand between the poet and the actual things of his experience. Yet for the Imagists the proper content of poetry was not really things described but the sensations of perceiving them, and so, in an important way, Imagism represents a retreat. It limits poetry to the narrow range of sense impressions and thus concedes that the autonomous material being with which science deals is outside the poet's range. Indeed, it is not hard to see in Imagism the same division between poetry and science which had been proposed by Bacon and Hobbes—that between sense experience, which is subjective, and the realm of actual being, which is comprehended by reason. The Imagist distrust of ideas in poetry is indicative. It was to be Symbolism rather than Imagism which would provide the more satisfactory answer, and the Symbolist verse of Pound, Eliot, and Yeats represents the dominant mode of modern poetry, one which seems even more characteristic of the age in that its basic techniques are reflected in the major contemporary novelists. The apparent difference between Frost's verse and Symbolist poetry makes his work seem out of place in contemporary literature. Yet if "modern" is a meaningful term, it is neither fair nor accurate to deny his modernity. He is not only a poet of the twentieth century, but one who, in his own way, deals with the very problem which is the concern of the Symbolists.

The connection between his art and the more characteristic modern poetry can best be seen by noting their structural resemblance. Both Frost and the Symbolists tend to view reality through the perspective of contrasting levels of being. In Frost's nature poems this technique quite obviously results from his desire to recognize the validity of science. Thus, despite his indebtedness to Romanticism, he must be seen as essentially anti-Romantic. By insisting on the gulf separating man and nature, he directly opposes the Romantic attempt to bring the two together. While the Romantics sought a place for sensations, feelings, and values within physical nature, he conceives of the physical world as a distinct level of being. And just because of this, he is able to avoid the assumption that the physical world comprises the whole of reality. He can accept nature as the limited, purely physical world which science depicts and yet place it within a larger context which includes the realities of purpose, feeling, and value. His method is to unify scientific nature and the realm of human experience, not by blending them, but by viewing reality as a vista of distinct but parallel planes.

In Symbolism one finds much the same kind of perspective, though it is developed in a different way. While there is great diversity between symbolist poets, they do, I think, share certain common tendencies. Their use of a deep historical vista and their characteristic interest in archaeology, anthropology, and philology indicate their intent to find for intuitions of value a firm basis in scientific fact. The imaginative logic of Symbolism would seem to go as follows: Symbols are an historical reality, that is, we know them as actual works of art, and every society, past or present, has produced symbolic representations of some sort. Further, a symbol has meaning, it was made to express this meaning, and though meaning is concerned with mental and spiritual things outside of the scientific scheme, one can believe that it too is real, for the symbol which expresses it is real. It follows that the things the meaning reveals are also real in that they have had the power to create the symbol. The symbol transcends time. While it was made in a particular time, its meaning continues to reside in it and is available to men living many centuries thereafter. Furthermore, symbols indicate a universal pattern in experience, for anthropology tends to show that in the art of many diverse societies there are certain common symbolic patterns. The symbol, then, provides a basis for accepting the realities which science does not account for, not only through the meaning it expresses, but by the very fact that it does express meaning—its very existence tends to prove the truth of the things it represents. Admittedly, the logic of this reasoning is not impeccable, but it has sufficed to give the subjective aspects of symbolist poetry some of the authority of scientific fact.

It is quite natural that Symbolist poetry should involve both a very strong historical orientation and a critique of the concept of time. Poetry of this kind requires that the symbol be seen in its various manifestations, and this means a constant reference backward from the present to other periods more or less remote. Thus Symbolism creates a very acute awareness of the distance between the past and the present, and of the passing of time. But, paradoxically, it also leads to a denial of time and an historical sense which, in Eliot's words, "involves a perception, not only of the pastness of the past, but of its presence." [3] For the work of art, as we have seen, transcends time, and the emergence of the same symbolic forms in the art of epochs remote from one another represents the similarity of these epochs and the unchanging aspects of experience. Whitehead has pointed out that a linear conception of time is essential to pre-relativity science.[4] The historical consciousness of the Symbolist poets, like Frost's insistence on the remoteness of nature, indicates an acceptance of the prevailing scientific scheme, but such an acceptance is only possible when the lineal scheme is combined with its opposite, the concept of eternity. Yeats' cyclical theory of history and Eliot's analysis of time in "Burnt Norton" illustrate this well.

In *The Waste Land,* one can see how directly the dual conception of time leads to that technique of contrasting disparate contexts so characteristic of Symbolist poetry. Cleanth Brooks, in his well-known analysis of this poem, summarizes Eliot's method of poetic organization as follows:

The basic method used in "The Waste Land" may be described as the application of the principle of complexity. The poet works in terms of surface parallelisms which in reality make ironical contrasts, and in terms of surface contrasts which in reality constitute parallelisms. (The second group sets up effects which may be described as the obverse of irony.) The two aspects taken together give the effect of chaotic experience ordered into a new whole, though the realistic surface of experience is faithfully retained. . . .

The fortune-telling of "The Burial of the Dead" will illustrate the general method very satisfactorily. On the surface of the poem the poet reproduces the patter of the charlatan, Madam Sosostris, and there is the surface irony: the contrast between the original use of the Tarot cards and the use made by Madame Sosostris. But each of the details (justified realistically in the palaver of the fortune-teller) assumes a new meaning in the general context of the poem. There is then, in addition to the surface irony, something of a Sophoclean irony too, and the "fortune-telling," which is taken ironically by a twentieth-century audience, becomes *true* as the poem develops—true in a sense in which Madame Sosostris herself does not think it true. . . . The items of her speech have only one reference in terms of the context of her speech: the "man with three staves," the "one-eyed merchant," the "crowds of people walking around in a ring,"

---

[3] "Tradition and the Individual Talent," *Selected Essays, 1917-32* (New York: Harcourt, Brace & Co., 1932), p. 4.

[4] Whitehead. *Science and the Modern World,* pp. 118-30.

etc. But transferred to other contexts they become loaded with special meanings.[5]

Though Brooks is primarily concerned with the irony emanating from Eliot's symbols, his statement provides a valuable definition of the structure beneath this irony. Eliot's technique, as he points out, is that of movement from one context to another. In this way the poet reveals the full meaning of his symbols and brings out the underlying resemblances between the diverse persons, episodes, and objects, with the result that these disparate materials are united within a single vision. For instance, the symbols of the Tarot cards reappear on several different levels: in the literary context of Shakespeare's *The Tempest,* in the historical context of the fertility rites reported by Frazer, in the myth of the Fisher King, and in the scenes of the modern metropolis. It is obvious, then, that Eliot's method depends upon his exploring a series of discrete contexts.

In this we see a fundamental similarity to Frost's pastoral perspective. Both poets assume a world composed of isolated levels of being, and thus both tend to see experience and portray it as a totality of sharply differing contexts. Where Frost juxtaposes rural and urban life, the regional and the cosmopolitan, the human and the natural, Eliot contrasts the social classes and holds up disparate historical periods for comparison. In both, too, the contrasting planes are not only different but parallel. They are held together and made to interpret each other by a dominant sense of analogy. Thus in *The Waste Land* one finds ranges of correspondence similar to those evoked by Frost's symbols. The wealthy neurotic at her dressing table is reflected both in Philomela and the woman being discussed by her vulgar friend in a pub; Elizabeth, Cleopatra, a stenographer of easy virtue, and the Rhine maidens are ranged in a single perspective; biblical scenes parallel pagan myths; arias from Wagner blend with echoes from the *Divine Comedy.* Eliot is not simply balancing off disparate items. Each introduces its entire context, and, at the same time, each reflects within its context some element of the myth, which, as a key analogy, joins all the contexts together. Similarly, in Frost's poetry the regional world is kept quite separate from the everyday life of urban society, and nature from the level of human experience; yet the separate contexts, though never allowed to merge, are held together by the contrast between them, which creates a constant reference from one to the other and an awareness of ironic parallels.

[5] *Modern Poetry and The Tradition* (Chapel Hill, N.C.: University of North Carolina Press, 1939), p. 167.

In comparing the poetry of Frost and Eliot, I do not for a moment mean to suggest that their work is really quite similar. Obviously any such claim would be absurd. The comparison is of value, however, in that it shows a structural element which is fundamental to both and which in both seems to have developed as a means of coping with the problem posed by science. By noting this similarity we can see more clearly Frost's place in modern literature. It demonstrates that he is an intellectual as well as a chronological contemporary of the Symbolist poets and that his pastoral mode, while leading to a kind of poetry quite different from that of Symbolism, belongs in the same chapter of literary history.

So far I have discussed mainly the pastoral structure as it appears in the nature poems, since here the origins of this structure seem most apparent. But the link between the nature poems and the true pastorals is a strong one, and the typically modern concerns and methods which we have noted in Frost's treatment of nature tell us much about the origins of the pastorals themselves. The important connection between these two kinds of poetry becomes apparent when one observes their parallel development.

It is a significant fact that Frost wrote nature poems which display the kind of pastoral design we have been considering many years before he produced pastorals. "To a Moth Seen in Winter," which the poet dates "circa 1900," shows that even at that early date his characteristic conception of nature had already formed. In this poem he describes the futility of the moth which has emerged from its chrysalis in wintertime to seek a mate it will never find. As the moth rests momentarily on his hand, he muses:

> You must be made more simply wise than I
> To know the hand I stretch impulsively
> Across the gulf of well nigh everything
> May reach to you, but cannot touch your fate.

Then in the concluding lines, which follow directly, he draws an analogy between the moth's little tragedy and his own human fate:

> I cannot touch your life, much less can save,
> Who am tasked to save my own a little while.

Not only do these lines epitomize the view of nature characteristic of his mature verse, but, what is even more significant, they show that from a very early date the idea of nature's remoteness is bound up with the habit of seeing reality in terms of contrasting planes. It is in passages like these that Frost's mature art first begins to emerge.

The pastoralism of the New England poems represents Frost's most fully realized development of the way of thinking implicit in such early nature sketches. When *North of Boston* is compared with *A Boy's Will*, it becomes apparent that the poet found his true medium when he discovered New England. The earlier volume gives glimpses of what is to come, but it is not until his second book that he begins to portray regional life in earnest, and it is just at this point that he first shows complete mastery of the pastoral form. The sudden maturing of his pastoralism in *North of Boston* is paralleled by a simultaneous maturing of his treatment of nature. Frost has called *North of Boston* a "book of people," and it is largely devoted to pictures of regional life in which dramatic action and character analysis are the dominant interests. However, it does contain one nature poem, "The Wood-Pile," which is superior to any he had hitherto written. "The Wood-Pile" marks a distinct turning. The nature poems written after it are clearly superior to those which came before. Compare "Ghost House," "My November Guest," or "A Line-Storm Song" with "Hyla Brook," "The Oven Bird," or "The Onset": the latter have a new vigor, a tautness in the line of reasoning, a greater refinement of perception in the imagery. Of course, not all the later nature poems display this new vigor, nor do all the early ones lack merit. The point is that Frost did not write great nature poems until he learned to write great eclogues. One may find an occasional poem like "Misgiving" after *North of Boston*, but one will not find a poem like "The Wood-Pile" before.

In tracing this parallel development I do not mean to imply that Frost's pastoralism grew out of his nature poetry—certainly not that he gave up nature poetry when he had fully developed his pastoral method. He has written nature poems throughout his career, and indeed in his later years more poems of this type have come from his pen than pastorals. His simultaneous growth in these two kinds of poetry, like the similarity of their structural design, indicates that both grew up in response to the same intellectual stimulus. We have seen that his special way of depicting nature is a means of dealing with the problem which science posed for the modern poet. It therefore appears that his pastoralism provides a means of dealing with a similar problem. It is that of preserving within the disorganized world created by science the sense of order and unity a meaningful life requires. In his pastorals, Frost's dominant motive is to reassert the value of individual perception against the fragmenting of experience resulting from modern technology. They thus deal with one of the most fundamental concerns of twentieth-century thought.

It is an issue which has had no small effect on Eliot's and Pound's efforts to develop a concept of culture. One sees it too as a motive in Yeats' thought. It is the central theme of countless modern works of social criticism.

It is true that Frost's solution to this problem involves a withdrawal from the modern city to an agrarian world which belongs to the past. He has, in effect, found a retreat in one of those out-of-the-way places where technology has not yet complicated life by separating man from the land. But this retreat is of a special sort. He does not turn his back on the world of today, nor does he advocate a "return to the soil." There is in his regionalism no call for action or program for social reform, and as a matter of fact he insists over and over again that no program will ever resolve the basic conflicts in human life.[6] His withdrawal must be distinguished from agrarianism. It is the adopting of an artistic perspective. Regional New England—just because it is primitive and remote from modern life—is for him a medium for examining the complex urban world of today, a standard by which to evaluate it, and a context within which to discover the order underlying experience that modern life has obscured and confused.

This point deserves a good deal of emphasis, for there is a tendency, even among the poet's warmest admirers, to view his preoccupation with rural New England as merely an escape from problems too overwhelming to be faced. Those who judge him in this way fail to see the positive value of his retreat for the intellect. Indeed, one may say they have failed really to read him at all.

Granted that Frost's approach is indirect. His evaluation of the everyday urban world is implied rather than stated. Yet is not such indirection in the nature of all poetry? At its best poetry is always oblique, because it is properly concerned with issues so difficult that they will not yield to the frontal assaults of logical argumentation. The fundamental problems with which poets concern themselves are not limited to those they can state in simple, direct terms—one can see this as clearly in Milton, Pope, or Wordsworth as in Eliot. The indirection of poetry is perhaps most obvious in pastoral, since this genre has always been one which deals with major issues in a minor key. If Frost's regional poems are at fault because they are remote from the main problems of their time, then the great pastorals of the Renaissance can be condemned on the same ground. To appreciate Frost's modernity, we must have some knowledge of the special advantages which the pastoral vision offers. We

[6] For those interested in Frost's social views, "Build Soil" and the preface which Frost wrote to Edwin Arlington Robinson's *King Jasper* (Toronto: The Macmillan Company, 1935), pp. v-xv, are among the most important of his writings.

must recognize that in some respects the retreat to a remote rural world can provide the most trenchant analysis and the most subtle evaluation of the world the poet seems to be escaping from.

The nature of Frost's pastoral retreat can best be seen by observing the difference between his poetry and that of the Georgians. The comparison is instructive, for it was with certain members of this group that Frost was closely associated during those crucial months in England when he wrote the greater portion of *North of Boston*. The Georgians too were interested in a poetry of rural life and sought, like him, to bring the language of everyday speech into their verse. Their influence upon his development must have been of the most beneficial kind. Doubtless it was the encouragement of such men as Lascelles Abercrombie and Wilfred Gibson which gave him the confidence needed to discover that the rural life he knew was his real subject and his own way of speaking, with its Yankee qualities of understatement and playful irony, his proper medium. Yet for all this, there is a vital difference between the man from New Hampshire and his English friends. The Georgians, like other poets, were half-consciously groping toward a solution to the problem posed by scientific thought. At its best, their poetry represents an attempt to discover human values in the hard, realistic fact, but they had no very clear notion of the problem they faced and hence no definite program. It is inaccurate to think of them as a coherent group advocating a particular kind of poetry.[7] What they shared was a common sensibility, one which recoiled from the drab sameness of urban life and sought to find in the countryside the color, romance, and rude spontaneity which industrialism had banished from the life of the average Englishman.

There was a basic confusion in the thought of the Georgians, or, to put the matter less kindly, a failure to think. One gets the impression that they reacted mainly against the ugliness of industrialism and failed to see that it was not the mere lack of color that starved the imagination, but the fragmenting of experience caused directly and indirectly by science. They assumed that if the poet could search out those isolated areas as yet unblighted by the factory system he would also find a genuine poetry. They espoused a mild exoticism, turning from the everyday scene to the countryside they had known in boyhood or to the farm village and heath of their weekend rambles. Here, it seemed, they could avoid sentimentality, for in such settings there was an intrinsic charm in the matters of fact they reported. But out-of-the-way places are of little interest unless they are shown within a larger view of reality, and such a larger view the

[7] See Frank Swinnerton, *The Georgian Scene: A Literary Panorama* (New York: Farrar and Rinehart, Inc., 1934), pp. 272-77.

Georgians failed to create. As Samuel Chew rather harshly comments, "The 'Georgians' did not extend the boundaries of poetry, and it is obvious today that theirs was not a revolution but a retreat." [8]

Although it was under Georgian influence that Frost first began to write of regional life, the sentimental rusticity of their verse is quite unlike his vision of New England. The Georgians do no more than paint the rural scene; Frost discovered how to shape it into a mythic world within which he could express symbolically other ranges of experience. The Georgians retreat to the country is *only* an escape; Frost's is a fresh approach to reality.

We can see the positive nature of this approach by noting the forthright way in which he proclaims his desire to withdraw. He has adopted this as a major theme in his poetry, and he never justifies it on the grounds that urban life is uncomfortable or ugly. Rather, he makes it plain that the world he has escaped to is harder and more demanding. As "After Apple-Picking," "Two Tramps in Mud-Time," and a great many other poems show, one of the central elements in the appeal which back-country New England has for him is that there the life of the imagination can be made to coincide with the humble business of earning a living, in the same way that one's "two eyes make one in sight." The often-quoted line from his early poem, "Mowing"—"The fact is the sweetest dream that labor knows"—strikes the tonic note of all his regional verse. Obviously, there is much in the theme of retreat that reflects the poet's own experience in a literal way, but this does not mean that he presents the withdrawal to the agrarian life of the past as a practical course for others to follow. Indeed, he himself abandoned farming not long after he began to succeed in his literary work. We must remember that he is creating a picture of reality, not drawing up a program, and while the retreat is to be taken literally with reference to the fictional speaker's own life, in terms of the poem it is the symbol of an attitude toward experience, just as New England is the symbol of a way of life.

Frost's apparent lack of concern for the modern world as most readers know it is, then, a consequence of the indirection normal in pastoral, and more broadly, in all poetry. He neither describes the conditions of life in the industrialized urban world, nor has he written much about the specific political and economic problems which are the subject matter of the daily papers. But one may question whether any other major twentieth-century poets, in their best poetry, have done these things either. The poetry most directly concerned with contemporary events, most outspoken in advocating reform, most engaged in fighting out

[8] "Poetry in the Twentieth Century," in *A Literary History of England,* ed. Albert C. Baugh (New York: Appleton-Century-Crofts, Inc., 1948), p. 1579.

political battles and plumping for a cause has turned out to be rather second-rate on the whole, as one can see by looking at the poems protesting the horrors of World War I and the radical verse of the Auden circle during the thirties.[9] One finds in Eliot many scenes of drab residential London, Yeats has written of the Irish uprisings, Auden gives us glimpses of both "the peasant river" and "the fashionable quays"; yet in each of these poets the modern settings are merely parts of a larger picture, whose subject is not the world of 1916, 1922, 1939, or "the modern world" taken as a whole, but a wide historical panorama. It is characteristic of all three to place the modern and the historically remote in shocking juxtaposition, thereby persuading us that Babylon and Bloomsbury are much the same. The result is to deprive the modern materials of their exclusively modern character and to show in the debates of the current epoch the elements which have always been present in the human situation. Detachment from controversy and a lack of reforming zeal seem to be common characteristics of modern poets, and they result, not (as some popular reviewers would have us believe) from an inability to deal with modern problems or an indifference to them, but from the feeling that overt argumentation is not the proper function of poetry. It would be hard to demonstrate that Frost is more aloof from contemporary life than the other major poets.

Lionel Trilling, speaking at a dinner in honor of Frost's eighty-fifth birthday, refuted very effectively this idea of Frost's aloofness. While granting that Frost's "manifest America" seemed distant from the anxieties of our urban society, he found at the center of the poet's work a dominant quality of terror:

> I conceive that Robert Frost is doing in his poems what Lawrence says the great writers of the classic American tradition did. That enterprise of theirs was of an ultimate radicalism. It consisted, Lawrence says, of two things: a disintegration and sloughing off of the old consciousness, by which Lawrence means the old European consciousness, and the forming of a new consciousness underneath.
>
> So radical a work, I need scarcely say, is not carried out by reassurance, nor by the affirmation of old virtues and pieties. It is carried out by the representation of the terrible actualities of life in a new way. I think of Robert Frost as a terrifying poet. . . . The universe that he conceives is a terrifying universe. Read the poem called "Design" and see if you sleep

[9] In speaking of Auden, McNeice, Day Lewis, and Spender, I am here referring only to those of their poems written during the thirties whose primary concern is with contemporary issues. These poems of social conscience, as they may be called, are much less numerous and important than is now generally supposed. This point has been well made recently by John Lehmann in "The Wain-Larkin Myth: A Reply to John Wain," *Sewanee Review*, LXVI (1958), 580-81.

the better for it. Read "Neither Out Far Nor In Deep," which often seems
to me the most perfect poem of our time, and see if you are warmed by
anything in it except the energy with which emptiness is perceived.[10]

The same grim reality, Trilling goes on to say, is displayed in Frost's
characters:

> Talk of the disintegration and sloughing off of the old consciousness! The
> people of Robert Frost's poems have done that with a vengeance. . . .
> In the interests of what great other thing these people have made this
> rejection we cannot know for certain. But we can guess that it was in the
> interest of truth, of some truth of the self. . . . They affirm *this* of them-
> selves: that they are what they are, that this is their truth, and that if
> the truth be bare, as truth often is, it is far better than a lie. For me the
> process by which they arrive at that truth is always terrifying.[11]

One of the great virtues of Trilling's speech is that in it he has made clear
the essential way in which Frost's poetry reflects modern life. Frost
does not depict the outward events and conditions, but the central facts of
twentieth century experience, the uncertainty and painful sense of loss,
are there and seem if anything more bleakly apparent in that their social
and economic manifestations have been stripped away. More important,
Trilling shows us that the terror Frost expresses is the terror which comes
and must come with the birth of something new. It is the mark of a
genuinely modern poetry.

Subject matter is a poor measure of a poet's modernity. The question
is not whether Frost depicts the scenery of modern life, but whether
he deals with its major problems. It is a superficial view which would
equate these problems with the issues of political campaigns or the
questions settled by warfare—the burning issues of one decade are apt
to be different from those of the decade before or the decade after.
Obviously the poet, if he is going to be truly representative of his age,
will have to penetrate the level of social action with its constantly
shifting controversy and succession of practical choices to the broad
intellectual problems which remain unresolved. This I think Frost has
done, and done much more bravely, more adventurously, and more
perceptively than his readers are yet aware.

Failure to recognize the modernity of Frost's thought is larely due to
the fact that his verse lacks the traits of style which seem characteristic

---

[10] I am indebted to Mr. Trilling for supplying me a manuscript copy of his
speech, and it is from this that the quotations are taken. The speech has been
subsequently published in *Partisan Review*, XXVI, 445-52.

[11] *Ibid.*

of modern poetry. There is what one may call in a very general way a modern style, and although the more one compares poets—Eliot with Yeats or Auden with Cummings, for example—the more differences one sees, nevertheless they do share certain common qualities. Admittedly Frost's manner is different, but it would be absurd to claim that style (in this narrow sense) is the only standard. It is possible to write in the modern idiom and yet show little newness or originality in one's response to the contemporary world. And even among unquestionably fine modern poets one often finds the style a good deal more contemporary than the thought. Stevens' concept of the imagination is apparently derived from Coleridge, and Williams, though he pictures modern conditions very realistically, deals with themes which will not seem entirely new to anyone who has read Walt Whitman attentively. I do not mean that either is at fault. I would merely suggest that if these poets are to be admired for their freshness of manner, then Frost deserves to be admired for his freshness of thought.

The point can best be made by comparing one of Frost's finest recent poems with a sonnet by Dylan Thomas. Thomas' poem is justly admired:

> When all my five and country senses see,
> The fingers will forget green thumbs and mark
> How, through the halfmoon's vegetable eye,
> Husk of young stars and handfull zodiac,
> Love in the frost is pared and wintered by,
> The whispering ears will watch love drummed away
>
> Down breeze and shell to a discordant beach,
> And, lashed to syllables, the lynx tongue cry
> That her fond wounds are mended bitterly.
> My nostrils see her breath burn like a bush.
>
> My one and noble heart has witnesses
> In all love's countries, that will grope awake;
> And when blind sleep drops on the spying senses,
> The heart is sensual, though five eyes break.[12]

That the poem is characteristically modern in form needs no emphasis. The difficulties it presents are of two sorts, and both result from the style. The first arises from the obscurity of syntax. It takes some study to discern the grammatical function of certain words and phrases, for example the antecedent of "her" in "her fond wounds" (line 9). The second, and, I think, more formidable, is that of grasping the many-sided meanings

[12] *The Collected Poems of Dylan Thomas* (New York: New Directions, 1953), p. 90.

of Thomas' metaphors: "lynx tongue" is easy, but "the halfmoon's vegetable eye,/ Husk of young stars and handfull zodiac" gives one pause. The device of synaesthesia—"The whispering ears will watch" and "My nostrils see"—indicates the kind of compression the poem depends upon, and it is one which leads to a peculiar use of language.

But though the poem has the complexity one expects in modern verse, there is nothing specifically contemporary about what it says. Thomas is here weaving together several familiar and traditional themes. There is, to begin with, the idea that wisdom is the knowledge of death. When the "senses see" what they see is "How . . . Love in the frost is pared and wintered by." The imagery of the octet emphasizes this vision of life diminishing, shrinking back to the primordial seed; hence the tongue will "cry/ That her [love's] fond wounds are mended bitterly"— that is, through death—and the nostrils "see her breath burn like a bush." The last image suggests not only the perfume of a shrub "ablaze with bloom," but the burning bush of Exodus. The vision is of death— the bush is burnt—but the burning imparts a new insight, just as God revealed his will to Moses. This brings us to the second thematic strand, the idea of life growing out of death. Love does not die out completely; it merely becomes dormant, like the tuber in winter (see again lines 3-5). "And when blind sleep drops on the spying senses,/ The heart is sensual, though five eyes break." One gets the impression that life becomes more intense when it withdraws to its core; as the senses die out in sleep or death, the heart itself becomes "sensual." But the poem does not assert a belief in immortality, or if so, only in a very special sense. Its main theme—to which the other two I have mentioned are subordinate—is that of the unity between the individual (in this case the poet himself) and the natural world. Love binds man to the natural world, because it exists in and through the senses—"country senses," the heart's "witnesses/In all love's countries." To love is to see through the senses, to see the world of physical decay. In death one loses consciousness by losing the senses, but death is the consummation of love, for then the heart itself is sensual in that the body is merged with the earth. In essence, the poem asserts a monistic view of reality. It portrays man's being, thought, and emotion as organically united to the life-process of the universe, and the resolution which it offers for suffering and death is seen in his reunion with the sum total of things. The central thought is hardly a new one. What is distinctly modern is the way it is presented, most especially Thomas' technique of using images which fuse distant associations, as in "the halfmoon's vegetable eye."

Let us set beside this the two little poems—really one, for they are to be taken together—which Frost has placed at the beginning of *A Witness Tree*:

BEECH

Where my imaginary line
Bends square in woods, an iron spine
And pile of real rocks have been founded.
And off this corner in the wild,
Where these are driven in and piled,
One tree, by being deeply wounded,
Has been impressed as Witness Tree
And made commit to memory
My proof of being not unbounded.
Thus truth's established and borne out,
Though circumstanced with dark and doubt—
Though by a world of doubt surrounded.

THE MOODIE FORESTER

SYCAMORE

Zaccheus he
Did climb the tree
Our Lord to see.

THE NEW ENGLAND PRIMER

The style of this poem lacks the kind of surface complication we have observed in the sonnet by Thomas. The use of language is clearer and simpler, the manner more relaxed, and the approach to the reader therefore seems much more direct. The last three lines of "Beech" can be taken as a moral or message explaining what the poem means. As I have argued in previous chapters, Frost's method is not nearly so simple as it seems, but the effect *is* one of simplicity, and by comparing this poem with Thomas' one sees that its style is less characteristically modern. With respect to the content, however, the situation is reversed. Whereas Thomas restates traditional themes in a new way, Frost's theme is distinctively of the twentieth century.

The poem deals with the nature of conceptualization. Through the image of the "wounded" tree, Frost portrays both the necessity which leads man to form ideas and the loss which the process inevitably involves. The poem is built on the paradox that man, for the purposes of thought, and indeed for life itself, needs abstract symbols which may serve to divide and order reality, yet that these symbols cause suffering and set severe limits to his thought. The beech "by being deeply wounded" establishes the "imaginary line," thus fencing off the human world of the farm from the unordered wilderness beyond. Yet the tree not only, in a sense, creates the farm, it also imprisons man within it—it is the poet's "proof of being not unbounded." This, of course, illustrates the value and limitations of all the imaginary lines or concepts which man creates through symbols. Only by imposing his clear concepts upon the flux of reality can man arrive at certain knowledge, while in turn the hard precision of these concepts restricts his ability to understand.

The fact that Frost calls the beech "Witness Tree" indicates that the poem points beyond man's merely rational thinking to his conceptions of religious truth. Hence the relevance of the lines entitled "Sycamore," which Frost has taken verbatim from *The New England Primer*.[13] The story of Zaccheus serves as a perfect summation of the poem's theme. As presented in the Bible, it illustrates the weakness of man's understanding. Being a short man, Zaccheus climbed a tree in order to get a better view of Christ as he passed—he made the mistake of assuming that to see God meant to see him visibly.[14] Yet this was not entirely a mistake. By his nature man needs a Witness Tree, whether it be the cross, Zaccheus' tree, or the beech which marks the property line.

As I have suggested before, this poem bears the stamp of the present century in a way which the poem by Thomas does not. It bears it more deeply, for it bears it in the thought rather than merely in the form. Frost's view of conceptualization and the role of symbols in human life reflects important strands of thought in modern philosophy, anthropology, and psychology.[15] One feels that the poem could not have been written before the present century. However that may be, the problem with which it deals is relatively new and is still the concern of modern thought, while Thomas in his poem builds upon ideas which at least antedate the Christian era. In saying this, I do not mean to suggest that Frost's poem is better or that Thomas' is any the worse for the ancient

---

[13] There are slight variations among the numerous editions of the primer. I have not found one in which this verse appears in precisely the form Frost uses, and I do not know whether Frost altered the version he copied. At any rate, such alterations would not be of material importance. In *The New England Primer, Improved: or an Easy and Pleasant Guide to the Art of Reading* (Greenfield, Mass., 1816), the verse appears as follows:

> Zacheus he,
> Did climb the tree,
> His Lord to see.

[14] Luke 19:2-8.

[15] See, for example, Ernst Cassirer, *An Essay on Man* (New York: Doubleday Inc., 1953).

pedigree of its thought. Nor is this one illustration meant to establish that Thomas is seldom concerned with specifically modern themes, or that if he were this would be a fault. Modernity does not assure artistic merit. A poem can be typical of the period in which it was written without being good. But those for whom the question of whether or not a poet is representative of his time really matters should notice how consistently and in how original a way Frost has explored major issues of contemporary thought.

The reader will appreciate that the distinction I have made between style and thought in comparing these two poems is artificial and misleading. It seemed necessary here for the purposes of argument, but, as more than a few have pointed out, the style of a poem and the ideas it expresses are really inseparable. While one must concede that Frost's style does not involve certain obvious, characteristically modern techniques, this does not mean that it is not modern in a fundamental way. Style is the extension into language of a poem's basic structure, and Frost's style, growing as it does from the pastoral design of his verse, displays an indirection and analogical mode of thought which are much more fundamental to modern poetry than any combination of purely verbal devices. The question is not whether his style is modern in precisely the way that Thomas' or Eliot's or Cummings' is, but whether it is modern in its own way—whether it reflects the temper of the age and serves as an idiom for dealing with its most urgent concerns.

While modernity is not in itself a value, there is much to be gained by noting the contemporary nature of Frost's art. The idea of Frost as a poet of the nineteenth century who has somehow got into the twentieth seems absurd when it is brought out into the open, but this phantom image of the poet persists, even in the minds of experienced readers, and it has done much to prevent an intelligent reading of his poems. While the "Beech"—"Sycamore" poem has gone unnoticed, editors of anthologies constantly reprint such poems as "The Runaway," which is not only a much less successful piece, but is not nearly so representative of his thought. Many, in reaction to the popular image of Frost and encouraged by the two essays of Randall Jarrell,[16] have tried to justify their liking for him by picking out for special praise those few poems—mostly lyrics —which seem "modern" in a superficial sense. Thus currently fashionable ideas about Frost are based upon "Acquainted with the Night," "Design," "Canis Major," "I Will Sing You One-O," and others of this sort.

---

[16] Randall Jarrell, "The Other Frost" and "To the Laodiceans," *Poetry and The Age* (New York: Alfred A. Knopf, Inc., 1953), pp. 28-36 and 37-69. These originally appeared in *The Nation*, CLXV (1947), 588-92, and *Kenyon Review*, XIV (1952), 535-61, respectively.

These are certainly very fine poems, but they hardly have the scope of the great regional poems such as 'After Apple-Picking" and "An Old Man's Winter Night," nor are they so representative of his unique achievement. The attempt to remake him as a metaphysical or Symbolist poet is perverse in the same way as Eliot's preference of *Coriolanus* to *Hamlet,* and like the latter, it gives us a valuable insight. It shows how desperately intelligent readers wish to escape from the distorted image of Frost foisted on us by popularizers and sentimental gentlemen who view modern poetry with horror. It is time to exorcize the phantom by recognizing Frost as the major figure in contemporary literature that he is.

Whatever Frost's relation to his own age may be, his achievement, in the end, will be measured by the intrinsic value of the poems rather than their relevance to the contemporary world. The kind of poetry he writes can best be understood by observing the method by which he has sought to make the present moment represent all other times, and the particular place he describes, the human situation as it has always existed. His essential technique is that of pastoral. He has explored wide and manifold ranges of being by viewing reality within the mirror of the natural and unchanging world of rural life. Pastoralism, whether in Frost or in the poets of the Arcadian tradition, will always at first appear to involve an escape from the world as we know it, but actually it is an exploration upstream, past the city with its riverside factories and shipping, on against the current of time and change to the clear waters of the source:

> Back out of all this now too much for us,
> Back in a time made simple by the loss
> Of detail, burned, dissolved, and broken off
> Like graveyard marble sculpture in the weather,
> There is a house that is no more a house
> Upon a farm that is no more a farm
> And in a town that is no more a town.
> The road there, if you'll let a guide direct you
> Who only has at heart your getting lost,
> May seem as if it should have been a quarry— . . .
>
> Your destination and your destiny's,
> A brook that was the water of the house,
> Cold as a spring as yet so near its source,
> Too lofty and original to rage.
> (We know the valley streams that when aroused

Will leave their tatters hung on barb and thorn.)
I have kept hidden in the instep arch
Of an old cedar at the waterside
A broken drinking goblet like the Grail
Under a spell so the wrong ones can't find it,
So can't get saved, as Saint Mark says they mustn't.
(I stole the goblet from the children's playhouse.)
Here are your waters and your watering place.
Drink and be whole again beyond confusion.

("Directive")

Chronology of Important Dates

1874	Born in San Francisco, California, March 26. Son of William Prescott Frost, Jr., and Isabelle Moodie Frost.
1874-1885	Boyhood in San Francisco.
1885	Moves to Lawrence, Massachusetts, with his mother and sister, after the death of his father.
1885-1895	School years and young manhood in Lawrence, Massachusetts.
1892	Graduates from Lawrence High School. Co-valedictorian with Elinor Miriam White. Attends Dartmouth College for a few months.
1894	"My Butterfly" published in the *Independent,* November.
1895	Marries Elinor Miriam White.
1896	Birth of first child, Eliot.
1897-1899	Attends Harvard as an undergraduate.
1899	Birth of daughter, Lesley.
1900-1910	Farms (near West Derry), writes poetry, and teaches school (Pinkerton Academy, Derry Village) in New Hampshire.
1900	Birth of son, Carol.
1903	Birth of daughter, Irma.
1905	Birth of daughter, Marjorie.
1907	Birth of daughter, Elinor Bettina, who died in infancy.
1911-1912	Teaches psychology at New Hampshire State Normal School, Plymouth, New Hampshire.
1912-1915	Goes to England with wife and four children. Writes and farms in Buckinghamshire and Herefordshire.
1913	*A Boy's Will.*
1914	*North of Boston.*

1915	Returns to America from England. Settles on a farm, Franconia, New Hampshire.
1915-to present	Years of fame.
1916	*Mountain Interval.*
	Elected to National Institute of Arts and Letters.
1917-1920	Professor of English, Amherst College.
1919	Moves to new farm, South Shaftsbury, Vermont.
1920	Co-founder, Bread Loaf School of English, Middlebury College.
1921-1923	Poet in Residence, University of Michigan.
1923	*Selected Poems.*
	New Hampshire.
1923-1925	Professor of English, Amherst College.
1924	Pulitzer Prize for *New Hampshire.*
1925-1926	Fellow in Letters, University of Michigan.
1926-1938	Professor of English, Amherst College. John Woodruff Simpson Foundation.
1928	*West-Running Brook.*
1930	*A Way Out* (One-act play, first printed in 1917; produced at Amherst College Northhampton Academy of Music, February 24, 1919).
	Collected Poems.
1931	Pulitzer Prize for *Collected Poems.*
1934	Death of Marjorie Frost Fraser.
1936	*A Further Range.*
	Charles Eliot Norton Professor of Poetry, Harvard University.
1937	Pulitzer Prize for *A Further Range.*
1938	Death of Elinor White Frost.
1939	*Collected Poems.*
1939-1942	Ralph Waldo Emerson Fellow in Poetry, Harvard University.
1940	Death of Carol Frost.

1942	*A Witness Tree.*
1943	Pulitzer Prize for *A Witness Tree.*
1943-1949	Ticknor Fellow in the Humanities, Dartmouth College.
1945	*A Masque of Reason.*
1947	*Steeple Bush.*
	A Masque of Mercy.
1949	*Complete Poems.*
1957	Litt. D.'s at Oxford and Cambridge Universities and National University of Ireland.
1958	Consultant in Poetry to Library of Congress.
1959	Eighty-fifth Birthday Anniversary.
1961	Reads "The Gift Outright" at Presidential Inauguration, January 20.

Notes on the Editor and the Contributors

JAMES M. COX, the editor of this volume, is an Associate Professor of English at Indiana University, where he is also a Fellow in the School of Letters. He was awarded an American Council of Learned Societies Fellowship for 1960-61 to complete a critical study of Mark Twain. Among his other works on Robert Frost are "Robert Frost and the Edge of the Clearing" and "Robert Frost Alone in Space," both published in the *Virginia Quarterly Review,* and "The Gestures of Robert Frost," which appeared in the *Kenyon Review.*

MALCOLM COWLEY has long been a prominent figure in American letters. Not simply a critic and reviewer, he is an embodiment of literary history, and his most well-known book, *Exile's Return,* is at once autobiography and literary history.

RANDALL JARRELL is one of the most versatile writers of our time, having excelled in poetry, fiction, and criticism. For his most recent volume of poetry, *The Woman at the Washington Zoo,* he received the National Poetry Award.

JOHN FAIRBANKS LYNEN teaches English at the University of Illinois.

MARION MONTGOMERY has published essays, short stories, and poems in quarterlies and the little magazines. He has been managing editor of *The Western Review,* and now teaches English at the University of Georgia.

JOHN T. NAPIER has written drama and poetry. He is at present working for the Atomic Energy Commission.

GEORGE W. NITCHIE is Associate Professor of English at Simmons College.

W. G. O'DONNELL is Professor of English at the University of Massachusetts.

LAWRANCE THOMPSON, author of *The Young Longfellow* and *Melville's Quarrel with God,* is Professor of English at Princeton University.

LIONEL TRILLING has probably reached a wider audience than any other literary critic writing today. In addition to his major study of Matthew Arnold, he has published three collections of essays—*The Liberal Imagination, The Opposing Self,* and *A Gathering of Fugitives.*

HAROLD H. WATTS, Professor of English at Purdue University, is author of *Ezra Pound and the Cantos* and *Hound and Quarry,* a study of modern literature.

YVOR WINTERS, author of *Edwin Arlington Robinson, Maule's Curse: Seven Studies in the History of American Obscurantism,* and *In Defence of Reason,* has been one of the foremost figures in the emergence of modern literary criticism.

Selected Bibliography

Baker, Carlos. "Frost on the Pumpkin," *Georgia Review,* XI (Summer 1957), 117-31. An excellent record of an encounter with Frost.

Cook, Reginald L. *The Dimensions of Robert Frost.* New York: Holt, Rinehart & Winston, Inc., 1958. A critical description of Frost's character and work. Contains records of Frost's speeches and conversation.

Cox, James M. "Robert Frost and the Edge of the Clearing," *Virginia Quarterly Review,* XXXV (Winter 1959), 73-88. An attempt to describe the myth of Robert Frost.

Cox, Sidney. *A Swinger of Birches: A Portrait of Robert Frost,* with an introduction by Robert Frost. New York: New York University Press, 1957. A record of a forty-year friendship, containing many quotations from Frost's casual conversation.

Hopkins, Vivian C. "Robert Frost: Out Far and In Deep," *Western Humanities Review,* XIV (Summer 1960), 247-63. A general description of Frost's achievement.

Lowell, Amy. "Robert Frost," in *Poets and Their Art.* New York: The Macmillan Company, 1926, pp. 56-62. A good early estimate.

Munson, Gorham B. *Robert Frost: A Study in Sensibility and Good Sense.* New York; George H. Doran, 1927. The first full-length critical appraisal.

Ogilvie, John T. "From Woods to Stars: A Pattern of Imagery in Robert Frost's Poetry," *South Atlantic Quarterly,* LVIII (Winter 1959), 64-76. An interesting analysis of the development of Frost's imagery.

Pearce, Roy Harvey. "Frost's Momentary Stay," *Kenyon Review,* XXIII (Spring 1961), 258-73. An excellent judgment of Frost's limitations as a poet.

Sergeant, Elizabeth Shepley. *Robert Frost: Trial by Existence.* New York: Holt, Rinehart & Winston, Inc., 1960. The only detailed, full-length biography. An indispensable account of Frost's life.

Thompson, Lawrance. *Robert Frost.* Minneapolis: University of Minnesota Press, 1959 (University of Minnesota Pamphlets on American Writers, no. 2). A careful and judicious appraisal of Frost's poetic stature, this volume provides a fine introduction to Frost's poetry.

TWENTIETH CENTURY VIEWS

Forthcoming Titles